CLASSROOM READING INSTRUCTION

ALTERNATIVE APPROACHES

D1501177

Patricia Marr Cunningham   Alamance County Schools, North Carolina
University of North Carolina, Chapel Hill

Sharon V. Arthur   Ohio University

James W. Cunningham   University of North Carolina, Chapel Hill

Classroom Reading Instruction

Alternative Approaches

D.C. HEATH AND COMPANY   Lexington, Massachusetts   Toronto

Acknowledgment is made to the following publisher and individual for permission to reprint from their publications:

p. 53: "When Johnny's Beginning," by Miona Wilkinson, from *Elementary English,* January 1958. Copyright © 1958 by the National Council of Teachers of English. Reprinted by permission of the publisher.

p. 139: "The Three-Toed Sloth," by Dabney Stuart. Reprinted with permission of the author from *Friends of Yours, Friends of Mine,* © Dabney Stuart (Rainmaker Press, 1974).

pp. 171–172: "Individualizing Book Reviews," by Arlene Pillar, from *Elementary English,* April 1975. Copyright © 1975 by the National Council of Teachers of English. Reprinted by permission of the publisher.

For Dr. George E. Mason, major professor *exemplar*, and the many children and teachers whom we have taught and from whom we have learned.

Preface

Classroom Reading Instruction, K-5: Alternative Approaches is different from other reading texts in many ways. It does not contain separate chapters on readiness, word identification, comprehension, critical reading, children's literature and methods of teaching reading as most introductory or supplementary reading texts do. It does not present various theoretical viewpoints and cite research which supports or fails to support these theories. The most important distinction between *Classroom Reading Instruction: Alternative Approaches* and other texts is that it serves a different purpose. The purpose of this text is to show alternative approaches to elementary reading instruction as carried out daily in classroom settings.

While working with preservice and inservice teachers in several states, the authors continually have seen the need for models of good reading instruction. Many elementary teachers were not happy with the instructional program they were following in their classes but had "never seen it done any differently." While we were able to "tell" the teachers what instruction would look like in other approaches, we were seldom able to "show" them. Our greatest successes in helping teachers try alternative approaches to reading instruction usually occurred when we were able to arrange for them to visit classrooms where these alternative approaches were being used. These visits to "model" classrooms were hard to arrange within the school day, however, and even when possible showed only a slice of the program. If teachers visited in September, they had an idea how to begin but did not really know what that program might look like in January. If they visited in January, they saw a smooth-running program but wondered how it got started.

Classroom Reading Instruction, K-5: Alternative Approaches makes extensive, year-long visits to model classrooms continuously available for anyone who desires them. As you read this book, you see a class of twenty-four children develop from kindergarteners to fifth graders at Merritt Elementary School. The children are intended to capture the interest of the reader and to show the varying reactions different children have to different reading approaches, but they are not the focus of the book. The focus of the book is on the various approaches used by the teachers.

Each year the class has a teacher who follows a different approach to reading instruction. The teachers record, month by month, in journal fashion their teaching strategies, classroom organization and reorganizations, successes and failures. The book communicates the belief that any major approach to the teaching of reading will succeed if it is well executed by a capable teacher. The reader sees capable teachers organizing their instruction and their classrooms to achieve a successful match between whatever approaches they have chosen and whatever types of students they have been given to teach. The *teacher* makes the difference, not the approach.

The approaches described are not new nor are they necessarily the only viable ones. They are, however, approaches which all three of the authors have successfully used or seen successfully used and which we feel are good models for reading instruction. More important, they are, in most cases, *adaptations* on the original approaches. Mrs. Wright, for example, uses basically a language experience approach to reading, but it is not a language experience program *à la* Stauffer or Allen. It is Mrs. Wright's version of language experience. These adaptations were intentional; it is not our desire that the reader who decides to try the language experience approach will do it exactly as Mrs. Wright does it but rather that the reader will further adapt it so that it becomes language experience *à la* that reader.

Because various reading approaches are described as they might function in actual classroom situations, we were able to include some practical topics not ordinarily considered in texts on reading education. These topics deal with the practical requirements of implementing reading programs in real classrooms, and include among others, discipline, classroom management, ways of communicating with and involving parents in the reading program, and problems faced by a new teacher. The principal advantage in presenting these topics is that they are directly related to the tasks teachers are asked to perform in the course of their duties.

While we feel that this textbook does show what classroom reading instruction is really like, we did have to make some compromises to keep the book to a reasonable length; the reader will have to consider, therefore, some limitations to the book's "reality." First, we do acknowledge that it would be most unusual in this mobile society for a class of children to stay together in one school for six years. This "unreal" situation was devised so that you could watch how the children grow and interact and could observe their different reactions to different approaches.

Second, we are *not* suggesting that children should have a different approach to reading instruction every year or that the approaches shown are only appropriate at the grade level at which they are placed. Any teacher could do an individualized program modeled on the program Mrs. Wise followed in third grade or a basal program like the one Miss Nouveau developed in second grade. While the language experience approach is probably not appropriate when a reader has achieved some sophistication in reading, it is appropriate for a beginning reader of any age. A fourth grade teacher who had a child who was not reading at all could use the language experience approach with that child. While Ms. Maverick's integrated curriculum approach does require some reading facility, it could be used by any teacher whose children have achieved that facility. Mr. Dunn's study-skill, critical reading program is also appropriate for any class in which most of the children have mastered the basic reading skills.

Third, we were not always able to clearly describe how each individual child was progressing in reading and how individual needs were being met. Often a teacher describes a teaching strategy or lesson and the reader knows that not all children would be ready for that activity at the same time. While each strategy or lesson is usually described in detail only once, the reader should realize that this lesson would be repeated at various times as various children were ready for it. *Kindergarten* and *Third Grade* contain end-of-year reports on the children while the other chapters do not. These reports are designed to show how different teachers might report student progress to parents; they are not designed to summarize in detail each child's learning.

Finally, the reader should remember that this is a reading textbook. Other areas of the curriculum are included only as they support and enrich the reading curriculum. The teachers' journals, therefore, describe only that part of their instruction which directly or indirectly relates to their reading program.

In fact, *Classroom Reading Instruction: Alternative Approaches* can serve as a core or a supplementary text in a graduate or undergraduate first course in the teaching of reading. Each chapter contains two types of activities—*For the reader to do* and *For readers to do together*—which are invaluable to students especially those enrolled in field-based reading courses. Activities titled *For the reader to do* provide an opportunity for the individual reader to apply knowledge gained from this book. Some of these activities suggest lessons to be carried out with one or more children. Other activities suggest instructional materials which the reader can create. Still other activities suggest tasks the reader may complete to demonstrate an understanding of specific content.

For readers to do together offer opportunities for groups of readers to talk about concepts presented in the book. Many of these activities require problem-solving and critical thinking. Groups of readers may be asked to work together to evaluate a particular teaching strategy. Often these activities are simulations of actual classroom situations. In these cases, the instructor or leader models a teaching strategy used by one of the teachers in the book. Both *For the reader to do* and *For readers to do together* provide readers with opportunities to develop a level of understanding of the material—beyond merely being able to discuss the content—to the point where they can apply the content in their teaching. These activities also present instructors with opportunities to evaluate the degree to which such understanding has been gained by their students.

Additional aids include a short bibliography, *Further Readings,* and four appendices. The *Further Readings* contain selected articles and books for each chapter which, based on their quality and relevance, will take the reader beyond the content of this book. The appendices contain valuable reference items for reading teachers; namely, a list of professional organizations and addresses, Revised A and P Sight Word List, Dolch Basic Sight Words, Kucera-Francis List.

In summary, all topics traditionally covered in most core texts—word identification, comprehension, critical reading, children's literature, reading methods—are covered in *Classroom Reading Instruction, K-5: Alternative Approaches.* The topics, however, are not separated and arranged in different chapters, but are presented in the context of a total teaching situation which more accurately reflects the actual classroom. The major topics in each chapter are listed in *Highlights,* a page which begins that chapter. The reader can use this page to preview the materials, techniques, and other concerns dealt with in the chapter. The index will allow readers to locate all parts of the book which deal with a specific topic if they want to, but they are not limited to that topical arrangement.

In short, other core texts present the pieces of a puzzle; our book presents the total picture these pieces fit into. Our goal is that as you read each chapter you will feel, "I could teach using that kind of approach. I know how to get started now. I can see what it would look like from day to day and month to month." We hope that you will find an alternative approach which seems to suit your personality and beliefs about children, that you will try that approach, and that you will write us and let us know how you adapted it to your own unique style.

We believe that you will enjoy this book! We know that teaching is hard work, but we also know that it can be fun and we are sure that reading can be fun. When we decided to write this book together, we made a pact that we would have fun writing it. For the most part, we have kept that pact. Now, we sincerely wish you will have fun reading it!

P.M.C.
S.V.A.
J.W.C.

Acknowledgments

No book is solely the work of authors. We would like to thank Jean Greenlaw and Bob Palmatier for the encouragement and support they gave us while we were in the initial stages of writing. We would like to thank Bob Palmatier and George Sherman for their careful, thoughtful review of the manuscript. Their critical suggestions resulted in a stronger book. We are deeply indebted to Harry Hultgren for the many hours he spent proofreading the manuscript and to Jennifer Ferguson, Donna Springer, and Ernestine Windle for their excellent typing. Finally, we are grateful for the many friends and colleagues who read our manuscript offering suggestions and encouragement.

Contents

Good-by Mr. Topps   1

MISS LAUNCH   The Parent Meeting   7
Monthly Logs   11
The Kindergarten Meeting   53

MRS. WRIGHT   The Parent meeting   61
Monthly Logs   65
The First Grade Meeting   93

MISS NOUVEAU   The Parent Meeting   101
Monthly Logs   104
The Student Teaching Seminar   142

MRS. WISE   The Parent Meeting   151
Monthly Logs   154
The Third Grade Meeting   195

MS. MAVERICK   The Parent Meeting   203
Monthly Logs   206
The Professional Meeting   245

MR. DUNN   The Parent Meeting   251
Monthly Logs   254
The Meeting at the Middle School   283

FURTHER READINGS   289

APPENDIX A   Professional Organizations and Addresses   294

APPENDIX B   Revised A and P Sight Word List   295

APPENDIX C   Dolch Basic Sight Words   298

APPENDIX D   Kucera-Francis List   300

Good-by, Mr. Topps

As Ms. Maverick surveyed the half-packed boxes in the office, she felt a twinge of anxiety about moving into the office—and position—that Mr. Topps was vacating. Both because she felt such a strong attachment to the school and the community, and because she was afraid of who else might be hired, Ms. Maverick had rejected a more lucrative offer for a principal's position in another school to take on the principalship of Merritt Elementary School. Mr. Topps had been appointed to replace the principal who was retiring after thirty-one years at the combined middle-secondary school. That middle-secondary school was badly in need of some new ideas, and Mr. Topps was just the man to get things moving.

Now, with the farewell party over, Mr. Topps and Ms. Maverick sat in the box-strewn office reminiscing about the past and planning for the future. Ms. Maverick once again congratulated Mr. Topps on his new appointment and expressed her faith that he would be able to make a real difference in the education of so many children. Mr. Topps, while admitting that he was pleased and excited, also expressed doubts about his or anyone's ability to make a *real* difference in the operation of a secondary school.

"There are so many confines," he explained, "Forty-five minute periods, teachers more committed to their subject matter than to students, graduation and college credit requirements, many more teachers and students to deal with, parents who seem not as interested as when their children were younger—there are those restrictions plus the other limits of tradition. I just hope I can make a contribution. I have told myself that it will take time and have given myself three years. If I can't make some real changes in that time, Ms. Maverick, I may come back here looking for my old job!"

"Well, I know that you will be a huge success at the high school, but I just may be ready to give someone this job in three years! If you think it will be hard for you at the high school, it will be even rougher having to follow you here. Did you see Mrs. Flame at your farewell party? She looked like she might cry at any moment. And the parents are sure the sky is going to fall in next September. I am seldom insecure about my abilities, but I'm just not sure I can deal with people as well as you have."

Mr. Topps assured Ms. Maverick of his confidence in her abilities. He went on to describe some of the history of Merritt School and at the same time provide some details on his teaching career. Upon graduating from college, he had taught first at the junior high school and then in the sixth grade for several years. He had tried several teaching methods that other teachers seemed to use with great success, but it had taken him several years to develop a teaching approach and style which seemed natural and comfortable. In the meantime he had taken many graduate courses and soon had been convinced by the research he read that the teacher rather than the method makes the difference.

"When I became principal of this school, I vowed that I would support and help all my teachers to become the kinds of teachers they wanted to be. I soon found, however, that this theory was not easily implemented. There were constant pressures from administrators and supervisors to adapt whichever teaching approach was in vogue at that particular time. The teachers, too, seemed to want to be all alike. The more traditional teachers wanted to initiate the new teachers into their ways of doing things, and the fresh-out-of-college teachers wanted to implement whole school innovations. Parents were also not very tolerant in the beginning. If parents had a first grader in Mrs. Wright's class and that child did well, they wanted all the teachers to use her language experience approach to reading! I spent much of my first several years here talking with school and community people about my beliefs concerning the need for different teaching styles and approaches.

"I found that the teachers needed more than just the freedom to teach in the way that they were most confident in—they also needed recognition of their accomplishments and encouragement to try out innovative ideas. I tried to provide this recognition and encouragement by visiting regularly in their classrooms and prompting teachers to share the good things I saw going on there. Mrs. Wise, for instance, had been scheduling daily time for uninterrupted silent reading for years. When I saw the value of this I simply called a meeting and had her explain this practice to the other teachers. Then, under her direction, we began school-wide SQUIRT—Sustained Quiet Reading Time. Mrs. Wise also gave me the idea for the beginning-of-school classroom meetings and the twice-yearly parent-teacher conferences.

"Another way in which I tried to provide encouragement for and recognition of good instruction was to open up the school to community members and parents. When I first came here, you never saw a person in this school who was not employed or enrolled here. Gradually, I began to enlist the help of parents and other community members as volunteers and resources. Some of the teachers who had not been putting forth their best effort became more conscientious when I or someone else was in and out of their classroom each day.

"I really don't know all the answers to running a good school and I don't expect I ever will, but I do know that for me, allowing each teacher to pursue his or her own approach and then seeing that that approach is well executed has proved to be a good administrative policy."

Ms. Maverick asked Mr. Topps if he did not *really* believe there was a single best way to teach.

"When, after several years, you found an approach to teaching which worked best for you and your children, didn't you feel that if all teachers could learn to teach in that way, they would do a better job? I'm afraid I'm not as tolerant as you are, Mr. Topps. I would give the teachers the freedom and support to teach as they want to, but I would also try to help them to see the advantages of the integrated curriculum approach. I think many teachers don't use it because they don't know how, but I am convinced that teachers, like children, can learn new skills."

Mr. Topps admitted that he had feared Ms. Maverick would feel this way about it. "You had a fine program and, yes, I do believe other teachers could learn to teach as you did. But first they must want to, and if they did, they would give up other fine programs."

Seeing that Ms. Maverick remained unconvinced, he reached into a half-packed box and pulled out a stack of notebooks. Ms. Maverick recognized these as the journals which Mr. Topps required all his teachers to keep and turn in to him each month.

"As you know, Ms. Maverick, I don't believe in having my teachers turn in lesson plans each week as many of my colleagues do. I know that when I was teaching the plans I turned in bore little resemblance to what I was actually doing in my classroom. I do, however, insist on knowing what each teacher is doing. This is especially important when you have as many different approaches to teaching as we have at Merritt School. During my second year here, I began having the teachers keep journals. In these journals, they recorded the major events which had occurred in their classrooms each month and kept a running account of their instructional program. Here are the journals for the class which has just finished Grade 5. In fact, this is the group which you yourself had and which you turned over to Mr. Ditto when you went to the university to teach that seminar. I wish that you would take these home and read them over the summer.

"This class was lucky to have had Miss Launch as their kindergarten teacher. She had a rich and varied program of experiences for them. She was especially concerned with increasing their oral language facility. You will see that Mrs. Wright does basically a language experience approach to reading, although she includes some basal readers and some individualization in her program. In the second grade, this class had Mrs. Flame, who was Miss Nouveau then. Poor Miss Nouveau! It was her first year in the classroom, and she was ready to quit at Christmas! She used a basal reader approach to reading instruction, and at the beginning of the year didn't use the basal very well. You will see what remarkable growth she made during the year. By the end of the year she had quite a good program. In third grade, this class had Mrs. Wise. What a great loss it was to this school when she retired! As you know, she had an individualized program in which she used children's literature as the base around which she built her instruction. I'm sure you will recognize this journal, Ms. Maverick. It records your integrated curriculum program and shows how Mr. Ditto adapted to it and then modified it after you left. Finally, here is Mr. Dunn's journal. For a second-year teacher, he did a masterful job. He was particularly dedicated to making the children independent learners and worked very closely with Miss Page in helping the children sharpen their critical reading and study skills.

"It will not surprise you, I'm sure, to observe how well these students were reading when they left here. Many were reading well above grade level and almost all were reading at grade level. Many people are amazed that so many of our children read above grade level when they enter the middle school, but I think it is just an indication of what good instruction, year after year, can accomplish. Read these journals carefully, Ms. Maverick, and I think you will see that each teacher's program has unique strengths. After that, make your decision about whether your approach to teaching alone would be best for all teachers."

At that moment, Mr. Topps' secretary interrupted them. Mr. Topps had an urgent call to turn to, leaving Ms. Maverick to gather the six journals. She motioned good-by to Mr. Topps, and journals in arm, left the office for the summer. She was eager to begin reading the journals, and grateful to have the long vacation to gather her thoughts for her upcoming year as principal.

Miss Launch

HIGHLIGHTS

Learning Centers

Field Trips

Oral Language Development

Dramatization and Storytelling

Comprehension Readiness

Reading to Children

Writing

Reading Readiness

Grading (reporting)

Parents as Volunteer Aides

Children's Literature

Self-concept

Language Experience Method

Vocabulary

Directed Learning

Integrated Curriculum

SQUIRT

Activities to Stimulate Interest

Poetry

Summary

Games

Diagnosis

Grouping

Alphabet

Miss Launch

The Parent Meeting

Over at last! Miss Launch glanced at her watch and noted with surprise that it was only 9 p.m. It seemed much later to her. As she moved about the room collecting materials and getting out other supplies for the next day, she thought over her first parent meeting in this new school. Her former school, where she had taught kindergarten for three years, had not held these meetings, and she had *not* looked forward to this one!

She had talked formally for approximately half an hour, including a period for the parents to ask questions. To her surprise, many parents had stayed longer for a private chat. But now, even they had gone, leaving her alone to reflect on this important night.

She knew that it would be one of the most important encounters she would have with parents this year, and that this meeting would set the tone for all future parental cooperation. She was also grateful to Mr. Topps for permitting her to hold her meeting before the school year began. The teachers in this school usually scheduled their parent meetings at various times in the early fall to avoid the problem of parents being forced to choose which meeting to attend if they had several children in the school. Mr. Topps had also told her to relax—these meetings went much more smoothly if they were informal and casual. To Miss Launch, with her penchant for food, that meant cookies and coffee!

While the parents were assembling in the classroom, she had announced that the coffee and cookies were in the rear of the room for anyone who wished a little refreshment. As they were waiting to get the food, she asked them to sign in on a sheet of paper so that she would know which parents had attended and which parents would need to be informed of her program later.

Miss Launch firmly believed kindergarten to be an essential and integral part of the total school program. She had told the parents that kindergarten was *not* play time, and that she was not merely a well-paid babysitter. Further, she had emphasized that in kindergarten the foundation for all future success in school was laid.

She had outlined some of the experiences that the children would have in her room and the reasons for them. This had been an important part of her presentation, for she wanted and needed parental support and cooperation. She had pointed out to the parents the various centers for learning. In addition to the traditional block, art, and house corners of the classroom, she had included other areas that she felt would enhance the educational program for the children. There was an "animals" area, an area for "puppets and plays," one for "reading," and a "things to do" corner that would include activities ranging from math to science to cooking and other topics. Much of the learning would take place in these centers.

Learning, however, would also occur outside of the classroom. Miss Launch had told the parents that she had planned two field trips a month to various places in the school and community. Follow-up activities for these field trips would include making thank-you cards, drawing pictures, and dictating stories.

Miss Launch also had informed the parents of her concern with oral language development. She said that there would be many and varied opportunities for the children to talk. One of the mothers questioned the validity of the program.

"Miss Launch, I don't know much about how they do school now, but when I was in school they didn't take learnin' time for talkin'. I don't see how that can help Chip learn to read! Readin' and talkin' are two different things as I see it!"

Miss Launch had replied calmly to Mrs. Moppet. "Not so different as you might think! Children are already speaking many hundreds of words when they enter kindergarten. They will be able to read all of those words within the next few years. In addition, they will be reading other words which they do *not* yet say. But almost without exception, those new words which they will learn to read will also have been words which they have used in speech. If they do not learn to *say* new words, or if they do not learn to use old words in new ways, then they will only read at the level at which they now speak. That is why I do so much with oral language development. In reading I want to build from what the children know to what they need to know. That is another reason, by the way, for the two monthly field trips we will take. Not only will the children become more familiar with their community, but these trips will also expose them to new words and new ideas which they need later for reading."

She had gone on to say that there would be much dramatization and storytelling. Some of the children's stories would be written on chart paper, some might appear in individual story books, and still others might become part of one of the classroom books of original stories. Each day, before the children left, she would sit with them and discuss all the activities engaged in that day. She felt this discussion would help them develop a sense of sequence, the recognition of main ideas, and a memory for things they had accomplished, all important requisites for reading. Besides, she had said, when parents ask children what they had done in school all day, she wanted to prevent the old "Oh, nothing!" response that children often give!

Miss Launch explained she wanted to give the children many experiences in sorting, classifying, and identifying. They would work with colors, letters, numbers, their own names, and myriad other concepts that would help them build the foundation for success in reading.

She intended to read to the children a great deal, and she expected them to "read" to her. For some children, this would consist of picture interpretation, while for others, actual words would be read.

Everyone would be reading during schoolwide SQUIRT (Sustained QUIet Reading Time). They would all read silently for two minutes initially, though she was certain that they would be sustaining their reading for four or five minutes by the end of the year. She explained also that she had planned a good many "literature/response" activities for the children—she would read a story and then relate many other curricular areas to the story.

Miss Launch indicated that she would use a variety of techniques to prepare children for the important notion that one reads to obtain meaning. They would construct charts of their animals' activities, of the weather, and of other things they knew about, and they would be "reading" their dictated stories to her and to one another. She, in turn, would read to them from works in children's literature. The children would be following "written" directions (e.g., picture writing),* and they would cook in the classroom, following simple recipes. The important factor, she reiterated, was that each child would have purposeful work to do. While she would not initiate wholesale reading instruction in the class, she would provide reading instruction for those who were ready and interested.

Horace's mother held up her hand.

"Could you explain that in a little more detail, Miss Launch? I'm not quite sure that I understand what our children will do if they are not ready to read. And how will you know if they are ready?"

MISS LAUNCH: Mrs. Middleman, isn't it? Well, Mrs. Middleman, children first of all need to develop a desire and purpose for reading. Reading is a difficult task at best, but without proper motivation, it is even more so. We're all going to read, read, read in this class and not just during SQUIRT. I will read to the children and they will "read" to me and to one another. Even if they're only reading pictures, they are still acquiring skills such as main idea, sequence, and making inferences. We will write and, I hope, receive letters. We will label things around the classroom and set up a post office for messages. We'll make books of all kinds—some will only have pictures like Mercer Mayer's "Frog" books and others will have words. We'll follow recipes for purposeful reading. In addition, we'll be working with rhyming

---

* See pp. 37–38 for a description of picture writing.

patterns and the shapes of letters. As I said earlier, I feel that a firm background of oral language is the most important contribution I can make to your child's future success in reading, so I will do much with that. I have lots more planned, but I hope that you have the general idea. As to the determination of readiness, we don't yet have tests that can accurately tell us when children are "ready to read." There are many factors—physical, emotional, and intellectual. Research has shown teacher judgment to be just as effective. Trust me.

MR. MOORE: You've mentioned cooking in kindergarten a couple of times now, and I can't for the life of me figure out what cooking has to do with this pre-reading program you've set out. Can you explain it to me?

MISS LAUNCH: Would you believe that it's really because I like to eat? (Chuckles around the room). Actually, I can justify it educationally, though I must admit that I enjoy the food, too! (Chuckles again). Cooking in this room will be done for several reasons. First, since children eat what they prepare, they learn that it is important to follow directions carefully; second, the food produced is the incentive to do the work well, so there is meaning to doing it; third, there is always more language produced as we discuss why a particular sequence is necessary, and why certain ingredients are added, what they do to-gether; and fourth, new concepts are observed and dealt with, such as the evaporation of liquid, or the nature of change as we observe it with popcorn. And, maybe I should add a fifth one—because it's fun, and if learning can result from an enjoyable activity as well as it can from a pencil and paper task, well, I'm all for it!

MRS. SMITH (aghast):   Do you mean that you're not going to have work papers and workbooks? My friend's son was in kindergarten last year, and he had all kinds of those papers done with purple ink and he had a reading readiness workbook, too. I think that with those you can tell what the children are learning, but with your method, how will you know?

MISS LAUNCH: I strongly feel that workbooks and ditto papers stifle creativity and encourage conformity. I assure you that I will know what your children are learning even better than if I used those materials. I use charts to keep track of those things which all of the children will be dealing with. For example, this chart over here has skills on it like "Can tie own shoes" and "Can say own phone number" as well as other kindergarten learnings. In addition, I keep an anec-dotal record on each child on which I note other observations of interest, such as social development or emotional upsets. I also keep monthly samples of the children's creative "writing" so that I can observe vocabulary and sentence structure growth. These are the devices which I use to give me the greatest possible information about your child, or, as in your case, children. I assure you that I will know as much or more about Roberta and Betty as the teacher of your friend's son knew about him last year.

Miss Launch then explained that there would be at least two parent conferences this year, and that at the end of the year parents would receive a written appraisal of their child's performance in various areas. She then summarized the scheduling she had completed for the staggered entrance of the children in school.

Miss Launch asked if there were any further questions.

PORTLY GENTLEMAN IN THE REAR: I have no questions as such, but I just want you to know that I am amazed that so much can be done with kindergarteners! You have a very ambitious year mapped out! Is there anything we can do to help you?

MISS LAUNCH: Is there ever! Thanks so much for asking, because my next statement was to be a pitch to solicit your help. I can use mothers and fathers to help with field trips, cooking, and all sorts of things. I'll be sending a request-for-help letter home soon, giving you the opportunity to volunteer. Some of the jobs can be done at home or are ones that consist of gathering scrap materials for special projects, so that even if you don't have a lot of time, you can still make a valuable contribution. As to all that the children can do, I have found that many adults tend to underestimate the capabilities of children, and for that reason, we do not help them to attain their full potential. I hope to help them do so without the attendant pressure that we sometimes place on children.

As Miss Launch evaluated the evening, she found that the meeting had gone rather well. Many of the parents had remarked to her that they were pleased that the emphasis would be on learning through creative means. She was certain that she would have a great deal of support from the parents whenever she might need it. She hoped that she had convinced them that kindergarten was "real school." Oh, well, if not now, then by the end of the year they would be aware of it! She glanced around the room. Yes, all was in readiness for tomorrow morning. She allowed herself the luxury of a stretch and a yawn; then she turned off the lights and left for home.

Monthly Logs

SEPTEMBER

September is always a bit of a shock to my system. Each year I am taken aback at how small and shy the entering kindergarteners are. I quickly realize that I am using the children of the previous spring as my criteria. How much they do grow and change in one year's time! There are so many obvious physical differences among them from the beginning. Some children, like Mitch and Daisy, don't seem to need to grow anymore this year, while others, like little Chip, may never completely catch up.

I asked Mr. Topps if I might stagger the children's entrance into kindergarten. I felt that each one of this group of twenty-two children would be better able to make the adjustment if he or she entered with a small number of other children. I could give more personal attention to each child while I tried to deal with some of the school socialization processes—such as how to use the water fountain and what "line up" means! Those can be difficult areas for children to deal with for the first time. Fortunately, most of them were already "housebroken"!

The following chart shows how I managed the staggered attendance. It was somewhat confusing for the parents, but as they each had a copy of the chart there were very few mix-ups. I suggested that they go through the schedule and ring their child's group with red or some other color to make it readily visible so that they could see, at a glance, the days he or she would attend. We also allowed the twins, Roberta and Betty, to attend the same sessions so their parents wouldn't have two sets of classes to keep track of. This attendance procedure has the added advantage of gradually acquainting children with the school. Even the half-day sessions we run can be tiring for children who are unaccustomed to remaining in one place for more than ten minutes.

Kindergarten Attendance Plan

Group 1	Group 2	Group 3
Mike	Joyce	Pat
Steve	Mort	Jeff
Rita	Butch	Alex
Mitch	Carl	Paul
Daisy	Larry	Manuel
Chip	Mandy	Daphne
Betty	Horace	Hilda
Roberta		

	Monday	Tuesday	Wednesday	Thursday	Friday
1st Week	Group 1	Group 2	Group 3	Group 1	Group 2
2nd Week	Group 3	Groups 1, 3	Groups 1, 2	Groups 2, 3	Groups 1, 2, 3

Another reason that I like the staggered attendance is that children come to know a few classmates well in a short time, rather than being lost in a sea of faces. It's important to feel a part of a group, no matter how small.

Getting started is the difficult task, and as I look over the list of all the things I hope to accomplish this year, even I am appalled. I went through my list a second time, this time indicating with a star those areas which are to be emphasized.

At the top of my starred list is the development of oral language skills. If children cannot listen with understanding, they will not be able to read with understanding. It is my job to aid children in building the oral language skills of listening and speaking.

In order to insure that children have a broad base of literary experiences, I use many children's books. One of the best ways to teach creative writing is to provide children with models which they can emulate. If children hear and/or read, "Oh, oh! Look, look!" then that is what they will tend to write. If, on the other hand, they hear and/or read "lovely liquid drops gliding through the air," then *that* is what they will tend to write. If they also have a firm foundation in children's literature, they will have a whole world of words and ideas readily available to them. Years of reading to children and of providing them with fine books to read will undoubtedly go far in helping children develop a love of words and of reading.

Also starred on my list is relevance. Children need to see some sort of relationship between what they do in school and what is going on in the world. Seeing the relevance of the various learning tasks which we set for children is often the only impetus needed for them to take advantage of—and learn from—them.

Finally, I want children in my class to feel good about themselves and others, and so we work very hard on positive self-concept. We touch one another a lot, so that a touch from me can be a very positive thing. There are two full-length mirrors on the doors which enable the children to see themselves as others see them.

Due to the extra-ordinary mixture of children I have this year, I really don't know how I could have managed with all twenty-two on the first day. Working with groups of seven and eight at a time was so much easier for me, as well as for them. One child was so withdrawn that I was immediately aware of the fact that his problem was more than fear of coming to school for the first time. Paul wouldn't speak to me or any of the others for three class sessions, and then he merely uttered his name in a group game. When this happened, we were so excited that we gave him a "silent cheer" (that is, we raised our hands into the air, shook them up and down, and formed our mouths as though we were cheering). Paul cried often during those first two weeks, but they were strange, silent tears that rolled down his cheeks. There was no sobbing or screaming—just a sad, sad look and those tears running down his cheeks. (I have asked the school social worker to investigate the home situation. Something is drastically wrong; perhaps we can discover what it is and then remedy the situation.) Alex and Daphne began to sniffle when they saw this (tears are among the most contagious of childhood afflictions), but Hilda simply told them to be quiet, that she had looked around and it was obvious that there was nothing to be afraid of! The sniffling subsided, but Paul continued his silent crying, despite all my efforts to comfort or distract him.

Some of my "distractions" are really fun. The first day that each group came to school, we all sat on the floor in a circle. (I do a lot of my teaching on the floor—I feel that it's important to be at eye level with the kids.) I moved into the center of the circle, pulled my ear, and said, "My name is Miss Launch." Then the child to my left moved into the circle, made some other sort of gesture and said his or her name. After all had participated in this way, I went back into the circle, pulled my ear, and said, "My name is ——," and let the children supply it. Each child in turn moved into the circle and repeated his or her gesture so that we could all guess the child's name. Mike is a character; his gesture was to lean over and stick his derrière high into the air! Nobody forgot his name, needless to say! It helps for children to have some further association when learning names, for seven or eight names is a lot even for adults to remember at one time, so certainly we should expect that children would find it difficult. Later on, right before they went home, we played the game again to reinforce their gestures and to practice the names. At intervals, I would look at someone and say, "Let me see—don't tell me now. Your name is ——. What is my name?" That helped, too. For the ones who had trouble, I simply pulled my ear, and they were very often able to recall my name. The next time the group came to school we played without the gestures to see if they could remember. Some of us (yes, me, too!) needed the help of the gestures to recall some of the names.

I read to the children every day, and sometimes the whole session was built around one book. First the story was read to them, and then we did other activities to tie the book into the other curricular areas. As an example, one of the first books I read to them was Mirra Ginsburg's *Mushroom in the Rain*. After reading it, we talked about their favorite parts of the story and they drew with crayons or painted at the easel the one thing they had enjoyed the most. We hung these up and let children tell what the part was and why they had chosen it. The fox section was the most popular of all, for children like to be scared just a little. Then we dramatized the story by playing the parts of the various animals. I sometimes had to play, too, to have enough actors for all the characters. When I asked the children what we could use for a mushroom, they cleverly decided to use an umbrella that they would open out more and more as the various animals came under! In addition, we counted the number of animals in the book. We looked for certain colors ("Find all the red things on this page"). We made up a song that we could sing to the tune of "Are You Sleeping?":

Is it raining,
Is it raining,
Little Ant?
Little Ant?
Hurry to the mushroom!
Hurry to the mushroom!
Drip, drop, drip.
Drip, drop, drip.

Is it raining,
Is it raining,
Butterfly?
Butterfly? (*etc., for all the animals up through the rabbit. Then:*)

Here comes Foxy!
Here comes Foxy!
Poor Rabbit! (*two times*)
"No, he is not here, Sir." (*two times*)
"Go away." (*two times*)

See the rainbow (*two times*)
In the sky. (*two times*)
Now the sun is shining (*two times*)
Warm and bright. (*two times*)

We also tested the hypothesis in the book that mushrooms grow in the rain. We planned more stories for the book, such as what might happen next, or who else might have come to the mushroom, or where Ant went after the rain stopped. I also did a "lap story" with them (compliments of Anderson, 1969). The lap story requires a small board which will fit in the lap, some paper to tear into the shapes of the story characters (or clay for molding), and several children willing to participate. First we talked about what we would need to tell the story—the characters and the props. I like to have them tear paper rather than draw or cut the characters, for it is not as confining to the children. They may feel that they can't draw well enough or cut straight enough to make perfect characters, but with torn paper there's no problem, for it's nearly impossible to tear an accurate reproduction of a character, so the pressure is off and they all laugh at what they have done! After the characters and the props are completed, we began the story with the children acting out the parts of various characters using the "reproductions" they had made. It's a fun-filled activity, and one that certainly encourages language, since no one has yet told it exactly as it was written.

For the reader to do

Find a picture storybook that you like. Plan and carry out a lap story with a small group of your peers or with some children.

●　　●　　●

This lap story is an example of how I tie art, music, physical education, science, math, literature, and other curricular areas together to make a mini-unit work. Children rarely forget a book when we do this kind of activity, and Miss Page, the school librarian, tells me that there is always a great demand for the book for weeks afterward. My term for this is "literature/response activity," and I use it frequently.

For readers to do together

In groups of five or six, plan some literature/response activities for some other picture story books. Share them with one another so that you will have several mini-units you can use when you teach.

●　　●　　●

After the class has done a lap story, I place the characters, props, and book in my Puppets-and-Plays Center so that the children can retell the story by themselves or with a small group. They enjoy doing it over and over.

We have only had two weeks of regular school this month because of the staggered entrance of the children, but in those two weeks we established a daily pattern or schedule. The morning group arrives at 8:30 and leaves at 11:30, so I only have three hours in which to do a lot of things. The schedule, which is altered for special events, field trips, etc., is usually:

8:30　Attendance, sharing, read a story or poem
9:00　Work time—centers, SQUIRT, oral language lessons, etc.
10:00　Physical education—outside if possible
10:30　Snack, rest, story
11:00　Work time
11:15　Group together for summary of day, etc.

During the third week, at work time the children were to find pictures of red things in magazines and catalogues. Larry, who is already reading, I've discovered, found the word *red* also. We pasted the things they found on a chart labeled "Red Things." Most of the children could already identify the colors without help, but some could not. I paired up Joyce (who could) and Chip (who couldn't) so she could help him find the colors. Daisy, Jeff, Paul, and Butch also worked with other children to find red objects.

Also during work time, I've been having the children practice their phone numbers and addresses. It is essential that they learn those as soon as possible, so that if they should ever get lost, they can be reunited with parents quickly. As Chip has no phone, he has learned the phone number of a neighbor. Later on this year, we'll practice dialing the numbers on the toy telephones that I have acquired.

We began the first field trips of the year right in our own school area. It is important for children to become oriented to the building, the grounds, and the personnel as soon as is possible. The first day the children came to school, we spent part of the morning walking through those parts of the building which we *had* to know—restrooms, the office, and the janitor's room (yes, for *when*—not *if,* but when a child throws up I can stay with him or her while someone asks the janitor to bring a mop). We have our own kindergarten-sized playground equipment, and that also had to be shown. We went to the office on subsequent days and met the secretary, Mrs. Mainstay, and the principal, Mr. Topps. I prepared for these trips by first going there myself and making sure that someone who knew precisely what it was I wanted the children to learn about that particular place would be on hand. I prepared the children by telling them the highlights of each place, alerting them what to look and listen for, and urging them to try to remember everything so that we could talk and make up a story when we got back to the room. Upon our return, I asked them to tell what we had seen and done. As each child made a contribution, I wrote it down on chart paper with the child's name after it, so that he or she could see the very words contributed. Then I cut the words apart and with the children's help, I glued them back on another piece of paper in the proper order of occurrence. Finally I read it all back to them and they agreed that they had done a fine job!

Our cooking experience for September came near the end of our fourth week. I had made a large chart of the following recipe which I had posted in the Things to Do Center. Each child was assigned to bring part of the required ingredients on a specific day (a letter to Mother helped here!). On Thursday, we began our task during worktime in the early morning, and fruit salad was our snack for the day! Everybody did something to help out; when they weren't part of the cooking, the children did their other work (such as working with blocks, finding blue things, and so on). I used dull knives or table knives for safety.

FRUIT SALAD

We need:

8 apples
4 pears
1½ cups of grapes
1½ cups of raisins
3 cups mandarin orange
  slices
1 medium size jar of
  mayonnaise

We do:

Wash the apples, pears and grapes.

Dump the raisins, grapes, and drained oranges into a big bowl.

Cut the apples and pears into small pieces and put them into the bowl, too.

Mix in enough mayonnaise to make it gooey.

For the reader to do

Begin to collect simple recipes that you could make with young children in the classroom. Make a booklet containing at least fifteen of them.

● ● ●

OCTOBER

October is over—I didn't think Halloween would *ever* arrive, and neither did the children! Every day they asked if it were here yet! Well, at least I was able to channel some of that interest toward school activities. Many of the books which I selected to read to them and ones which they chose themselves were about Halloween, witches, or monsters. One of my favorites, *Where the Wild Things Are,* was one of those with which we did literature/response activities. The children made monster masks and we had a "wild things" parade. We also had a "word gathering" for scary words—I asked them to tell me all of the scary things they could think of. Since this was our first word gathering, the children had trouble getting started. After only a few suggestions by other children, everyone joined in. Even Paul gave me one—*night.* When they started to bog down, having given me several nouns, adjectives, expletives, and verbs, I asked them for scary colors, then for scary smells, sounds, and looks. This is their completed list—I am sure Dr. Herbert Sandberg of the University of Toledo, who had explained word gathering at a meeting I attended, would approve.

Scary Things

blood	monster	bad dream	nightmare
ghost	bloody	black	Boo!
howl	scream	witch	mummy
afraid	fear	scared	storm
giant	frightened	ghostly	red
orange	purple	navy blue	fire
dogs	growl!	blood on my leg	night

something touching me in the dark
when my night light is out
footsteps in the dark
my mom's closet without the light
my window with the curtains open

After we had completed the list, I told the children that we were going to write a poem together. I had read many poems to them and they had enjoyed them. Now it was our turn to produce! Poetry writing with children can be so enjoyable that I am amazed that more teachers don't attempt it. Poems need not rhyme in order to be poetry, and some of our first efforts were not poems at all in the traditional sense, though they did possess poetic elements. This concrete poem format is the simplest one I know to use with children, and it consists of simply drawing a random number and arrangement of lines on the chalkboard. The children then tell words or phrases to fill them in. Here's the first one we ever did:

One Night

Black cat scream, black cat howl
Why do you make that noise?
Growl, Purr, Growl, Purr
Dog and cat
fight.

For readers to do together

Have a word gathering of fall (winter, spring, or summer) words and make a concrete poem.

● ● ●

We also did a concrete poem on the color black. First we had a word gathering of black words, sounds, and smells to get them prepared.

Black

Black, black is the night,
         blacker than black
            is
                  my   window.

While we were gathering black words (which just happened to be the color chart they were working on that week) a discussion took place. The children were coming up with all kinds of black things, when Butch contributed two words: *Joyce* and *Jeff.* Some of the children turned around and looked at those two children as if they had never seen them before, and Alex said, "Hey! They are kinda black!" Others started murmuring as well—this *was* a revelation! Larry said, "No, I don't agree. They are called blacks, but I think they look more brown than black." Joyce and Jeff were asked what color *they* thought they were and Joyce said, "Well, what color do you think *you* are?" Jeff said nothing. After a little more discussion they all agreed that Joyce was brownish, but that Jeff was closer to black. So his name went up on the chart of black things, and though he tried to hide it from them, he smiled! Later I saw him tracing out the letters of his name on the chart. He was the only child to get listed on the chart!

By now I had labeled a lot of things around the room: window, door, mirror, desk, table, chair. Also I was working with each of the children so that they would recognize their own names. I wrote each name about three inches high on unlined paper. I then took each child's hand and traced over the name with his or her two fingers. All the time we did that, I said the name over and over with the child. Then, after we had done that a few times, I let him or her go to the scribble section of the chalkboard where he or she could write it, using the paper as a model. I stayed with each child until the name was mastered and then went to work with the next one. With that technique, almost all of the children can recognize their names when they see them in manuscript writing, and several can write their own names without looking at a model. As a further incentive, I labeled the bulletin board with their names and then asked them to make a picture of themselves and tell me where to hang it. Mort, Paul, and Daisy were the only three who needed extra help. Mort got confused because of all the names which began with *M,* as did Daisy with both of the *D* names. Paul just didn't have a clue! Another activity they like is to dip their one-inch brushes into clear water and write on the board with those. They have fun, they learn, there is no erasing to do, and, at the end, the chalkboard is clean!

We have charts all over the room now. Last month's "Red Things" and "Blue Things" have been joined by this month's "Green Things," "Yellow Things," "Orange Things," and "Black Things." The children are generalizing now about the colors and their close shades. We can play "I spy something green" now and not have someone guessing the white clock face! There are charts, too, indicating self-care skills that are important for them to know. A check mark by a name for a particular skill informs the child he or she is considered to have mastered that skill. One thing I no longer do is button jackets or sweaters or tie shoes. I told the children that I would help them during October and teach them how to do those things if they hadn't already learned. After that, they were to ask friends to help them or do it themselves. In my experience, other children won't put up with this for too long. After doing Carl's buttons three times, Manuel is quite likely to say, "Hey! Why don't you learn to do this. Here, I'll show you one more time. Now, *you* do it." I've found the other children to be better teachers and to provide more incentive than I can. Besides, I'm here to *teach* them, not to dress them.

The parents have been a tremendous help in freeing me to teach; they've helped with a lot of the detail work that takes up so much of a teacher's time. For example, they can check to see if Mitch can tie his shoes or button his coat, and help him record his successes on the wall chart. They also help with some of the ancillary tasks, such as cutting out paper shapes.

This month, we studied shapes—the circle, square, triangle, and rectangle, one per week. The shapes were pinned to a bulletin board entitled "Shape of the Week." For example, I put up circles of all colors, and sizes as well as gift paper printed in circle patterns. One mother found round objects in magazines; these also went up on the board. After discussing roundness, the children were sent off to work alone or in pairs to find three things that exhibited roundness. I set the timer so that they would only have three minutes in which to do it. Excitement ran high as they scurried around the room looking for round things. They gathered at the chart and we had a word gathering of round things. I called first on those children who were likely to have had trouble, and asked them what they had found. In this way, they were able to contribute something to the group, too. Several times children had selected the same object, and they would say, "Hey! That's *mine*! You can't say mine!" I took the tack of praising them for having been so clever to have discovered the same object and went right on! The children then searched magazines for pictures of round things and we put them up on the bulletin board also. I made available a box of paper circles of various sizes and colors (cut by a mother at home) for the children to form into pictures. Using this same procedure for all four shapes resulted in a good understanding and recognition of each shape by the end of the month.

Perhaps you'd be interested in the letter which the parents received from me at the beginning of October to solicit help.

Dear Parents,

As I told you at our September parent meeting, I am most eager to provide your children with a year full of good learning experiences. In order to give them the kind of program I have envisioned, I am asking for your help in many ways. Would you please put a check mark beside those things which you would be willing to do for us this year. The space for "other" is one that you might suggest to me any possible aid or special talent which you would like to contribute.

Thank you so much for your prompt attention to this matter. Your children and I will gain much from your participation in their education.

Sincerely,

Miss Launch

....

Please detach here and return.

I would be willing to help in the following ways:

_____ coming to school one hour a week

_____ typing at home (or school)

_____ cutting out paper at home (or school)

_____ transporting children for field trips

_____ helping with the monthly cooking project at school

_____ donating scrap materials (cloth, pretty paper, etc.)

_____ tape-recording stories, music, etc.

_____ making puppets

_____ contributing art materials

_____ contributing materials for house corner

_____ contributing books, records, pictures, etc.

_____ contributing scatter rugs, pillows for floor, etc.

_____ other:

Name: _____

Telephone: _____

Parental response to the letter was overwhelming. For the most part, parents want to be involved in their children's education and will volunteer if there is something specific that they feel confident in doing. In some cases, parents prefer to or *must* do things at home. For example, Chip's mother must stay home to take care of an elderly aunt and uncle who live with them. She thus offered to cut out things for me if I would send the materials to her, since they don't have any magazines or newspapers. *Where* it's done matters not to me! I'm just delighted that parents are willing to do it at all!

Our two field trips this month were to those places which supply us with food—the store and the farm. I had gone to these places prior to the children's visit, and I made extensive notes to myself about the kinds of things I wanted them to notice and learn about. As the store didn't open until 9 a.m., I made arrangements for the manager to show us around at 8:45. I planned to spend half an hour there so the children would be able to observe some shoppers, but the store wouldn't be too crowded. I prepared the children for this trip by discussing with them the various services and goods which the store has to offer. Daisy was the greatest contributor, for she had spent a good bit of time in stores with her mother. I put down anything the children said, so after the trip they could look at their list and add to it. From the amended list we made up a story about the store which hung on the bulletin board surrounded by all of the children's pictures. Here it is:

We went to the store. (Daphne)
We saw lots and lots of food. (Daisy)
The fruits and vegatables are called *produce*. (Larry)
Lot of meat. (Chip)
There were sweet things to eat. (Carl)
The store man showed us many things. (Pat)
We had fun and learned a lot. (Rita)
My mother and Larry's mother drove. (Roberta)

In addition, the children drew pictures which I mailed to "the store man" along with a copy of their story and personal note of thanks from me.

We did the same kinds of activities for our visit to the farm. So many children do not associate the farm with the store that I made a special effort to talk about where butter, milk, meat, and vegetables come from. When I first asked them where milk comes from, Butch replied, "From the carton." But where did the milk for the carton come from, I persisted. Jeff told me that it came from the store! In my whole morning group, only three—Larry (no surprise!), Steve (the science buff), and Daphne (who lives on a farm)—knew that cows give us the milk we drink.

A concern I have when taking my children on these trips is that the guide will speak loudly enough for all to hear. Because I prepare them so well for their trips, they have plenty of questions to ask and are willing to listen to the answers, but too often the guide is unaware that he or she should wait until they are all quiet and close enough to hear, and that he or she should speak loud enough to overcome background noises.

Both the grocery store and the farm people gave us pumpkins for our room, so after the carving was all done, we fixed pumpkin seeds for our cooking experience. Everyone helped to clean them.

PUMPKIN SEEDS

We need:	*We do:*
Lots of pumpkin seeds	Wash off all of the stringy stuff on the seeds.
Some butter	Drain the wet seeds on a paper towel.
Some seasoned salt	Melt butter in a small pan.
	Put in the seeds and turn them over until they are all covered.
	Place them on a cookie sheet and sprinkle with seasoned salt.
	Bake at 350° until they start to get brown—about 15 minutes.

NOVEMBER

Finally! Colors are finished! Our room looks like a rainbow gone crazy. Because some of the children had decided that Joyce was a "brown thing," I changed the order of the colors we were working on. We did brown the first week in November. They remembered their "discovery," and when we began to gather "brown things" for the chart, her name was the first thing mentioned. She helped me spell it, too, which made it even more important to her. We did purple and white things during the second and third weeks. The children seem to have enjoyed this exercise, and I note that they choose to play the "I spy" game with one another often during their time at work. Larry is able to read a great many of the things we have listed on our charts. I'm amazed that he can read so well so early! He often chooses the reading corner in which to spend his free time.

The reading corner is furnished with an old bucket seat from the car of a friend of mine. (My friends are well trained—they never throw any unusual items away without checking with me first! Over the years I have asked them for odd items, from popsicle sticks to eggshells!) The children love it—two can sit together cozily, reading or looking at books. There also is a small rug remnant, some pillows donated by parents, and a small table with three chairs. A shelf contains a variety of books, with a range of those with pictures only to those with quite a long story line. The children choose books which they want me to read to them, and often we do literature/response activities with these books.

The blocks area is another one that the children enjoy and use frequently. It lends itself to all sorts of language experiences as the children build and discuss what they have done and why. Sometimes they ask me to write signs for them or write down stories that the constructions trigger. By the end of November we had enough of those stories to make a book which we placed in the reading corner. The children were really pleased that I valued their work enough to put a cover around it and give it a title. Nearly everyone in the class had contributed something to the book, and even those who hadn't had worked in the block corner and could enjoy the stories and illustrations.

The art area has paint, easels, clay, crayons, colored chalk, *lots* of paper, odds and ends for constructions, and various other materials for art work. I have a section of the bulletin board reserved for paintings and a small table nearby for the display of constructions. Very often, art work acts as a stimulus for story writing. One of the children might ask me to write down his story about the horse he or a classmate had made of clay. I am often asked to label their work; not only is there further language concept development, but this labeling also seems to add value to the work.

We went to the local fine arts gallery on one of our field trips this month. The children were intrigued by the variety and quantity of art represented there, though it is rather small by many standards. They kept asking me (or Larry) to read the attached signs. Mike found the nude! He came running back to the group and began whispering excitedly to some of the boys. Soon Butch, Carl, Mitch, Mort, Alex, Manuel, and Horace started to follow Mike down one of the corridors. "Where are you going, boys? Remember the rules we made—you can't go off alone." They stopped and all blushed except for Mike.

"Well, come on with us then," he said.

I asked the twins' mother if she would mind staying with the rest of the group for a few minutes while I went with them to see what was up. The nude was quite lovely, but it was wasted, for the most part, on these five-year-old boys. Mike watched my face attentively—for signs of shock, I suppose. I merely commented, "Didn't the artist do a nice job? Notice how well he blended these colors here. Why do you suppose he chose to make her hair blond?" That did it—no more snickering. They began to see the painting and not just the subject. Without haste, I ushered them all back to the main group. I wondered what the repercussions of this little episode might be.

After we returned from the gallery there was a flurry of art work as there never had been! Everyone had decided to be an artist when he or she grew up—well, *almost* everyone. Mort, however, didn't find one thing that excited him, and Paul—poor dear—was hardly aware of where he had been. Daisy was interested in a huge banana that was painted in shades of purple—she talked about it for days! Steve showed particular interest in the bird paintings and the photography montage of nature scenes and his paintings reflected that.

As many boys as girls play in the house corner. They spontaneously act out the kinds of things they see and hear at home. It's easy to tell whose father helps clear the dinner table and whose mother spends a good part of the day on the couch watching television. The re-creation of some of these day-to-day details helps children to get their lives in focus. Sometimes, by acting out the harsh realities that they encounter, they find that they are better able to cope. I remember one child who acted out a rape scene on the floor of the house corner, though, thank goodness, not replete with all of the sordid details. That was during the first year I taught, and I didn't know what to do or how to handle it. I sat down near the child while he was working later and asked him to tell me about the story he had made up in the house corner. That's when I found out that he had been awakened by noises one night in their one-room apartment and had observed what he acted out. "My momma, she cry real hard afta' that. She say, you go back to sleep now, so I did." He never acted it out again and never seemed to refer to the matter. I can only assume that he acted it out to get rid of it.

I have never called the house corner the "doll corner" or "doll house" as some of my colleagues do, for lots of boys don't want to play there if it has that name. They learn too soon to shun the so-called feminine play things. By calling it the *house* corner there is a greater opportunity to draw boys in. They experiment with all sorts of housekeeping experiences, even arguing over whose turn it is to vacuum the floor. Of course, they get real cooking and dishwashing experiences from the cooking sessions we have.

As for cooking, I don't know that I will ever again let the children make what we made this month! We were to participate in a Thanksgiving feast. My morning group and Mrs. Wright's first grade prepared food and ate together; my afternoon group did the same with the other first-grade teacher's class. The first-graders made cornbread and churned butter; *we* prepared cranberry-orange relish. I may never eat it again! Juice all over the floor, little seeds in everything—and then some children didn't even like it much! Perhaps if I had used a blender rather than my old-fashioned food grinder it would have gone better.

Because this is "turkey month," we went to visit a turkey farm. We saw lots of live turkeys and then saw how they were processed for shipment to our local stores. This was one of the hardest field trips to get ready for, because I knew that there would be a possibility that some children might be upset by the "murder" of the turkeys. Carl and Betty were the

CRANBERRY-ORANGE RELISH

We need:

4 cups
   cranberries
2 oranges
2 cups sugar
a large bowl
a big spoon
a food grinder

We do:

Wash the cranberries; throw away the mushy ones.

Wash the oranges and cut each into four pieces.

Pour cranberries into top of grinder. Turn the handle. Make sure that the bowl is catching the ground-up cranberries.

After grinding some of the cranberries, grind up two orange sections. Then grind more cranberries. Keep doing this until all the cranberries and oranges are gone.

Add the sugar and mix well.

Put in the refrigerator overnight (after letting them sample it, of course!).

Makes enough to give everyone a dab.

only two with whom I had trouble—there were many tears from these two! Daisy only made it worse by hovering over the birds and smacking her lips. Chip asked me what turkey tastes like. How can that be explained to a child? If only there were some way that we could be having turkey instead of cranberry-orange relish!

We also learned to play some new games. I wrote out six copies each of the capital letter forms *P, H, A,* and *R.* I made each one about six inches high so that the children could readily see them from across the room. They are on sheets of oaktag and covered with clear plastic adhesive paper so that they are durable. The first game was one that the whole class played together. I shuffled the cards and dealt out one to each of the children. I told them to find the other children who had the same letter shape. When two children got together they had to stay together while searching for other children who matched them. If they thought that they had found one that was a match, they carefully looked at the parts to see if they were correct. After all groups had been formed with no leftovers, I checked them. Perfect the first time, just as I had known it would be, for the abler ones helped those who could not yet match! (I had set the timer for three minutes. They enjoyed the timing since it gives games a little added excitement.)

It was interesting to observe the differences among the children as they formed their groups. Paul stayed put and was found by Mandy and Horace, who were also *P*'s. They dragged him along with them until they found or were found by the other *P*'s. Daisy dashed wildly around the room, ostensibly looking for the other *A*'s, but in fact making it only more difficult for them to track her down. Mort sat in a chair, apparently not wanting to exhaust himself, being fully confident that the *H*'s would get to him in time. Chip and Manuel held hands and went from group to group checking the letters, even though Chip was an *A* and Manuel an *R*. I suppose they just needed the extra confidence that they gave one another. The children begged to do it again, so we shuffled the cards and went through the same process. This time, Hilda tried to organize the thing a little more by shouting out "A! A! A!" apparently as a clue to those who might know the name of the letter. Larry formed his hand into the letter *P* and said "Do you look like this?" Ingenious children I have!

For another game which I played with them that day I placed three cards of the same letter on the chalkboard tray with one that was different. I arranged the cards like this for ease the first time: *A A A N*. I then asked Rita to come find the ones that were the same. She chose the first three. "Terrific! Let's all give Rita a silent cheer!" (The silent cheer is a good reward for children and it's also easy on the teacher's eardrums.) I continued the game with other children making the letter combinations harder or easier depending on a child's capabilities. I then put the cards into the "Things to Do" center and suggested that they might like to play with them sometimes.

For readers to do together

Form groups of four or five. What are some other gross discrimination games you could have children play with the cards? Share your group's ideas with your class.

● ● ●

DECEMBER

Despite the holiday rush and clamor, we did manage to accomplish some things this month. It does seem to me, though, that the holidays can't come a minute too early, for we have been in a holiday whirl since Halloween!

Two of the skills I've concentrated on this month are left-to-right and top-to-bottom orientation. I've been combining several of the skills which I want to work on, and give the children oral directions to follow. I have a cube with an open end, and I tell a child to place an object "in the box," or "by the box." Then, as an alternative, I let one child place something and then tell us where he or she has put it. Or I let one child place it and another tell where it is in relation to the box. I notice them repeating this activity in centers and on the playground.

Left-and-right were harder to deal with. We talked about how some of us use left hands and others of us use our right hands to do things with. I asked if anyone knew which was the right hand—several did, notably Larry, Pat, and Roberta. I asked them for ideas that would help us to remember which was which.

Alex said, "Well, once my Mom, she said she had to 'member sumthin.' So she put a string on her finger."

"Good idea, Alex. How about if we tie a blue piece of yarn around the wrist—see, this is the wrist—and then we will know that it is connected to the right hand."

"But what about the other one? How will we know what *it* is?" Daphne wanted to know.

"How, indeed? What is the other one and how will you know?"

"Well," said Hilda, "anybody can see that the one without the yarn must be the other hand, the left one. Hey, that's funny! The left one is left without yarn! Ha, ha, ha!"

We all chuckled over that one, and I am sure that Hilda's joke helped to establish yet one more association for left and right.

Learning to give and follow oral directions is a difficult but important task. One activity which the children enjoy (and so do I) is for a small group with which I am working to select a picture from a book and then tell me what to draw. They are to select a picture of a single object, such as an animal, and then, without giving me clues as to what it is, they tell me how to draw it. I work on the chalkboard with my back to them so that I cannot see what they are looking at. They will tell me to "hook circles together" and I will perhaps end up with the caterpillar which they are describing from *The Very Hungry Caterpillar* by Eric Carle. Or they might start me out with directions like, "Make a square. Put four skinny rectangles along the top edge from each corner. Hook them together in the middle with two small rectangles and a circle in the middle of them. Hook the top of them together with a fat rectangle. Draw a worm on the top rectangle. Make loop-like things along the sides of the worm."

For the reader to do

Can you guess what the picture is? Try to draw it, and then compare it to the picture on the sixth page of the text in *Duffy and the Devil* by Margot and Harve Zemach.

● ● ●

When children see my renderings of their oral directions, they begin to realize how extremely important it is to give explicit directions. One advantage this exercise has is they can see immediately where they have not been explicit enough and can tell me what to correct. They can see if I haven't made the rectangles the right size, for example, or placed them correctly so that they can rectify their errors. They can say, "No, on the bottom." Later on, after we have played the game this way for some time, I will pair the children and let them play it with one another. They enjoy this activity and it is an enjoyable way to get across the idea that they must be precise with the language. Even later, I will pair them so that they sit back-to-back. One will give directions and the other will follow, just as before, except that this time the one giving the directions cannot see what his or her partner is doing. After one has finished describing what to do, the two children compare the illustration just drawn with the original. I have found that this is an excellent way for the children to monitor their own progress in giving and following directions, for the two often will talk about what was done and see where they can improve.

Still another exercise I use to develop skill in giving and following oral directions is a "sculpture" game. I select four children to assume the roles of sculptor, imitator sculptor, clay, and observer/reporter. The rest of the children form a living wall. The sculptor and his or her lump of clay (another child) stand on one side of the living wall; the imitator sculptor and his or her "clay" stand on the other; neither can see the other. The reporter sits where he can see *only* the sculptor and his clay. The sculptor begins to move the clay around, forming it into whatever shape he or she has in mind. While the sculptor is "molding," the reporter tells the imitator sculptor what needs to be done to form an identical sculpture. When the sculptor is finished and the reporter has given the last of his or her directions, the living wall dissolves and the children observe the two supposedly identical sculptures. They compare and contrast, and determine where errors were made. The children beg to do this over and over, and some of them become fairly accurate at both giving and following the oral directions.

For readers to do together

Do one of the three preceding exercises for giving/following directions. Develop some similar kinds of exercises. Duplicate one of them per person and distribute to each class member.

● ● ●

This month we took our field trips to the police station and to the post office. I thought it would be a good idea to familiarize the children more with the law enforcement agency since some children get lost when they are shopping with their parents. By acquainting them with police officers on an informal basis, I hope that they will be comfortable with them if a need ever arises.

The post office trip was taken during our last week at school before the holidays so that we could mail letters to Santa. Each child, except Mort, dictated a letter to Santa Claus telling him how good he or she had been and what it was that he or she would like in return. The letter was then read to the child, just as it had been dictated. Here are some sample letters:

Dear Santa,

I been good. Please bring me big bag peanuts.

Chip Moppet

Dear Mr. Claus,

I am well. I hope that this finds you the same. I have tried very hard to be a good girl, though I sometimes have trouble with that!

I would like very much for you to bring me some new pencils, some blue writing paper, and a lot of books.

Thank you very much for your time.

Pat Penn

The trip to the post office inspired the children to ask for a post office in our room. It sounded like a good idea to me, for very often children like to find little surprise notes in their boxes and to send notes to other children. (Also, any note which I wanted carried home to parents could be placed inside and would be less likely to be forgotten.) The children and I decided that round oatmeal containers would work very well for our mailboxes (I was to get one too, for they said, "Well, what if we want to send *you* a note?") The children began to decorate their boxes as soon as my cry for help to the parents had brought in enough boxes for us all. We glued them together, pyramid-style, and attached the name of the child from the upper edge of his box. They looked like this when finally assembled:

Even in the short time we had before vacation, the children used their boxes often to send and receive notes. They were fascinated with the idea, and I noticed that some of the children who had trouble identifying their own names in the past were able to find their own mailboxes with little difficulty.

Another device we started this month to help the children identify their own names and also to help develop responsibility is a *job chart.* There are always many tasks to be done in a classroom, and by this time of the year I try to involve the children even more than previously. There are enough jobs for everyone, even though several children have the same job simultaneously at a particular time, as the cleaners do. So that children have a variety of jobs during the year, the job assignments rotate weekly. There are jobs that can be done by the children only if their teacher instructs them. For instance, they must be told how much water to give the plants. One tip that I found helpful was to color-code plants to soup cans used for watering. Draw a line inside the soup can with waterproof paint to indicate how much water is needed for a plant. A small square of color on the plant container that matches the line drawn in the can will clue children so that they will have a hard time going wrong. Be forewarned, however, that if you have a color-blind child like Butch, you may have a drowned cactus and a droopy ivy! Using this kind of a coding system is the beginning of learning to follow "written" instructions. Though no words are used, children learn to decode the meaning of the symbol being used (in this case, color) in order to follow some specific instructions.

Here is the job chart for one week. Every week new assignments are made:

Water plants	Chip	Paul			
Room cleaners	Betty	Butch	Daisy	Rita	Hilda
Messengers	Manuel	Daphne			
Mailman	Larry (he knew all of their names)				
Line leader	Mort				
Group work leaders	Roberta	Horace	Carl	Alex	
Feed animals	Pat	Mike	Steve		
Special helpers	Mitch	Joyce	Mandy	Jeff	

We've also been doing some gross discrimination listening exercises. I play middle C on the piano and the children stand up. When I play higher than that, they are to get up on their tiptoes; lower, they squat down. I always go back to middle C, though, so that they always make their move from a regular standing position. They must listen carefully and respond accordingly. Other times I say, "Stand tall; stand small" and they must go up or down depending upon what word is used.

Plan five listening/response activities. Duplicate them and share them with the class.

● ● ●

We did another very easy poetry format this month. First, I asked the children if they knew what opposites were.

Horace volunteered, "That's when my Mom puts money into the bank."

"Pretty good guess," I replied. "That is called a *de*posit."

Larry said, "You know, they're words that mean just the different thing, just the, well, *opposite,* like hot and cold, wet and dry, up and down."

"Very good, Larry. Can you think of any other opposites, children?" They came up with several pairs: warm and cool, summer and winter, big and little. I asked them to choose a pair so that we could make up a poem. They chose "up and down." I told them that this time we would start and end the poem with those words and fill in with others. We would put the words in one long column, one word per line. There were an uneven number of words, for the middle word, the transition word, had to have something to do with both of the opposites. Here is what they came up with:

Up,	Larry
Sky,	Joyce
Clouds,	Pat
Flying,	Mike
Swing,	Hilda
Falling,	Butch
Dirt,	Mitch
Rocks,	Steve
Down.	Larry

I read their poem to them, phrasing it to make the most of the poetic elements. Notice that the middle word is the one where the transition is made between the opposites. The words from the top to the middle build images for the top word; the words from the middle down build images for the bottom word. As the children become more sophisticated, they learn to anticipate the middle and start to build images for it, too.

Form groups of five or six. Choose a pair of opposites and make an "opposites poem." In order to create poems with richer imagery, use at least fifteen words. Don't forget to build up the transition word. Share your poem with the class.

● ● ●

December seemed like a good time to make hot chocolate for our monthly cooking experience.

HOT CHOCOLATE

We need:	*We do:*
1½ cups cocoa 3 cups sugar Salt 27 cups milk Marshmallows Hot plate and pan	Mix dry cocoa with sugar and a sprinkle of salt in the pan. Add 1 cup of milk and stir to make smooth. Pour in 26 cups of milk and heat until very hot. Don't boil! Dip into cups and put a marshmallow in, too.

JANUARY

The children seemed really glad to be back at school—two weeks is a long time to be away. I find, too, that they have become bored at home and come to miss the routine which we have so carefully established. Furthermore, most of them are anxious to share their holiday "goodies" with the other children. Pat got her wish, and received some new books, which she assured me she could read. I asked her to bring them in and show them to us and perhaps read them to the class. Pat brought in one of those commercial, early reading books (*Ten Apples Up on Top*) that she had received for Christmas. First she read it to me, and then I let her read it to her small group. After she finished, I asked her to bring the book to me and I went through a procedure similar to the one I had used to determine if Larry had, indeed, been reading. I turned to a page, isolated a word, and asked her to identify it. I find that many children can recall words in phrases or sentences or identify them from picture clues, for they are good memorizers. This method indicates real learning if they can identify the words without those clues. Many parents have told me that their child can read when actually the book had been read so often that the child had memorized the text. Pat stumbled on a few of the words, but for the most part she read them correctly. I had to agree with her—she *was* reading.

Reading to others is one of the favorite activities of the children, even of those who cannot read! It works this way: when one of the children indicates to me, as Pat did, that there is a book he or she would like to share with his or her group, I ask the group leader to get the group together. (Group leaders are appointed each month and are listed on the job chart.) The group leader informs the others in the group when they are to work together, and is also responsible for this work being turned in to me. In addition, he or she must get the group together for special things, as when a member of the group wants to "read" to them. At an appointed time the group meets together and listens to the story. Most often the children "read" pictures to one another and make up a story. This story, while generally plausible, is often quite different from the original. This doesn't concern me, for they gain so much from the experience. They learn to hold a book so that all can see the illustrations and to speak loudly enough for all to hear; they are also gaining in their ability to sustain interest and to determine the main ideas of the story so that it makes sense in the re-telling. They are developing the notion that they need to be able to recall the sequence of the story and the support-ing ideas that make up a story. Since it can be terrifying for young children to try to "read" to the entire group, I found this method of sharing books with a small number a good alternative.

Occasionally, there are some children who want to "read" to the entire class. I always determine in advance whether the experience will be traumatic. Larry, for instance, can actually read words, and has read a lot of the Dr. Seuss material to the others. He has no fear of working with the class as a whole, and conducts himself amazingly well for a kindergartener. Alex feels confident enough with one book to do it for the class—he loves the story *Nobody Listens to Andrew* by Elizabeth Guil-foile, because he admires the main character. He would tell that story to the class ninety-two times if he had the chance! Carl likes the A. A. Milne stories, so he will tell again and again about the adventures of Pooh, Eeyore, and Piglet. My efforts to increase the range of his interests have not been successful so far. Daphne will start to use the child's version of *The Wizard of Oz* by L. Frank Baum and then revert to tell the story as it occurred in the movie. There are several striking differences between the book and the movie, but Daphne is doing what she can with it.

Now that both Pat and Larry are reading, I often pair them on tasks. They learn from one another and free me to work with other children. The first thing I had them do was an alphabet book of their own in which to keep their words. Any word which they wanted to learn to read was written there on the appropriate beginning-letter page. I wrote the words on a sheet of paper so that they could trace over them, just as I had done earlier with their names. They would go to the chalkboard, write the words, and then teach them to one another. Sometimes they would look up a word in the picture dictionary, so that they could identify the meaning of the word, and practice with one another.

I have added materials to the Things-to-Do Center. I placed wooden beads, long strings, and pattern cards there. Each of the fifteen cards had a different pattern of beads drawn full-size so that children could check their own work against the pattern card. The children try to match the pattern on the cards by stringing beads of those exact same colors, sizes, and shapes.* For example, one card had this pattern: green triangle, blue circle, yellow square, purple rectangle. After the children complete the stringing of the beads, they hold them against the pattern card and see where they have made errors. In addition, I cut replicas of the beads from colored construction paper so that the children are able to form their own pattern cards.

Another kind of pattern card which I intend to include later requires the children to predict which bead will come next in an established sequence. One of the cards will show a pattern such as: red circle, green square, orange rectangle, red circle, green square, orange rectangle, red circle, green square, and so on. The answer to what bead comes next in the sequence is drawn on the back so that the children can check their own work after completing the task. It is my hope that children will transfer this skill to anticipating when I read a story to them. I will teach this transfer of making predictions with beads to predictions with stories by doing several of the bead pattern cards with the group before beginning a story. I will tell them that they can do the same thing when I read to them; that is, they should be alert to the facts given in the story, and on that basis, make a prediction as to what will happen next. I will stop reading at a crucial point and ask them to think back to what they have heard and then try to guess what might happen next— "Just like using the beads," I will tell them.

There was a flood of stories to be dictated and typed for the children after our field trip to the fire station this month. *Now* everyone wants to be a firefighter! They tell gory stories to be written down about how brave firefighters save helpless women and little babies—the influence of television, I think, for the Fire Chief certainly did nothing that would have aroused such stories.

Our second trip, a visit to a restaurant, couldn't compare with the excitement of the trip to the fire station. The children were fascinated with the huge appliances in the kitchen, and informed the chef that they, too, were cooks. He asked them what they could cook and they proceeded to catalogue our entire year of cooking for him, complete with the description of the mess we had with the cranberry-orange relish!

This month we fixed No-Bake Cookies. A real treat!

---

* The child creates a three-dimensional model with beads to reflect the two-dimensional pattern on the card.

NO-BAKE COOKIES

We need:

6 oz. semi-sweet chocolate bits
3 tbsp. white corn syrup
⅓ cup orange juice
3½ cups confectioner's sugar (sifted)
3 doz. crushed vanilla wafers
Hot plate, pan, spoons

We do:

Mash vanilla wafers.

Melt chocolate over hot water in top of double boiler; remove from heat.

Stir in corn syrup, orange juice, 3 cups sugar, and vanilla wafers.

Form into one-inch balls; roll in ½ cup sugar.

FEBRUARY

This month I began to have the children follow "written" directions. The written directions consist of a series of pictures which show the children each step to take in finishing a figure. They particularly enjoyed the one shown here.

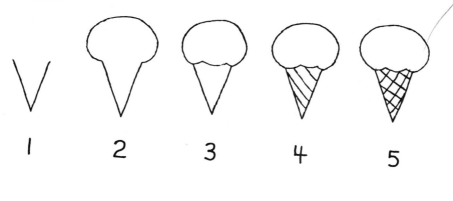

I begin the exercise by handing out paper with an oblique line already drawn so that they know what size to make their drawing. My instructions are given from the chalkboard, where I draw a similar kind of picture in various stages. I ask them what to do to make the picture on the board look like drawing #1 (p. 37). What do we do to make it look like drawing #2? And so on, until we have a completed picture. Some of the more mature children like to create their own sequences for their friends to do.

For the reader to do

Plan a "following written directions" lesson like the one above. Share your lesson with your class.

● ● ●

Roberta has become so envious of Pat's reading that she has decided she, too, can read. I've known that she has been ready to do so, but in keeping with my policy of not pushing children, I didn't want to give her instruction until she expressed a desire to learn. It's strange how Pat inspired her. I suppose that Larry's reading was so much a part of him that she never saw it in relation to herself, but Pat's reading hit home! Suddenly she saw reading as something that could be done if she wanted to, and she *wanted* to! She does not read nearly as well as Larry and Pat, but she has made a good start.

This month we have been studying clothes—namely, choosing, styles, colors, and care. We went to a department store and to a combination laundry/dry-cleaning establishment. I noticed a greater sense of responsibility on the part of the children when we finished the unit; there are far fewer coats on the floor of the closet. That could be because on the day of the field trip I asked the dry cleaner what it might cost, typically, to clean a child's coat. She gave me a price, and I then proceeded to drop a pile of pennies totalling that amount on the counter. When the children saw that pile of money (and, no doubt, thought of all the bubble gum that it would buy), they gasped! My point was made!

This month, too, I have been trying a technique that John Warren Stewig suggested using when I attended an International Reading Association meeting at which he spoke. He suggested using different artists' interpretations of the same subject and asking children to go through the following three-step sequence. First, ask them to describe the object being viewed in clear, concrete terms. Next, have them compare and contrast objects being viewed. Last they are to value one of the objects, explaining why they prefer one interpretation over another. I used the three books, *One Fine Day, Mushroom in the Rain,* and *In the*

Rabbitgarden. Each of these has an illustration of a fox. I held up one at a time and allowed the children time to describe what they saw. I tried to elicit clear, concise statements that showed thought, observation, and conclusion. I asked them to tell me how all three foxes were alike. Typically they said that all had four legs, a nose, a mouth, and so on. Then we got into contrasting elements which brought on comments about size, color, and ferocity. In the valuing step, I asked them to tell me specifically what kinds of things made them prefer one of the foxes. Then I asked which one seemed to be the most gentle or the most fierce.

Stewig says that the same thing can be done by using varied interpretations of the same story so that children can see the various ways in which different artists deal with *The Three Pigs,* for instance. We have been doing this twice a week for three weeks now, and I plan to continue that schedule for the remainder of the school year. One thing that I have noticed lately, though, is that whenever I am reading a story that has a character similar to one of those in Stewig's visual/verbal literacy lessons, the children will comment. Mandy recently said, "Look at that snake [in *The Crows of Pearblossom*]! I don't like him as much as the one in *In the Rabbitgarden.* Doesn't he look scary and mean, Rita?" The children agreed that they much preferred the gentle snake of *In the Rabbitgarden.* Some stated that the snake in *Crictor* was their favorite because he could come to school!

The children are telling more and more stories, just as I am, because of another new storytelling method we are using. I find a book with illustrations that I think the children will like, and I place a sheet of clear acetate over the pictures. I then trace those pictures and fill in with color. It's important to use permanent magic markers, because water color doesn't adhere to the acetate. After they have dried, I seal the side I drew on with clear adhesive plastic in order to protect the ink and give the acetate substance. I cut them out carefully, close to the edges, and place them on an overhead projector! I have just created transparencies which can be used to tell or re-tell stories. I don't try to make pictures of everything in the book—just enough pictures to carry the story along.

For the reader to do

Choose a picture storybook that you especially like. Create a set of acetate pictures to tell that story according to the directions above. Tell your story to or with a group of children.

● ● ●

Another way that I have encouraged storytelling is by having the children play with cutouts from storybooks sealed with some of the clear adhesive plastic (I've been accused of having stock in the company, I use so much of it!). I attach a small bit of sandpaper to the back of the little cutout, and it is ready for use on a flannel board.

Our poetry writing is coming along so well! I read Mary O'Neill's *Hailstones and Halibut Bones* to the children and discussed with them that Miss O'Neill thought colors could represent things and feelings, as well as thoughts. Then we did a poetry format (again as a group) that has this configuration:

> I feel ——————
> I see ——————
> I hear ——————
> I smell ——————
> I taste ——————
> I feel——————

The unifying factor here is the repetition of the phrase "I feel." To help the children recognize the five senses the poem deals with, I told them that I would give them several days to work on a collage of pictures from magazines, newspapers, and other sources that portray the five senses. They were to find as many pictures as they could that would finish the phrases I listed. It was a messy assignment, but the children helped to create several poems and collages. In addition the children were proud because the collages described *them* as individuals. I had the children work individually on this project, so I did have to help out some of the more unsure children such as Paul and Chip. Paul struggled—with my help—to find one example for each phrase; Chip kept asking the others to save any pictures of peanuts that they found for him—he wanted to finish each phrase the same way! When some of the children wondered if they could finish the phrase with just one word, I told them that they could. Others complained that they couldn't do that—they needed to say more! I told them that the only rule was that they finish the phrases, no matter how many words they used.

In deference to Valentine's Day, we baked heart-shaped cookies that the children decorated using paintbrushes dipped in food coloring mixed with water. These are rolled cookies, so I have many cookie cutters available for them to use. These cookies are nearly indestructible—kids simply cannot roll too much flour into them!

NURSERY SCHOOL COOKIES

We need:	*We do:*
½ cup oleo (*not* butter) ¾ cup granulated sugar	Cream sugar and oleo. Add egg and vanilla; mix well.

1 egg
½ tsp. vanilla
2 cups flour
¼ tsp. salt
½ tsp. baking powder
½ tsp. soda
2–3 tbsp. milk
Food coloring

Sift dry ingredients and add some to the oleo mixture. Add some milk and stir. Then add dry ingredients, then milk. Keep adding that way until both are gone.

Chill at least an hour (overnight is better.)

Roll out dough on a floured surface. Cut with cookie cutters and decorate with paint brushes dipped in food coloring and water.

Bake at 350° about 7–8 minutes, or until edges start to turn brown.

MARCH

When Dr. Link, the college supervisor, was here in January, she asked me if I would accept a student teacher for the spring quarter. I told her I would be delighted if she had a male interested in kindergarten. I have so many boys with special problems that I thought a male figure in the classroom would be a big help.

"Sorry, Miss Launch," she told me, "but we're having a hard time drafting young men into the primary grades in general. Chances are pretty slim that we can find one interested enough in kindergarten to want to spend a whole quarter there."

So much for that hope, I thought. Imagine my surprise when Dr. Link brought over Mr. Mutatus and introduced him as my new student teacher! I know the shock on my face must have shown because Mr. Mutatus said, "I know. I look a bit old to be doing this kind of thing. It's just that my children are nearly grown and I have worked as an accountant for many years to support them. Now it's time for me to do what I want to do with the rest of my life."

"Then you're not a faculty member from the university?"

"Oh, no. I'm a 45-year-old man about to be reborn! I always did want to be a teacher, but I got sidetracked and am just now getting back to it."

Well, that was the beginning! Mr. Mutatus and I have been working closely together to plan the remainder of the school year for the children. He's a real joy to have in the room. He seems to anticipate what needs to be done before the need arises. I tell him that it is his paternal instinct coming out! We are now Helen and Ed to one another, for it seemed so silly for a man almost old enough to be my father to continue calling me Miss Launch. Ed has many fine ideas from his experiences with his own children. Now when Steve brings in something that creeps, I can admire it from a distance and let Ed take over! What a relief!

After school every day, as we plan for the next day and for the rest of the quarter, we also share our ideas about education. He agrees that we need to saturate the children with literature. Since he has just finished his children's literature course, he has introduced me to many fine books of which I was unaware.

One of Ed's really good ideas was to gather the children around him as usual for the morning opening exercises, and then announce that they would be playing a game that might take all morning to finish, but that it didn't matter because they could play the game while they worked! Surprise, surprise! Each child was going to have the picture of an animal pinned on his or her back, and they were to guess the animal. They could ask only two questions of each classmate, and the questions could only be answered yes or no. The purpose of this restriction was to encourage a maximum use of language on the part of the one guessing, and to discourage unnecessary hints and clues. The children seemed very excited by the idea and were ready to begin immediately! Ed reminded them that they were to continue their work while trying to guess, and that it would be a good idea to think carefully before asking questions so that the questions wouldn't be wasted. He gave the following demonstration: "Miss Launch, will you please pin the picture of an animal to my back?" I did so, and he turned so that his back—and the picture—were toward the children. There was much giggling from some of the children.

"Okay. Steve, do I have hair? No? Hmmmm. Steve, do I have six legs? No? Thank you. Let's see now—Rita, do I have wings? No. All right, do I have scales? Ah, ha! Now we're getting some place. Mandy, do people catch me to eat? No, that means that I'm not a fish. Do I crawl? I thought I might. Horace, am I a snake?"

The children were amazed that Ed guessed the animal so quickly. He explained that animals are in groups and that he was trying to find which group he was in. One large group that includes bears, cats, dogs, beavers and people was the one he was asking about first—they all have fur or hair. When he knew that the animal didn't have fur or hair, he knew that it had to be an insect or an amphibian (living both on land and in water) or a bird or a reptile (an animal with scales). "Listen carefully" was his last injunction before pinning on the animals.

"Mr. Mutatus, can we ask you and Miss Launch questions, too?"

"You most certainly may," he answered. And the game was on! Larry, Hilda, Roberta, and Steve guessed theirs rather quickly, for they had paid attention to what was told to them and tried logically to figure out what to ask next. Daisy used up all her questions by running from person to person asking questions like, "Am I a deer? Am I a goat?" rather than trying to find the category and proceed logically. It took most of the children the entire morning to determine what they were. Paul managed to find out that he was a dog, though his guess was based on luck, rather than system. Mitch never figured his out because he kept trying to start arguments with those who answered his questions. He wanted so much to own a horse that he was convinced that a horse must be the animal pictured on his back. Whenever the children would give him an answer that didn't fit his mind-set, he would argue with them, insisting that they must be wrong! Carl guessed "deer" fairly early, partially, I think, because he likes deer so much. And so it went—an interesting exercise for the children. They've already asked Ed to let them play it again soon.

I asked Ed why he had chosen animals to concentrate on. He explained that it would be much more difficult for the children if they had several categories to choose from. If, for instance, they knew that they might be either a form of transportation, an animal, or some kind of food, they would waste several guesses trying to discover the general category. Ed chose animals because children are attracted to animals and would probably respond best in the initial game if they enjoyed the chosen category. Later on we could use other categories.

One of our field trips this month was to the office of one of our local dentists. He explained all of the equipment to the children and let them take turns sitting in the chairs in the work areas. I am sure that he allayed many of the children's fears, or, at least my own! However, the best trip this month was to the Young People's Library at the University.

Ed and I had talked about my plans to take the children to a library, and he had suggested that instead of the town library which many of these children have already used that we take them all to the University Library and get cards for the children to use. The University Library has many more books for children to choose from. I hadn't planned to have Ed supervise a field trip until May, but since he is so familiar with the children's library at the University, I let him go ahead. He didn't seem to be the least bit concerned about the planning or the execution of this trip, so I asked him about it. His explanation: "Look, Helen, if you had taken as many Girl Scouts, Boy Scouts, church groups, and 4-H'ers on trips as I have, you wouldn't be worried either!" He did a terrific job!

The children have been working all year on matching upper-case letters to upper-case letters, and more recently they have been matching lower-case to lower-case letters. At last we're ready to begin matching upper- and lower-case letters. One of my tricks is to tell them that while they were outside an elf came in and mixed up all those nice letters we had been playing with—could anyone help us to get them straightened out again? Of course, there are always several volunteers! We concentrate on three pairs at a time, which is a workable number for them. Also, I always begin with those upper- and lower-case letters which tend to resemble one another except for size (such as Ss) to further insure success.

I also play a game of "concentration" with the letters that we are currently working on. I shuffle the six letter-cards and place them face down in a two-by-three array. The children take turns selecting two of the letter cards to be revealed. They are then turned over. If they match, they keep the cards. If they do not match, the cards are turned back over to be chosen at a later time by someone who can remember the position of the letters.

Another game for group work after all of the upper- and lower-case letters have been studied is a game like "Go Fish." We have two different groups of cards, one each for upper- and lower-case. The cards are shuffled together, and three cards are dealt to each player. If the player has a match of letter forms, the cards are put on the table. After everyone is given a chance to do this, the player to the left of the dealer asks another player if he or she has a particular letter. If the answer is "yes," the card must be relinquished. The player continues to ask for cards until he is told to "Go Fish" by a player who doesn't have the card asked for. The first player then picks a card from the remainder of the deck which has been placed in the center of the playing area. The first player to have all his or her cards matched and on the table is the winner.

An individual activity for matching is played with the bottom of an old ditto master box. All twenty-six letters of the alphabet, upper-case form, are written on the bottom of the box. The lower-case forms are on separate cards which can be placed over the upper-case forms. In the lid of the box is the answer key showing which forms match, so that children can check their own work and correct errors immediately.

The third-graders from Mrs. Wise's class have been making books for the children as well as coming down to take dictation so that the kindergarteners can get *their* stories into print as well. The third-graders have been studying book binding and have made some very handsome books for the children to take home or to put in our classroom library. To thank them for all their help, we invited them to come help us eat the results of our next cooking effort—popcorn!

POPCORN

We need:	*We do:*
Large bag of popcorn	Put enough oil in bottom of popper to cover.
Cooking oil	
Popcorn popper	Put in enough popcorn to cover the bottom, too.
Salt	Plug in the popper.
	When the popping stops, put on the salt and eat it up!

APRIL

Spring is in the air! What a beautiful spring we are having! Much of the exuberance I feel is due to having Ed Mutatus in the classroom. Dr. Link has been here several times, and each time she just sits in the back of the room watching and smiling. She has confided to me that Ed is one of the strongest student teachers she has worked with; professionally and personally, he is quite well-adjusted and very competent. Dr. Link did admit that she had had some initial concerns about this placement, for when they had sent out a bulletin asking if any men would be willing to work with kindergarten children, Ed was the only one who had shown interest. Dr. Link was afraid that, due to his age, he might be too rigid and nervous to work with very young children.

"Ha!" I said. "That man can work *circles* around me and still have enough energy left for a rough-and-tumble game with the children!"

Dr. Link smiled and said, "I know. He comes to the afternoon seminars as full of pep and energy as when I see him here at 9 a.m. I asked him how he does it, and he told me that he loves it! For the first time in many years, he is excited to get up in the morning and begin a day."

Well, it shows! He has implemented a good many activities which *I* was hesitant to do. For example, he has the children working regularly at the workshop in a far corner of the room, learning to hammer and saw correctly (something which I need to learn, too). The children have created little tables—somewhat rickety!—shelves, and sculptures. There has been a lot of language activity back there, as well as the noise of all the tools.

The children have been creating greeting cards all year long, but some of the birthday cards for Jeff were just too much! Someone got the notion that even if he couldn't give Jeff a present, he could *wish* to give him a present. I don't know who began it, but both Ed and I were swamped with requests like "Please write, 'I wish I could give you this for your birthday!'" In walking around later, I noticed that they were cutting pictures out of our catalogues and magazines. The picture of a bike, swimming pool, motorcycle, or some other luxury would appear at the bottom of the written message, which was then passed over to Jeff for his birthday. Jeff was grinning from ear to ear all day long!

This was the perfect month for both of our field trips—one to a small farm owned by the grandparents with whom Daphne lives, and the other to the local greenhouse, which is within walking distance of the school. Even more exciting than the farm itself was the ride to get there, for Daphne's grandfather came to get us in a hay-covered wagon pulled by his huge old tractor. The children talked and wrote stories for weeks about the farm and the tractor.

We've been working with rhyming words, and one of my favorite books to use for this is *The Hungry Thing*. The children in the book meet the Hungry Thing and find that he will only eat silly rhymes for real words, so that if they want to feed him "noodles," they tell him he is eating "foodles"; "soup with a cracker" is "boop with a smacker," and so on. As we read the story, the children try to guess what the Hungry Thing is eating throughout the book. When we finish the book I tell them it is our turn to feed the Hungry Thing. I tell them to think of their favorite food and then to try to find a silly rhyme for it so that the

Hungry Thing will eat it. It's fun to play with words, and if children realize that when they are small, I think they will be more likely to enjoy words as they grow up. A love of words also will help make better readers.

The poetry we composed this month used an "I wish" format. I told the children that they were to think of four different things they wished for. The poem was to have five lines beginning with the words "I wish," but the first and the last lines were to be identical. Here is the large group poem that we did before breaking up into small groups for more poetry writing.

> I wish spring was here. (Steve)
> I wish that the sun was warm. (Manuel)
> I wish that the frogs would make noises. (Butch)
> I wish I could go out without my coat. (Alex)
> I wish spring was here. (Steve)

The group work this month consists of sorting objects according to sounds. I have a large collection of the little plastic baskets that cherry tomatoes come in which I have labeled with upper- and lower-case consonants. Each of the four groups gets five baskets with letters on them and one marked with a question mark. The group's task is to sort out a paper bag full of odds and ends such as rubber bands, a toy car, and a favor from a birthday party into the baskets that have those beginning sounds. If there are any objects in the bag which do not fit into any of the baskets (and there are some of those), then they are put into the "question mark" box. The children must decide where something belongs, for a toy firefighter's hat could be placed in several different baskets: *f* for *fire hat*, *h* for *hat*, *r* for *red*, *p* for *plastic*. I give them five minutes to complete the task, and check the work of the groups after the timer rings. Again, most of them seem to enjoy racing against the clock, though it seems to make Betty nervous. She wants plenty of time to make absolutely certain that everything has been correctly placed. Mort works at the same pace whether the timer is on or not, which is somewhat infuriating to his group.

Ed Mutatus has been responsible for the "Things-to-Do" Center this month, and I think that his "boxes" project is worth reporting on. He had constructed a "feely" box by cutting a hole in one end of a shoebox and attaching to the hole a sock with the toe end cut off. He then placed a comb in the box and permitted the children to reach in through the sock and into the box where they could feel the object but not see it. Each child was permitted a few seconds to feel the object and then report to Ed what the object might be. Ed changed the objects frequently so that the children would have many opportunities to use the sense of touch. The next project was somewhat harder for the children, for he had arranged the experiences in order of difficulty. This time a single child would feel the object, describe it in three different ways, and then guess what it was. The third kind of experience that Ed gave them was to let a child see an object, describe it to the other children, and let *them* guess what was being described. The fourth task was even more complicated, for this time the child felt an object, described it to the other children, and they had to guess what it was that he or she had felt. Occasionally, as a variation, Ed would let several children feel the same object so that they could help one another with the description. The rest of the group had to try to guess what it was that was being felt. This worked out very well particularly, when Paul, Chip, or Joyce, who have a great deal of difficulty verbalizing, described the object. However, it is obviously easier for the group if the clues given are clearly stated, a skill these three were unable to master.

The three gained from listening to the descriptions given by the more verbal children, however, for they experienced the same object and could compare their own perceptions with what was being said. The fifth task with the "feely" box was to have a child feel an object and then give a one-word clue. After a guess was made, he or she gave another one-word clue, and so on. A particularly interesting game was one that took place this week. Steve reached into the box and felt the object. He said, "Prickly." There were guesses of *porcupine, cactus,* and *pins.* The next clue was "Woody." The children were stumped for a moment, until Larry guessed that it might be a plank from the workshop. The next clue: "Tree." Something from a tree that is wooden and prickly?

"Oh, I know, I know!" exclaimed Hilda, who had been putting all the clues together. "It's bark from the tree!" She sat back smug and confident.

"No, that's not it. Seeds."

The crest-fallen Hilda began muttering, "Seeds? Seeds. Seeds! It's a pine cone! Am I right this time, Steve?" Steve's nod reassured her that her deduction skills had been well-utilized.

The most difficult of all was the last project—identifying the object within a wrapped box by asking questions of Mr. Mutatus. They found this to be a very challenging task. They knew that it could not be a chair, for instance, for the package would not accommodate that large an object. The questioning techniques of the children had increased with the readiness activities (described above) which they had been doing for the few weeks prior to this exercise, and they soon guessed that the object was a shoe. Ed got the idea for this project from one of his field experiences prior to student teaching: the teacher he had observed presented a wrapped package to the children for them to determine the contents. The task was too difficult for them because they had not had exercises leading up to this game. As a result, the children were unable to figure out what was in the box, the teacher was frustrated and embarrassed, and Ed had tried to figure out what had gone wrong. He concluded that the activity was incomplete and useless until he set up the activities that he had our children do.

It's been a busy month, and I thought that we needed a special treat so I told the children that we were going to make a "Crazy Cake." As you read along, you will find out why it has that name!

CRAZY CAKE

We need:	*We do:*
3 cups flour	Sift flour, sugar, soda, cocoa, and salt into an un-
2 cups sugar	greased 13 X 9″ pan.
2 tsp. soda	
6 tbsp. cocoa	Make three holes in the flour mixture.
1 tsp. salt	In the first hole, put the oil.
12 tbsp. salad oil	
2 tsp. vanilla	In the second hole, put the vanilla.
2 tbsp. vinegar	In the third hole, put the vinegar.
2 cups of water	Pour the cold water over this and mix.
10 tbsp. cooking oil	
	Bake at 350° for 30 minutes.

MAY

I'm not sure that I could have survived this past month without the aid of Ed Mutatus! He has taken more and more responsibility for the instructional program, freeing me to catch up on some of the things which I must do.

He made arrangements for, and supervised, the trips this month. The first was a day trip to the zoo with children from both kindergarten sessions, as well as many parents. They took sack lunches. Everyone returned exhausted but exhilarated (and only a few of the children got sick on the bus).

Ed had a fine idea for the last field trip—he asked the two first-grade teachers if they would permit our children to visit their rooms to acquaint them with the teachers and also to give them some idea of what they could expect to see in first grade. Both teachers agreed, and gave the children a fine overview of the first-grade program. Mrs. Wright had one of her students act as guide around the room, and she had others who explained the various things that they were working on. The kindergarteners were quite impressed with the "big" first-graders who were so helpful to them, and all of them said that they wanted to be in Mrs. Wright's room next year.

After the children had finished their tour, Ed asked them how they would feel about doing something similar for the kindergarten class who would be arriving next fall.

"You mean that Miss Launch is going to have *more* kids here? I thought she just taught us," said Daphne.

"Now you know that there is an afternoon class, too, Daphne. You know that I teach other children."

"Yes, but we thought . . . I thought . . . I mean . . ."

"I will remember all of you. You don't have to worry about that. We care about one another, and when we care about people, we don't forget them. But you can't stay with me forever. You are ready to go on and learn more. You don't want to do the same things again. First grade is so exciting! You'll love it, but remember to say 'hello' to me once in a while!"

Ed listened to this with some interest, but now he got them back to the point of discussion. "You still haven't answered. Shall we do something for the next kindergarten class like what they did in first grade?" Amid cries of "Yes! Yes!" there was one, Larry, who commented that that would be difficult, since we didn't know who the children would be.

"How about this?" Ed began, and outlined the plan for creating a mural depicting the various kindergarten activities. The children would put it up on the bulletin board and leave it there. When the fall classes came in they would see some work done by "big" kindergarteners telling them what to expect. The children loved the idea, and so did I. One of my pet peeves has always been that I begin the school year without any art work from children on the walls—now there will be.

SQUIRT has been highly successful this year. We're up to five minutes a day as a class. However, some children continue reading after the timer rings. Mandy told me that she enjoys the idea of everyone reading at the same time.

Ed asked if he could plan the final cooking experience for the children, explaining he wanted to have them prepare breakfast at school. Nothing too complicated—just French toast, juice, and milk. We each brought in an electric skillet from home and breakfast was ready rather quickly. It was enormously successful. I didn't think Chip would ever stop eating, and I was sure that Daisy wouldn't, though she informed us that she had a huge breakfast before arriving at school! Even Mort seemed to show a flicker of interest—I suppose because it was not our normal routine (he seems so bored by routine).

My routine lately has included writing reports about each child. This is something new to me, and it has taken me a while to get in the swing of it.

ALEX: Alex enjoys sharing his creative stories with the others in class. He has a fine imagination and has been working hard to develop the oral skills necessary to communicate his ideas. He is a very responsible child, one whom I can count on to work hard at a task. He can tie his shoes and do other self-care tasks.

BETTY: Betty is a delightful, responsible child. She has had a few difficulties adjusting to being in the same class with Roberta, but I think that she has come to accept that. She has worked very hard to produce stories that are creative, but they do not come easily to her. She entered school with all of the requisite self-care skills. She is on the verge of reading.

BUTCH: Butch has many discipline problems that interfere with his learning and, unfortunately, the learning of others. He and Larry seem to have a special antipathy for one another. His stories tend to be less creative and with fewer vocabulary words than I hoped. He can tie his shoes with no difficulty. He does need some further experiences at home to help him accept responsibility.

CARL: Carl's active imagination and the stories he has shared with the class about his imaginary friends have delighted us all. He is a verbal child who is ready to begin reading instruction. He accepts responsibility well and is quite capable of accomplishing the self-care skills.

CHIP: Chip is speaking in sentences now, even though they are not always complete. He tells stories that are factual and does his best to complete whatever task is assigned to him. He has mastered the self-care skills which we have worked on. He needs further vocabulary enrichment before he begins the actual process of reading.

DAISY: Daisy still has many problems. She tends toward egocentricity to an extreme degree. She has trouble accepting responsibility and is highly distractable. She has all the self-care skills, but rarely uses them on her own. Her language skills have not developed very much this year. She has much potential that we must try to help to develop.

DAPHNE: Daphne, though not highly creative, is very responsible and makes many efforts to contribute to class discussions. She has a large vocabulary. She dresses herself and was one of the helpers for other children who could not yet do so.

JEFF: Jeff is of great concern to me. He rarely speaks unless spoken to, and does not become involved often with the activities in the classroom. He has a vocabulary deficiency which we have worked to overcome this year. He came to school completely able to care for himself. He is one of the most responsible children I have ever taught.

JOYCE: Joyce, though very quiet, shows flashes of wit and ingenuity. She has a great deal of interest in words. When she does speak, she exhibits a large vocabulary, many experiences, and a highly developed imagination. She completes her work, though must sometimes be reminded that it exists, for she daydreams frequently. She has not expressed great interest in reading yet, but when she does, she should learn easily.

HILDA: Hilda uses her natural sense of logic to deal with many classroom situations. She has had a fascination for words during the entire year and is ready to begin reading instruction in the fall. She is quite responsible, though she has little patience with those who have not yet attained skills that she considers important, such as self-care. She always had imaginative stories to tell and used her strong vocabulary to do so.

HORACE: Horace is one of those children teachers love to have: he's cheerful, friendly, cooperative, and willing to learn. He has a good vocabulary and uses it to tell interesting stories. He was one of my best helpers with teaching other children how to "button up" clothing. He is most eager to learn to read and write.

LARRY: Larry entered kindergarten already reading. He has an excellent memory and vocabulary. He does not flaunt his knowledge, though, and the other children take his abilities for granted and seek his help nearly as often as mine in reading things for them. His stories reflect his excellent vocabulary and imagination.

MANDY: Mandy is quite ready to begin her reading experiences next fall. She is a very capable, creative, and unusual child. She tends to daydream some, but always manages to complete her work. She has an excellent vocabulary and talks frequently of the many unusual experiences she has had. She needs to develop more confidence in herself and her abilities, for she tends to underrate herself.

MANUEL: Manuel has been one of the hardest workers in the class this year. He takes his responsibilities seriously, and he endeavors to complete tasks accurately. He makes frequent contributions to the class discussions. He has increased his oral language so that he now speaks in entire sentences.

MIKE: Mike is an extremely active child; he is constantly involved in something and has no difficulty keeping busy! He is a creative child with a fine oral language background. He means well, but does not find it easy to carry through on assignments. He needs to develop more of a sense of responsibility for his own actions; when that occurs, he will be able to face the task of learning academic material.

MITCH: Mitch needs to learn to accept responsibility and to bear up under the teasing of others. Sometimes, no matter how hard he is trying, circumstances prevent him from being as good as he would like to be. He responds well to praise, but negatively to criticism. He has a fine vocabulary and an active imagination which we should help him channel.

MORT: Mort doesn't seem to be involved with ideas or materials in school. He has a good understanding and speaking vocabulary, and I think he could come up with some fine stories and contributions to class if he would get involved. I hope that he will be encouraged to find reading materials that interest him so that he will learn.

PAT: Pat began reading instruction in January. She has a great deal of interest in the process and should experience few difficulties. She especially enjoys trying to write down her stories. She is helpful and extremely reliable.

PAUL: Paul is a kind, unselfish child. He is still unable to button his coat or to tie his own shoes. He is still the victim of many fears, and sometimes doesn't even want to go to the playground because of some fear he cannot verbalize. He is not yet speaking in whole sentences, and, indeed, often does not respond when spoken to. When Paul does say something, there is nothing creative about it—it is always a reflection of something that has just happened.

RITA: Rita is ready to read! She should have a fine time next year, for she has a good vocabulary, a rich background of experiences, and is a diligent worker. She has expressed quite an interest in letter sounds and was always a leader within her group during work on them.

ROBERTA: Roberta is a delightful child to have in the classroom. I can depend upon Roberta to brighten a gloomy day. She is highly verbal and imaginative. Very little goes unnoticed by her. She was spurred on to reading by noticing that another child had begun; that was all she needed.

STEVE: Steve has been our science consultant-in-residence! He is the most knowledgeable child of his age I have ever encountered. If his reading instruction next year can focus on this interest, reading should come easily to him. He is totally self-reliant in the self-care skills. He has helped other children attain this same independence. His stories tend to be factual and less imaginative. I hope that he will learn to express himself in this way, too.

The Kindergarten Meeting

As elementary supervisor, Miss Kurt was intrigued with the curriculum that Miss Launch had implemented in her classroom. It was her job to make certain that children received the best possible education. At first she had been concerned that these children would be behind the others when they entered first grade because Miss Launch had told her that she could not in good conscience implement a whole-class reading program. Miss Launch had told her supervisor that she would give instruction to those children who were ready, but that she was not about to try to teach them *all* to read. Miss Kurt visited the classroom throughout the year and was impressed with the progress that she had observed. As the months went by, she came to have a great deal of respect for Miss Launch's program. Therefore, it was a credit to Miss Launch that she was selected to address the spring meeting of kindergarten teachers for the school system.

Miss Launch was nervous at the prospect of her address. She knew these teachers only slightly from other meetings held during the year, and she knew from those times that many of them did not agree with her. She decided that she would need to be well-prepared if she were to make any impact. To that end, she dug out a copy of a poem which had appeared in *Elementary English*, called "When Johnny's Beginning," by Miona Wilkinson:

> Johnny will learn, and Johnny will grow
> Johnny will read and love it;
> But don't tear apart the pretty word
> 'Til Johnny's seen the beauty of it.
>
> The snow, the bird, the flower, the cat,
> The puppy, the pony, and Mother—
> These are so much better
> Than $\bar{a}$ and $\breve{a}$ and $\bar{e}$ and $\breve{e}$ and $\bar{o}$ and $\breve{o}$,
> Or the sound of any letter.

What's pretty about a beginning *c*;
or a short *a* or an ending *t*,
To cause a fellow to love it?
But a *cat*, a whole *cat*, with
its fur and its purr—
He'll remember the softness of it.

Johnny must love it
If Johnny's to grow
And who ever loved
A long or short *o*?

She thought that this poem summed up many of the things which she felt, and reflected the kind of classroom which she had finally developed. Miss Launch opened the meeting with the poem and began to summarize the activities her class had engaged in for the past year. She showed several of her class charts and told the group that several areas had been emphasized: following and giving directions (both oral and written), dramatization of stories and poems, creative story-telling, listening, observing, oral language development, poetry, self-care skills, literature/response activities, field trips, and learning that reading is for a purpose. She brought with her samples of some of the group poems that had been done during the year. She also showed them some of the "lap story" characters which had been placed in the story center. The teachers expressed considerable interest in this technique, and she went through the steps of a lap story with them by having them create one based on the story of Little Red Riding Hood.

She told the teachers that virtually every classroom activity was geared toward the attainment of one major goal: acquisition of oral language skills, because children who are handicapped by vocabulary deficiency experience much difficulty in school and in society. The greatest single indicator of intelligence in our society is vocabulary. Success in our culture is dependent upon how well one can manipulate the language. In addition, judgments about a person's character and capabilities are often based upon the language that a person employs.

For the reader to do

Miss Launch's chart (on p. 55) is incomplete. Make a duplicate chart and write in the rest of the children's names and more areas to be evaluated. Include social, academic, physical, and self-care skills. Indicate mastery of these skills with a check mark, and be prepared to defend your decisions.

● ● ●

	attends to stories read	responds when spoken to	knows address	knows phone number	can recognize own name in print	can match like forms	can match upper- and lower-case letters	follows two spoken directions	follows three spoken directions	knows color names	can name other children in class	follows three written directions	follows four written directions	ties own shoes			
Alex	★	★	★	★	★	★		★		★	★	★		★			
Betty	★	★	★	★	★	★	★	★	★	★	★	★	★	★			
Daisy		★	★	★		★											
Jeff	★	★	★	★	★	★		★	★	★	★	★	★	★			
Butch		★	★	★	★			★		★	★			★			
Chip	★	★	★		★	★		★						★			
Carl	★	★	★	★	★	★		★		★	★	★		★			
Daphne	★	★	★	★	★	★		★		★	★	★		★			
Hilda	★	★	★	★	★	★	★	★	★	★	★	★	★	★			
Horace	★	★	★	★	★	★	★	★	★	★	★	★	★	★			
Joyce	★	★	★	★	★	★	★	★	★	★	★	★	★	★			
Pat	★	★	★	★	★	★	★	★	★	★	★	★	★	★			

Miss Launch's talk was followed by a question-and-answer session. One of the first, and one of the most predictable, questions asked concerned the academics in kindergarten: "Why aren't you preparing the children for what they will be doing in first grade, Miss Launch? We all know that they will be further ahead if they start reading early. They need to be working in workbooks and doing ditto papers or they will never be disciplined enough to carry out first-grade assignments. Besides, parents insist that their children read earlier and earlier. I can't fight that kind of pressure."

"As a matter of fact," replied Miss Launch, "research seems to indicate that an early start on reading does *not* produce gains which hold up over a period of time (Gans, 1963; McCormick, 1966; Spock, 1965). Just because very young children can read, does not mean that they *should* read. It seems to me that these youngsters have so many things to learn that are important prerequisites for successful reading, that we should build a firm foundation of experiences and vocabulary so that when we *do* teach reading it will be accomplished much more easily. As to the use of workbooks and work papers to teach children, I can only reply that I would be bored stiff grading all those papers and books for the fifty children in my two sections! Every night! No thank you! I'll spend my evenings preparing materials for class centers and planning group and individual activities. I think that you would find the groups I have worked with to be as responsible as any other class group. In my room I expect the children to begin to accept some of the responsibility for their own learning. And that, after all, is what it's all about—they must learn to be independent learners. I handled the parental pressure by carefully explaining my program to the parents, and then getting them involved in the classroom."

"Well, I for one am glad that somebody is standing up to all these parents who think that they can dictate what goes on in the school," spoke up one elderly teacher. "I think that we had better get kindergarten back to what it was meant to be—a time for the children to play with other children and see the inside of the school at the same time. We provide our greatest service to parents by taking care of the children so that Mother can work or run around to club meetings!"

Miss Launch looked startled for a moment. "Oh, I'm afraid that I must have created the wrong impression! I *do* feel that we must provide a strong academic program for the children, but not in some of the more standard or traditional ways. We worked with letter sounds and "read" and "wrote" stories. In my class, however, I will not pressure children to perform identically. Larry, Pat and Roberta were the only three who received formal reading instruction; the rest of the class had readiness activities."

"How do you answer parents who want to know how you will determine if their children are 'ready to read,' Miss Launch?"

"Well, I can point to Guszak (1972) as support for my contention that standardized reading readiness tests cannot be considered reliable predictors of reading success, nor can they provide the teacher with any clear direction in helping children to attain readiness. Guszak's work shows that the teacher is as reliable as reading readiness tests in predicting how children will perform. *I* am the one who sees their children on an academic basis; *I* am the one who sees how they respond to stimuli; *I* am the one who must find the 'teachable moment.' "

"Thank you, Miss Launch, for your interesting talk. Having been in her classroom a dozen times this year, I have come to know that one of her weaknesses is food! I suggest that we all sample some of her children's cooking efforts, together with coffee, at the back of the room. May I also suggest that you visit Miss Launch's classroom to see her approach in action."

References

Anderson, Paul S. *Language Skills in Elementary Education.* Toronto, Ontario: The Macmillan Company, 1969.

Gans, Roma. *Common Sense in Teaching Reading.* Indianapolis: Bobbs-Merrill, 1963.

Ginsburg, Mirra. *Mushroom in the Rain.* New York: Macmillan, 1974.

Guszak, Frank. *Diagnostic Reading Instruction in the Elementary School.* New York: Harper and Row, 1974.

McCormick, Nancy. "The Countdown on Beginning Reading." *The Reading Teacher* 20 (1966):115–20.

O'Neill, Mary. *Hailstones and Halibut Bones.* New York: Doubleday, 1961.

Sendak, Maurice. *Where the Wild Things Are.* New York: Harper and Row, 1963.

Slepian, Jan, and Seidler, Ann. *The Hungry Thing.* New York: Scholastic Book Services, 1971.

Spock, Benjamin. "Why I Don't Believe in Speeding Up Primary Reading." *Redbook,* October, 1965.

Wilkinson, Miona. "When Johnny's Beginning." *Elementary English* 35 (1958).

Zemach, Harve. *Duffy and the Devil.* New York: Farrar, Strauss and Giroux, 1973.

Mrs. Wright

HIGHLIGHTS

Whole Class Stories

SQUIRT

Group Stories

Independent Activities:

   Listening Center

   Math Center

   Magazine Center

Rhyming Words

Individual Stories

Auditory Discrimination

Vocabulary and Classification

Initial Consonants

Objects Have Many Names

"I am Thinking of" Game

Consonant Substitution

Consonant-Plus-Context Clues

Picture-Word Cards

Chart of Christmas Words

Word Bank

Flannel-board Stories

Basals for Independent Reading

Story Parties

Digraphs and Blends

Parent Conferences

Revised A and P Sight Word List

Writing Center

Dictionaries

Two-syllable Words

Taba "List, Group, and Label" Lesson

Dialect Differences

Mrs. Wright

The Parent Meeting

September 13: Mrs. Wright sat in her first-grade classroom awaiting the arrival of the parents for their meeting. She remembered her first parent meeting and felt the same tightness in her stomach as she remembered that first night. One problem, of course, had been that although she was perfectly at home with groups of youngsters, she had been quite uncomfortable talking to adult audiences. The major problem was not knowing what to talk to them about! Mr. Topps had explained to her that the purpose of these beginning-of-school meetings was for each teacher to greet the parents and give them an overview of the program their children would be participating in during that year. He had gone on to say "Of course, first-grade parents are always most curious about the reading program. They want to know how you are going to transform their little ones into bookworms!" Mr. Topps had then volunteered to be present at her session, but Mrs. Wright had declined. The only thing worse than trying to explain her reading program to parents was having to explain it when she herself didn't understand it! And the only thing worse than both of those would be to have the principal there as a witness to her ignorance!

The first parents began to arrive. "Oh, Mrs. Wright, it is so good to see you again. Do you remember me? I'm Pat's mother, and I was Kate's mother. Well, I mean I still am, but she's in the third grade now. She did so enjoy your class." Mrs. Wright realized that she had reminisced for fifteen minutes and rose to greet the parents who were now streaming through the door.

"Welcome, parents, to first grade," Mrs. Wright began. "I have only had your children for a week now but I must say they are an exceptional group! I am sure we will have a busy, exciting year, and as the year goes on, I will want to talk with each of you about the progress of your children individually. Tonight, however, I would like to describe our first-grade reading program and respond to any questions you may have.

"If you will look around the room you will see some experience charts. These charts were dictated to me by your children and reflect the experiences we have had in this first week of school. This chart, titled 'George the Gerbil' is one we did on the first day of school. First, we sat very quietly and observed George for several minutes; then we talked about our observations. Finally, several of your children told me some things they had observed and I wrote them on the chart."

George the Gerbil

George lives all alone in his cage. (Daphne)
George is brown and furry and cute. (Betty)
George is always on the go. (Roberta)
George likes to eat vegetables. (Manuel)
He looks a little like a miniature rabbit. (Horace)
Gerbils are rodents. (Larry)

Mrs. Wright turned to the second chart on the wall. "This chart was written today," she continued. "It outlines all the things we do in order to get lunch in the cafeteria. To make this chart, we first made a list on the board and then decided which we had to do first, second, and so on."

How to Get Lunch

1. Remember to bring your lunch money. (Betty)
2. Give your lunch money to the teacher. (Pat)
3. Line up and walk quietly through the halls. (Alex)
4. Go to the cafeteria. (Steve)
5. Wait in line again. Then pick up your napkin and fork. (Mike)
6. Get your tray off the stack. (Mandy)
7. Walk by and let the ladies put food in your tray. (Rita)
8. Pick up your milk. (Carl)
9. Go way over to the other side and sit down. (Hilda)
10. Eat your lunch. (Mitch)

"As you can see, I write the sentences just the way your children say them and put each child's name after the sentence. In this way, most children have an immediate initial success with reading. They can remember what they said and can find the sentence with their name after it. They can then 'read' that sentence.

"We will be using whole class experience charts to record classroom events and to use as reading material all year. Starting next week, I will divide the children into four heterogeneous groups and do group stories with them. Since these groups will have only five or six children in each, every child will have a chance to contribute something to each story. Still later in the year, your children will be dictating individual stories to me and making up individual books. In fact, I would really appreciate the help of any of you who could volunteer an occasional morning to help write these stories since it is difficult for me to get around to twenty-two children. It is quite simple and enjoyable. You just never know what will pop out of a first-grader's mouth, as I'm sure you are more aware than I! Don't worry about their revealing family skeletons. They sometimes do, but they spin wild tales of fantasy and your skeletons would be lost in the tall tales. I'll make a deal with you. I'll promise not to believe anything fantastic they tell me happens at home if you promise not to believe their tales of what's happening at school!

"Many of you may be thinking that although it might be a good idea to write stories, that shouldn't comprise the total reading program. 'How are they going to learn the words they must know?' and 'What about phonics?' are questions you must have. Well, you can be sure that I will be teaching sight words and phonics. Each child will have his or her own individual word bank. Here is one left by a child who moved away unexpectedly last year and didn't take his with him. As you can see, he had quite a stack of words that he knew when he moved in February.

"These word banks are started when we begin the individual stories. Each child comes to that back table there and tells me his or her story. Sometimes the stories are thought up by the children, but more often, they are inspired by a picture, a display on the flannel board in the corner, or an activity going on in the room. As the child dictates the story to me, I type it. I then read the story aloud to make sure it is accurate. Then we talk about things like how many sentences a story has, which is the longest sentence, which is the longest word, why there is a period here and a question mark there. In this way, the children learn about the conventions of writing.

"Each child then goes back to his or her seat, reads the story and often illustrates it or pastes a magazine picture above it. Children usually read their stories to other members of the class. The last part of the project is for the child to underline each word he or she knows in the story.

"The next day, when this child comes back to dictate another story, I use a little card like this with a hole cut in it to isolate an underlined word. If the child can pronounce that word, it is a known word. I then write the word on a half of an index card and that card goes in the word bank. At first most of the words in the word bank are tangible, important-to-children words like *snake, hamburger* and *football*. Later, however, as certain words are used again in the stories, the child learns to recognize intangible frequently used words like *the, and, to*. In this way, each child learns a sight vocabulary which includes those words usually found in basal readers.

"The words in the word bank are then used to develop phonics skills. First we start out to develop the relationship between the consonants and their sounds. Once each child has some words in his or her bank that begin with *b*, for instance, the children sort through their banks and pull out all the words they have which begin with the letter *b*. I write *b, B* on the chalkboard and while individual children are dictating their stories to me, the rest are looking at all their words to find those that begin with *b*. This also helps keep them meaningfully occupied when I can't be with them.

"Just before lunch, we have our phonics lesson. Each child tells me the words he or she has collected beginning with *b* and I list them on a *b* chart. In this way we use the words the children already know to help them learn the sound of the consonants, the digraphs (*sh, ch, th, wh*) and the blends (*bl, st, cr,* and so on). We also develop many other sound-letter relationships by having children sort through their cards looking for something specific. We look for all the words which end in *s, ed,* or *ing,* or we look for all the compound words, or all the words which can be used to describe a boy, a car, a gorilla. From the individual stories, each child develops a personal bank of sight words. As a class, we then draw on these sight words to make generalizations about sounds and words.

"Well, it seems that I have talked most of our thirty minutes away and haven't left you much time for questions. But, let's use what little time we do have for questions."

A TALL MAN: This experience story method has some advantages, but will the children ever read real books in class?

MRS. WRIGHT: Oh, yes. I got so carried away explaining about language experience, I forgot to tell you about the rest of the program. The children certainly read. In fact, we have in this school something called SQUIRT—Sustained Quiet Reading Time. Every day at 1 p.m. a bell rings and the whole school reads—everyone from kindergarten through fifth grade. The cooks, secretary, custodian, and principal go to different rooms on a rotating basis so the children can see that they, too, are reading. This is crucial since the theory behind SQUIRT is that adults always talk about the importance of reading, but many children seldom see an adult read. We hope that by providing a daily time for free-choice reading and by reading with the children every day for six years that they will develop the habit of reading.

During SQUIRT everyone starts reading at the same time but different classes read for different amounts of time. In first grade we start with five minutes. I use this little timer to time it. Gradually, as the children become more able to sustain their silent reading we increase the time by one minute at a time. Last year, my first-graders got up to thirteen minutes! During this time, children and adults read whatever they choose.

In addition to this daily SQUIRT time, once the children are able to, they read independently from many basal readers and library books. During the second half of the year, we have story parties every Friday. The children fix a snack and get together in three's or four's and read a favorite story to each other. This gives them meaningful practice in oral reading. That was a rather long answer to your question but I do want to emphasize that language experience is a route to books, not a substitute for them.

AN ATTRACTIVE WOMAN: Mrs. Wright, if all children are doing different things, how are they going to be graded?

MRS. WRIGHT: We don't give grades in this school. We send home written reports with comments about the child's progress in each area. Twice a year, and more often if possible, we ask you to come in for an individual conference to talk about your child's progress. Most of our parents come to feel that this gives them a lot more information than a grade of *A* or *S* ever could.

Mrs. Penn: Mrs. Wright, I know we are about out of time, but I just want to say that this year you have my second child, Pat, and two years ago you had Kate. I think this is a fine way to teach reading. In fact, I requested that Pat be in your room.

Mrs. Wright ended the discussion by assuring the parents they were welcome to visit the class at any time, got the names of a few volunteer parents, and gave silent thanks that she had mastered parent meetings during her years of teaching.

Monthly Logs

SEPTEMBER

Now I understand why October is my favorite month—all month long I celebrate my survival of September! I have my groups formed and the children are learning about me, and I, about them. We have adapted quite well to one another. This class has a number of exceptional children on both ends of the scale. It is a rare day on which Paul doesn't return to his seat, put his head on his desk, and sob quietly. I have tried to contact his parents but there appears to be no father at home and his mother works. Miss Grant, the social worker, says his home situation is quite difficult so I will continue to do what I can for him here.

Daisy needs to be put on a diet! Her mother will be in next week; I wonder how I'll broach the subject to her. I guess it depends on her over-all reactions to the other concerns I have about Daisy. I'd like to say, "Your daughter is a spoiled, selfish child," but I'll restrain myself!

Poor Chip! I have managed to stop most of the taunts and snickers directed at his tattered clothes, but I know Butch and Mort still bother him on the playground. He goes his own way, however, and pays as little attention to them as possible. I do admire the child. He tries hard, but he knows so little about the world. The other day he made his first contribution to a group story. We were talking about fishing and Chip's sentence was, "You fry them up and they sure good." Joyce wanted to correct his sentence and I informed her that that was Chip's way of saying it and that was the way I was going to write it!

Larry, Roberta, and Pat are reading! Miss Launch tells me that Larry was reading when he came to kindergarten, and that Roberta and Pat learned during the year. Next month, when I begin the individual story writing, I will begin to confer with those three about their reading. Larry has more general knowledge than the other children. He is always adding some little-known (to the other children) fact to our stories. The others listen in awe and amazement. Yesterday Hilda said, "Larry, how do you know that?" He responded, "I read it in a book," as if that were the most natural thing in the world, and I guess it is for him.

Most of the groups seem quite well-balanced. They have chosen names for themselves: Roberta, Mort, Mitch, Jeff, and Daisy are the

Beatles. Rita, Paul, Pat, Horace, and Daphne are the *Bookworms*. Mandy, Mike, Manuel, Betty, Butch, and Alex are the *Mouseketeers*. Larry, Steve, Joyce, Chip, Carl, and Hilda are the *Beavers*. Roberta and Betty's mother called the other day to ask why the girls are in different groups and which one was in the higher group. I told her that no group was any better than any other, that these were not ability groups, but rather, groups heterogeneously formed to facilitate more participation in the stories. I told her that both girls were doing well and commented on how different their personalities were. She agreed that about the only things they shared were their brightness and common birthdates.

I have begun having the children work independently this month so that I can begin individual stories next month. Presently, I have three independent work centers in the room: a story center, a magazine center, and a math center. During the first two weeks of the month I worked with the groups in each of the centers. I made sure that they knew what they were to do in each center and how to get out and put away the materials. Each morning I do a brief orientation to the materials and activities in each center.

The four groups rotate through the four activities during the morning two-and-one-half hour block. On Mondays, the Beatles start off the morning in the story center. There, they put on headphones and listen to a story. Sometimes I have copies of the book in which they can read along as they listen if they choose to. They then complete a short listening comprehension exercise which they bring with them when their group meets with me. At 9:30 this group moves to the magazine center. Here they look through magazines and newspapers for a particular object, word or letter, cut it out, and paste it on a large chart on the bulletin board in that center. So far they have looked for "Things that Move," "Things to Eat," "Animals" and the letters *Bb, Ff, Mm, Ss, Tt*.

At 10:00, we have our morning snack. Each week a different child has the responsibility of setting the timer for fifteen minutes and giving us a one-minute signal just before time is up. During this one minute, the children clean up and try to get to their next activity before the buzzer sounds. This is a good system for getting us all back to our morning work.

At 10:15, the Beatles come to me. We go over the listening comprehension exercise together and then talk a little about the story they heard and their morning's activities. For the rest of the half-hour, we are busy either writing a new chart story, re-reading the completed ones, or doing word development exercises.

For the reader to do

Here is a listening comprehension exercise Mrs. Wright made for her children to complete after they had listened to *Hugh and Fitzhugh* (Goodspeed, n. d.).

The class listened to the story she had taped. One child held the book and turned the pages when the bell sounded. The children then read along as Mrs. Wright's taped voice read the directions and the other printed material on the listening comprehension exercise sheet:

"In the story you have just heard, three of the following things were said about Fitzhugh. Listen as I read all five statements. Put a circle around three statements which describe Fitzhugh. When you have finished, save your paper until your group meets with Mrs. Wright.

    1. He looks like a mutt.
    2. He sure is shy.
    3. He's a lazy old dog.
    4. Friendly.
    5. He's hard to handle."

Choose a picture-story book and construct a listening comprehension exercise as a follow-up to that story.

● ● ●

```
                 Giraffes
                 Giraffes

Giraffes have very long necks.   (Mort)
Giraffes have very long necks.

I saw a giraffe when my mother took me to the zoo.  (Daisy)
I saw a giraffe when my mother took me to the zoo.

Giraffes eat only leaves and plants.   (Mitch)
Giraffes eat only leaves and plants.

I think giraffes are the tallest animals in the world.  (Jeff)
I think giraffes are the tallest animals in the world.

If a giraffe wanted to come into this room, he would have
If a giraffe wanted to come into this room, he would have

to come in feet first.  (Roberta)
to come in feet first.
```

Yesterday I gave the Beatles two typed copies of their most recent story. I had left space between the lines so that we could cut the sentences from one sheet, mix them up, and paste them directly under the same sentence on the other sheet. The children enjoyed these individual matching activities. After we had done the first three sentences, Roberta wanted to know if she could cut the individual sentences into words and paste them. She had second-guessed my future plan, and so I let her go ahead. Her story is shown above.

At 10:45, the Beatles go to the math center. There they count, classify, measure, and manipulate objects. We use half of the allotted math time for these activities. At 11:15 we meet in a group and talk about how the morning went. New additions to the charts are discussed and praised; discoveries are shared and complaints registered. We are now more than ready for lunch!

Each day a different group begins the rotation, starting in the story center. Fridays, however, are "magic" days. We usually do something different first thing in the morning and write a whole-class story based on that experience. We then review our other whole-class stories and do word activities. There is only one possible way to keep all this movement straight—a chart the Beatles and I made to show their schedule.

Morning Schedule

Beatles

	Monday	Tuesday	Wednesday	Thursday	Friday
9:00	Story Center	Magazine	Math	Mrs. Wright	Whole Class Activities
9:30	Magazine Center	Mrs. Wright	Story	Math	Whole Class Activities
10:00	Break	Break	Break	Break	Break
10:15	Mrs. Wright	Math	Magazine	Story	Whole Class Activities
10:45	Math Center	Story	Mrs. Wright	Magazine	Whole Class Activities

The charts for the other groups are similar to this one. Each group rotates in order through the story center, magazine center, meeting with me and the math center. The difference is which center they begin in. On Mondays, for example, the Bookworms are in the magazine center first, then meet with me at 9:30. After break, they go to the math center and finish the morning in the story center. On Mondays, the Mouseketeers begin their morning with me, then rotate through the other centers. The Beavers begin their Mondays in the math center and end their morning with me. While this may seem confusing, the charts make it all quite clear.

To most first-graders, Halloween is second only to Christmas in generating excitement and distractions. I try to build on this excitement and channel their energies. Several of our Friday whole-class stories related to Halloween. We carved a jack-o'-lantern and then wrote down the steps in sequence. I read a newspaper article to them about some children being hurt on Halloween and we made a list of Halloween safety rules. We planned our Halloween party and made lists of what was needed and who would bring each item.

We also did a lot of work with rhyming words this month. I began by making sure that the children could hear if two words rhymed. All but Paul and Daisy now can tell if two words rhyme and pick out the one that doesn't rhyme in a series of three words (such as *jump, boy, pump*). We then began to make charts of words that rhyme. We chose Halloween-related words: *cat, witch, moon, trick, treat, owl, candy*.

We made these charts over several weeks and reviewed the words frequently until most of the children could read down the list of rhyming words. We also observed that most, but not all of the words, ended with the same letters as the word they rhymed with. Finally, we used our rhyming word charts to write a group poem. I made up the first sentence of each couplet and the children composed the second. In several cases, we had several suggested second lines. We wrote them all down and decided when we had the poem written which choice we liked best. Here is the final version.

Halloween Night

On Halloween night you might see a cat.
  A black cat riding high on a bat.

On Halloween night you might see a witch.
  When she sees you she ducks into a ditch.

On Halloween night you might see an owl.
  Whooo, Whooo is all he will howl.

On Halloween night by the light of the moon,
  If you watch, you might even see a raccoon.

This month we began our individualized story writing. In order to make time for this, we altered last month's schedule. On Fridays we continue to write whole-class stories and their follow-up activities. On Monday and Tuesday we follow the same schedule as we did in September with each group rotating through the four centers: listening comprehension, magazines, math, and meeting with me to write group stories. On Wednesdays and Thursdays, however, I do not meet with any of the groups. I sit at the back table and have each child come to me to dictate his or her story. On Wednesdays I meet individually with the

Beatles and the Bookworms. On Thursdays I meet individually with the Beavers and the Mouseketeers. While I am meeting with one child, the rest of the children rotate through the three centers. On Wednesdays, for instance, from 9:00–9:30, the Mouseketeers are in the story center, the Beavers in the magazine center, and the Bookworms in the math center. The Beatles are meeting individually with me or preparing for our individual conferences. Between 9:30 and 10:00, I finish with the Beatles and begin meeting with the Bookworms. The Beavers and Mouseketeers rotate into the magazine center and math center and the Beatles, who are finished with me, plus the Bookworms (who meet with me after the break) are in the story center. From 10:15–10:45, I finish my individual conference with the Bookworms. On my lucky days, I have a parent in to help with these individual stories and that makes a big difference.

So far, I have trained Mrs. Penn, Mrs. Smith and Mrs. Middleman to record the children's stories. First, I let them sit and watch me record them, and then I observe as they record one or two. Mrs. Middleman had to learn to print the letters correctly and Mrs. Smith was hesitant to record Chip's "bad grammar."

"How will he ever learn to talk right?" she asked.

It took some explaining but I believe she now understands that if Chip is to see reading as talk written down, we must write it down as he talks it!

If I don't have a parent in, I almost always end up with a child or two to squeeze into the afternoon schedule.

For the reader to do

Make a chart showing Mrs. Wright's October morning schedule.

● ● ●

Also this month we have begun our whole-class phonics lessons. We do these lessons beween 10:45 and 11:15 on Wednesdays and Thursdays. This month, we have worked primarily on auditory discrimination, hearing which words begin with the same sound and which begin with a different sound. We take objects in the room and put the ones which begin alike together. We also sort pictures and play the "I'm thinking of" game. One child starts by saying, "I'm thinking of something in the room that begins like balloon." He then calls on children to guess the object; the correct guesser then gets a turn to think of something. (Each child whispers the object to me so that I can be sure the game is honest! Some children love to say "No!" even to correct guesses.) We vary the game by guessing things to play with or things to eat. In addition to building auditory discrimination, this also helps improve their vocabulary and classification skills.

I checked out each of the children individually last week to see if they were discriminating the sounds at the beginnings of words. I had each of them sit with their backs to me and read ten pairs of words to them. Five of these word pairs began with the same sound; five, with different sounds. I then had each child tell me if the pairs began with the same or a different sound. All but Paul and Daisy were able to respond correctly to at least nine of the ten pairs. Now that they can make this discrimination, I shall begin to help them make the association between particular beginning consonants and their sounds.

For the reader to do

Make an initial sound auditory discrimination test like the one Mrs. Wright described.

● ● ●

The individual story dictation is off to a good start. At first, many children did not know what to tell a story about. I encouraged them to look through magazines, find pictures they liked and think of a story to go with the picture. Now many of them come to me with their picture, ready to talk. Also, during our afternoon science and social studies experiences, I point out possibilities for stories. Each child (except Paul) now has four stories.

For several (Chip, Joyce, Mort), their stories are really only one sentence, or in Chip's case, only a phrase. Chip's language development is like that of a four-year-old.

Joyce is strange! I think she has a good imagination because I occasionally watch her solitary play-acting in the theater corner on Friday afternoons. She is very nonverbal, however.

Mort just couldn't care less about the stories! He seems bored with everything.

Paul is a mystery. Each time it is his turn I talk to him or look at a picture book with him. He nods his head and occasionally utters a word, but certainly no stories. He is spending part of the morning with Miss Launch in the kindergarten. We both feel the language development activities she does every morning will help him.

Daisy will tell a story (which always begins with *I*). Part of the exercise is to underline all the words the storyteller knows—so Daisy underlines them all. When it comes time to put words in her word bank, I use my card with the hole in it to isolate the underlined words and see which ones she knows. She seldom knows a word, except, of course, *I*. I discussed this with her mother and then went on to the subject of her weight, but her mother informed me that Daisy had a healthy appetite and was "just growing."

Many patterns are beginning to emerge in the children's storytelling. Roberta and Mike have wild imaginations—their stories always have a strange twist in them. Larry tells only factual stories. Steve is a nature buff—his stories are all about animals and living out in the wild. Hilda fancies herself a young Nancy Drew-type, and Alex always spins fantastic tales and swears they are true.

Here are three of the Halloween stories:

THE CASE OF THE MISSING WITCH

It was Halloween and all the witches had gathered at the cavern to brew their evil stew. Just as they began chanting, Minerva Witch noticed that little Itch Witch was missing. The witches were furious. They must brew their stew before midnight or lose their magic powers and all members of the witch council must be present at the brewing. Quickly they decided to call on Hilda, the detective, to help them solve the case of the missing witch.

by Hilda

I like Halloween because you get lots of candy and stuff to eat. Last year I got two big bags. This year I hope to get three.

by Daisy

A TRUE HALLOWEEN STORY

My Aunt Sadie is a witch. Last Halloween she came to visit us and wore her witch's costume. Usually, she just wears regular clothes. She can cast spells and knows all kinds of magic. I was the only kid on the block with a real witch for Halloween.

by Alex

NOVEMBER

I am so pleased! We are up to seven minutes of SQUIRT time each day. The children now seem eager to read and when the bell rings at 1:00 most of them are already settled on the rug in the reading corner. Mike has the biggest problem sitting quietly for seven minutes, but last week one of the mothers brought in some comic books and he now sits and looks at them, especially the monster comics! Larry is reading a book about a boy detective.

Yesterday during sharing time Larry related a part of his book to us. I concluded that he is reading even better than I had suspected, checked it out, and decided he is at least on second-grade level. I have decided to put him on a more individual schedule. I will still have him meet with his language experience group on Mondays and Tuesdays. He contributes much to that group and seems to enjoy it. The children all like him now, except Daisy and Butch, and I don't want him to appear any more "different" than he is. I will continue to have him spend the allotted time in the math center. Although he's a genius with words, he's only average with numbers! I suggested to him that he might want to go to the library while his group is in the listening comprehension center, but he says he really enjoys the stories. He now will go to the library while his group is in the magazine center. He really didn't need to be there anyway.

This month they have been cutting out pictures of objects which begin with the consonants *Bb, Ff, Ll, Mm, Pp, Rr, Ss, Tt* and *Ww*. They have also looked for words which occur frequently: *the, is, and*. Roberta found *and* written in all capital letters in a very decorative type style and proudly placed it on the *and* chart. Just before lunch, when we were reviewing the new additions to the charts, she pointed hers out proudly and said, "I knew it was an *and*, even though it looked funny, because it is spelled *a-n-d*!"

While the children are in the magazine-newspaper center, I encourage them to cut out pictures of things they like and paste them on index cards. When they come to me (or one of the mothers) on Wednesdays or Thursdays, they bring these cards and tell us what they call the item. I then write the word on the other side of the card. Many of the children now have a stack of these cards and are learning to read them without any help. They sit down with the word-side of the card showing and try to think what that word is. If they think they know it, they turn the card over to see if they were right. If they don't know a word, the picture "tells" them the word.

I learned through experience to let each child tell me what each picture is called. There are very few things which have only one name. What is that thing in which you push a baby down the street? A stroller? A carriage? A buggy? A pram? The first year I taught, I had the children cut out pictures and paste them on cards and then wrote my word for that object on the cards. One day I observed a little boy going through his cards. He looked at the word *dog* and said *puppy*. He then turned it over, saw his picture of a puppy and smiled. On the next card, I had written the word *car*. He looked at the word, said *Volkswagen*, turned the card over and there was a car that just happened to be a Volkswagen. I stood there horrified as it occurred to me what he had just learned: d-o-g spells "puppy," c-a-r spells "Volkswagen." Well, we had to redo everyone's cards—I discovered that each child had at least one card, more often many cards, for which his or her word did not match "my word." Now I say, "That's a nice picture. What do you call it?" and write that on the card.

Our main focus in phonics this month has been to establish letter-sound associations for the consonants *Bb, Ff, Ll, Mm, Pp, Rr, Ss, Tt* and *Ww*. The charts with pictures of things which begin with these letters decorate the walls of the room. Since these are charts which the whole class uses, we must agree what these things are called. Each child writes his or her name under the picture he or she put on the chart and tells us what that picture is called. We check to see if it fits the letter at the top of the chart and begins like all the other pictures on that chart. Occasionally, a child puts a picture on a chart which begins with another sound. I then help look for another picture which begins with the sound to paste over the incorrect one. This doesn't happen often, however, because the children work in that magazine center in their groups and they help and correct each other.

We still play "I am thinking of." Now, however, we add the letter "I am thinking of something to eat that begins like *soap* with an *Ss*" and write the letter on the board. Even the children have begun to write both the capital and lower-case forms of the letter when they put them on the board. I do it so that they learn to associate the two forms. I guess they do it because I do it. Amazing!

We also have bags made out of donated pillowcases and dyed bright colors hanging under the windows. These bags have a large letter written in magic marker on them and contain objects beginning with the letter. The children and I have brought in many items for the bags—the *Bb* bag now contains a bow, a bag, bubble gum, a ball, a book, a battery, a bobby pin, a black crayon, a blue crayon, and a bra (Mike's contribution!).

Most of the children have achieved good facility with the consonant letter-sound associations. Chip, Mike, and Butch get half of them right most of the time. Even Daisy has a few and when I checked her on my auditory discrimination test, she was able to discriminate correctly for eight of the ten pairs. Her biggest problem is that she is so lethargic and that she expends much of her limited energy fighting with the other children who "pick on her." Paul has a long way to go before he will be able to make letter-sound associations.

I am now working with the children on the important step in phonics instruction—application. It took me a few years to realize that a child's ability to tell me that *dirigible* begins with a *d* and then suggest other words beginning with *d* wouldn't necessarily increase his or her ability to read unknown words. He or she must apply those associations to unknown words, but if they are not taught to make this application, they won't be able to. To help children transfer consonant letter-sound associations to their reading, I do two kinds of activities: consonant substitution and consonant-plus-context.

The first year I taught I followed the basal reader manual religiously. One of the exercises which it suggested on a regular basis was consonant substitution. I would put a word on the board which the children knew as a sight word, and then underneath it write other words which looked and sounded alike at the end. Prior to doing this the children had to know (1) what rhyming words are, (2) that two words which end with the same letters usually rhyme, and (3) the sounds of the letters beginning the unknown words. The children caught on very quickly. When I wrote the known word *man* with *ban*, *Dan*, *tan* and *van* right beneath it, they observed that all the words looked alike at the end and therefore probably rhymed. They then read the known word, *man*, and the four unknown words, *ban*, *Dan*, *tan* and *van*. We did exercises like that with all their regular sight words and all the consonants they knew. Later, we did the same thing with the digraphs and blends.

I assumed that because they could do these substitution exercises they could use their knowledge of consonant sounds to figure out the pronunciation of words which began with a consonant and ended like one of their sight words. This assumption turned out to be without basis in real reading situations. Directly after doing one of the *man*, *ban*, *Dan* exercises at the board, a child would be reading in a book of his or her choice and come across a word like *fan*. He or she would come to me and ask what that word was. I would be astonished and point out that it ended exactly like the ones which were still on the board and thus rhymed with *man*. The light would dawn and the child would say, "Oh, *fan*!" This happened regularly enough so that I began to realize that it was not the children but the teaching method that was deficient.

Finally I realized what should have been apparent from the beginning. When I wrote *man* on the board and put the words under it, the children had the model word, *man*. When they were reading along in a book, there was no model rhyming word above the unknown word. The child had to sort through the sight words mentally, a skill I was not teaching. Now I do consonant substitution exercises, but once the children catch on, I help them choose their own model words for an unknown word. This is a difficult task for many and I try to break it down into small steps and provide practice in it all year.

Currently, each child has five cards on which I have written the words *and*, *run*, *will*, *man*, and *boy*. I write a word on the board which ends like *and* and rhymes with one of these five words on their cards. They must then sort through their five words and find the "look-alike" word. At a signal from me ("Ready, Set, Show!"), all children show their look-alike word. We talk about where the words are alike (at the end) and where they're different (at the beginning) and what they will probably do (rhyme). Then someone volunteers to come up to the board, match his or her word to mine, and pronounce both words. In this way the children are having to search for the model, but from a tangible limited store of words. When the children show facility at matching these five words, I will add two more and then two more until eventually they have about fifteen words. These fifteen words will all be words that have many words which rhyme with them, and which the children recognize as sight words.

Imagine that you are teaching a first-grader who has a sight vocabulary of the following words:

my	jump	cat	five	sing
and	big	like	in	it
run	make	look	up	at
can	car	old	down	will

1. If you teach what rhyming words are, initial consonants *b, c, d, f, g, h, j, k, l, m, n, p, r, s, t, v,* and *w,* and how to substitute initial consonants, what words can he or she decode? List and total.
2. Teach the initial digraphs, *sh, th, ch, wh*. What words can be decoded? List and total.
3. Teach the initial blends *br, cr, gr, pr, tr, fr, dr, bl, cl, fl, gl, pl, sl, st, sk, tw*. What words can be decoded now? List and total.
4. Add all three totals. How many new words could be decoded using only the original twenty-word sight vocabulary?
5. Still using only the original twenty words, now teach the final consonants *b, d, g, n, m, p* and *t*. What new words can be decoded? (Remember not to include words already learned from initial substitution and not to include words in which the sound of the vowel is changed—*sing* cannot become *sip*.)
6. Teach the final digraphs *sh, ch, th*. What new words can be decoded?
7. Teach the final blends *mp, nt, nd, st, ft*. What new words can be decoded?
8. Get a grand total for final substitution by adding the totals for items 5, 6 and 7. What did you discover about consonant substitution? What is one problem with final consonant substitution?

● ● ●

One day, when all the children are matching one of their fifteen words to my unknown word on the board, I will suggest that maybe they could "think of" their look-alike word without actually searching through the cards. (I will know when to move to this stage because many of the children will have begun to shuffle through their cards when I place the word on the board looking for a particular word rather than looking to see which one matches.) We will then continue practicing by trying to think of which of the fifteen words is a look-alike word. At this point, the children are using the fifteen-word store in their head to provide a model for an unknown word. There are two more steps. First, I will extend this fifteen-word store to include all the sight words they know. This is easily done by saying one day, "Instead of just using the fifteen words we've been using, let's try to figure out some unknown words which don't end like those fifteen, but do end like other words you know. From then on, they practice using all the words in their heads and getting several "model" words. Occasionally, there will be words for which there are two possible models, only one of which rhymes. The word *grow*, for instance, may be matched by *show, blow, cow, now*. When the children suggest these, I put them in two columns and say something like, "The *ow* at the end of words sometimes has the sound you hear in *show* and *blow* and sometimes has the sound you hear in *cow* and *now*. Let's try both and see which match gives us a word we know."

The final step in this process is to encourage the children to use the process in their reading. When a child comes to me and asks what a word is, I ask if he or she can think of a word which ends like that word and which will help in figuring it out. I provide practice and experience all year with this process of comparing, contrasting, and finding a match, first with initial consonants, digraphs, and blends, and later with the final consonants, digraphs and blends. By the end of the year, many of the children are successfully figuring out hundreds of new words, and I haven't taught a single vowel sound!

There is another way I help the children apply their knowledge of consonant sounds to reading. I provide lots of practice in using the context plus the first letter so that the children will be able to make good guesses about what a word might be. From the beginning, I have encouraged the children to say *blank* when they come to a word they don't recognize and to go on to read the rest of the sentence. Most of them are now aware that doing this will often allow them to go back and provide the word they couldn't figure out.

Once they have learned some consonant letter-sound associations, I teach them to use those associations and the context to figure out unknown words. I use the overhead projector and let them help me read a sentence in which one word is covered up. We say *blank* when we come to that word. Then they guess all the words that might go in that blank and I make a list of these guesses on the board. I uncover the first letter of the unknown word. We then decide which words on the board are now impossible and erase them. Sometimes we add more words which begin with the uncovered letter and they guess which one they think it might be and explain why they think this. We uncover the word and discover what the word is. In this way, the children learn that the context will somewhat limit the possibilities for an unknown word and the first letter will limit it even more. These exercises are fun and I am beginning to see the children use these context-plus-consonant clues in their reading.

DECEMBER

Finally—two weeks vacation! Am I ever ready for it after this month! What an action-packed month! Thank goodness Mr. Topps now has the older children do the Christmas pageant—it has been hectic enough without that chore.

We have been making Christmas cards and learning to read the words of many carols. Most children wanted to write a letter to Santa although Butch and Hilda insist that there is no such thing as Santa Claus. They are constantly teasing the other children about it. Yesterday, Butch had Rita in tears and I decided to try to call a halt to it. I told them that I didn't know for sure that there was a Santa Claus but that someone always left presents under my tree at Christmas. Larry refuses to comment on the subject but he wears a knowing look.

Mort's mother came in one Friday morning and told us that in her family and many others Christmas is not celebrated. She then explained about Hanukkah, and the children wrote a whole-class experience story about Hanukkah customs. Typically, Mort was uninterested even while his mother was here.

Early in the month, we made a chart of Christmas words to help the children in card, letter and story writing, and reading. We have used these words for our consonant substitution practice and many children have added lots of Christmas words to their word banks. More and more now, they are taking it upon themselves to write their own words on cards and add them to their banks. Several children now need a second box to hold them all. They write their own stories sometimes by taking the words from their banks and arranging them in sentences. If they need a new word, I supply it. If they need a duplicate of a word they already have, they make a duplicate card. Soon I will begin to help some of the children sort their cards alphabetically and make their own personal dictionaries. Then they will be able to do much writing independently.

Larry is already writing his own stories. When he comes to me on Thursdays, we have a conference about the books he has read and he shows me the stories he has written. Often, his stories are summaries of the factual books he is constantly reading. Larry continues to amaze me.

We have made charts for the other consonants this month: *Cc, Dd, Gg, Hh, Jj, Kk, Nn, Vv, Yy,* and *Zz,* and are continuing our substitution and context exercises. The children are getting very good at making intelligent guesses at unknown words and at using words they know to figure out those they don't. Many of them are reading their own stories and those of others quite fluently. They are devouring the easy-to-read books they check out each week from the library. Next month, I shall make lots of pre-primers available for them to read and begin to individualize their morning activities more.

I used the flannel board extensively this month to motivate their experience stories. I found pictures of Christmas objects in a little punch-out book in a five-and-dime store and glued sandpaper on the backs of these pictures. I set up the display in the story center and told the whole class a story by placing the cut-outs on the board and moving them around appropriately. I then encouraged the children to make up their own stories and illustrate them with cut-outs. Next, I suggested that they might want to dictate a story to me about the cut-outs and then come back to the flannel board, read their story, and act out their story with the flannel-board figures. This was quite successful and even Daphne, who has a great deal of difficulty coming up with an original story, wrote a clever one. Each day now I see her at the flannel board reading her story and acting it out. Usually, she has an audience for these performances. This is the first time I have used my flannel board in this way, but it won't be the last.

good

As a Christmas gift, each child made up a book of his or her stories. Getting the books together took a lot of time. I wanted to be sure each child could read all, or almost all, of what he or she took home, so I paired up the children and let them take turns reading their stories to each other. I circulated and gave help as needed. Larry, Roberta, and Pat were a tremendous help. Last week I sat down with each child and listened to all the stories that each had written. We then selected five for each Christmas story book, decided on a title for the book, numbered the pages, made a table of contents, and stapled the stories together between construction paper. The children decorated the covers of their books, wrapped them in paper they had printed in art class, and made gift tags for them. None of the mothers were allowed to help because this was supposed to be the big Christmas surprise—each child had a book of stories he or she could read. Fortunately, I had the loan of two fifth-graders, so we made it. I guess I'd do it again!

This month, I have chosen Christmas picture books to read to the children. I read to them each afternoon after lunch. I always try to give them some purpose for listening as I read the story. When the story is over, we discuss the story in terms of that purpose. Before I read the book about Christmas in Australia to them, I asked them to listen so that they could list all the ways that Christmas would be different if they spent their next Christmas in Australia. We compared and contrasted Christmas in Australia and the United States. Later I will help them to transfer this skill in listening comprehension to their reading.

I also wrote a letter to parents in which I included book titles they might consider as Christmas gifts for their new readers. I listed the books as "easy-to-read" and "read-aloud," and stressed that most picture books are meant to be read to young children since they have a large uncontrolled vocabulary load. I also suggested ways in which they might talk about these books with their children, and cautioned them against demanding that their children read to them. As soon as children feel comfortable with a book, they will ask that parents listen to them read it.

Well, now I must get out of here. I expend so much of my Christmas energy with these children, I hardly have any left for my family. The stores are open late tonight, maybe I can start my shopping.

For the reader to do

Find a beginning reader to dictate some stories to you. Help make a word bank of known words. Help put together some of his or her stories to make a book.

● ● ●

JANUARY

This has been a most satisfying month. The children have become much more independent and mature. Sometimes I think that I spend all fall laying the groundwork for these long winter months. When the children came back on Monday, I had put out four sets of pre-primers. Two were from the series being used in this school and the other two I found in a corner of the book closet. These last two were a bit ragged around the edges, so I got Mr. Topps' permission to cut them up and I stapled the individual stories into construction paper booklets. I color-coded all the pre-primer story booklets. I had fourteen pre-primers out but it looked like more than that, because eight of them were cut up into little books. When the children first saw them they were impressed with the pile. They immediately began to open them and Hilda shouted, "Hey, I can read this whole book." She proceeded to do just that and many of the others followed suit! An exciting start to a new year!

For a while, I let the children experience the excitement of being able to read so many books. I then called them all together. They shared tales of their holiday vacations and a few had brought some of their treasures with them. I was so pleased to see that many of them had easy-to-read books from the list I had sent home and that they were proud of them. I promised that we would have a story party that very afternoon so they could read their books to the other children. I then told them that the books on the table were for them to read and that, as they had already discovered, they could indeed read most of the words in them. "Most of the books," I explained, "have a family or two in them and this morning we will get acquainted with the members of the family." I then introduced the family in one series by showing pictures in the four books and talking about the characters. We then wrote a group experience story about this family. That afternoon we repeated this procedure with a family from a second series, and the following morning I introduced them to the names of the family in the third series. The fourth series had fairy and animal stories rather than stories about one family.

The children were now truly ready to read fourteen pre-primers. With the exception of the names, most of the words were sight words for them because they had occurred so often in their group and individual stories. They were able to figure out the remaining words by using consonant substitution and context-plus-consonant clues. I gave each child a folder in which I had stapled a ditto sheet to each side with the title and color code of each book. Under that were the title and page numbers of the stories in the book. We spent a long time identifying each of the fourteen books and then finding the stories in them. During this time, we talked about what the stories might be about, and different children expressed the desire to read different stories. I then demonstrated how they would use this folder to keep a record of the stories they had read. They were to check off each story as they read it and write the date (copied from the board) next to that story. I further told them that they could read any story in any book and that since there were over 100 stories, I didn't think any of them could read all of them. (I saw several confident nods as I said this and realized that my challenge had been accepted.) I told them that they could read these stories by themselves or with a friend, and then let them get started immediately. About half the children chose books and read with a friend, and the other half read alone. I walked around and gave them assistance in finding and recording the stories they had read. Most of the children chose a book and read it from start to finish. Others browsed through the books to find a good story. Larry read the titles of the stories from the dittoed record sheet and then went looking for what he wanted! I think he will be back to his library books soon. But, as usual, he seems to have a natural instinct for not appearing too far ahead of the other children.

Our schedule is somewhat different this month. We still do our whole-class experience stories on Friday mornings, and on Friday afternoons we have story parties. The groups are meeting with me on Mondays only for group language experience stories. I have considered cutting out these group stories altogether, but have found that the children enjoy them and that through group stories I am developing with them notions about the conventions of writing.

We are now doing more individualized work with consonants and context. I plan activities so that I can find out which child knows what as I work with the small groups. Finally, I think it is important for their continued oral language development. (Paul, who absolutely never speaks up when the whole class is working together, will occasionally contribute something to this small group.) On Mondays, the children still move through the three centers—math, listening, and magazine—as they have all year.

On Tuesdays, Wednesdays, and Thursdays, I spend from 9:00–10:00 and from 10:15–10:45 meeting with individual children. With some of the children, I am still writing individual experience stories, listening to them read their already-written stories, and helping them add words to their word banks. Paul will now tell me one-sentence stories, usually about a picture he has cut from a magazine. Some days he can read all his old stories and other days he is in a fog. Jeff tells stories, but only about what is going on in the room. He never talks about his home or makes up any imaginary tales. Mike gets the prize for storytelling this month.

Larry's mother was in to help last Wednesday morning. Halfway through the morning, she came to me looking quite pale and disturbed. She asked if she could talk to me in private and proceeded to show me the story Mike had dictated to her. "I was absolutely shocked," she said, "but you had told me to write down exactly what they said, so I did. Now he wants it and I am afraid he will read it to the other children." She then handed me Mike's story.

MIKE'S MONSTER STORY

One day I saw a monster—a big, big ugly monster.
He had eyeballs hanging down on his cheeks.
The blood was dripping on my shoes.
It made me puke.
I ran home and puked in the toilet.
I looked out the bathroom window and there he was!
It scared me so much I crapped in my pants.
When he smelled that, boy, did he run away fast.

Mike was in the corner grinning. The other children were as still as mice watching to see what would happen. Obviously the word had spread that Mike had written a dirty story. I hesitated a moment, then walked over and handed Mike his story. I didn't say a word to him but did suggest to the rest of the class that they had work to do. Larry's mother was still quite upset, but agreed that what he had written was not really obscene. I explained to her that Mike was trying to shock us and that there would be some tittering for the rest of the morning and perhaps a few similar stories that week, but that the fad would soon pass. Fortunately, I was right, but poor Betty was scandalized! She went home and told her mother that "that awful Mike has really done it this time." Roberta then told her mother the story, Betty being too delicate to talk about it. Fortunately, their mother told them just to ignore Mike. Betty will, for sure, but I think Roberta is intrigued by Mike.

Some of the children are still dictating stories, shocking and not so shocking! I let them choose whether they want to dictate a story, read a story that they have written to me, or read a part of a book they have read to me. I check each individual folder when they come to me for their individual time and see which and how many pre-primer stories they have read. Hilda, Roberta, Betty, and Pat have read them all! Daisy has checked them all, but I know she hasn't read them. The other children have read varying numbers, and all but Paul, Daisy, Jeff, Chip and Butch are reading fluently in the pre-primers. Next month, I will put the four primers out! I will, of course, leave the pre-primers so the children can choose what they want to read.

The pre-primer reading has had a great effect on our SQUIRT time. We are now up to nine minutes. Mr. Topps was in the other day reading with our class during SQUIRT and told us that our first grade was sustaining our silent reading even longer than the second grades. The children were very proud and wanted to try for ten minutes next month. I told them we'd see if we could spare that much time from our schedule. I imagine we will find the time since real reading is my ultimate goal for them.

FEBRUARY

> Dere Mrs. Right
> I dream of you evry night
> Please be my valentine
> That wood be just fine.

As this anonymous Valentine shows, the children are becoming independent writers as well as independent readers! This month, as for other holidays, we have written whole-class and group stories around the Valentine's Day theme. We have also made charts of Valentine words and done our phonics substitution exercises starting with a Valentine word. In addition to the consonants, most of the children now know the sounds of the digraphs (*sh, ch, th,* and *wh*) and we are currently working on the blends. As we master the sound-letter association for each of these, we apply them immediately through substitution exercises and context exercises. I now can see the children beginning to use these word identification skills as they read.

I have added two more centers to our room. One is a writing center for independent writing. There I have put different kinds of paper (stationery, bright-colored paper, chart paper), envelopes, and colored flare-tipped pens. I have also put charts with the first 100 words from the revised A and P sight word list (Appendix B) arranged alphabetically. These are the most commonly used words and since the children now know the first letter of most words, they can find many of the words they need to know how to spell on this list. For other words, they spell them the way they sound or ask someone for help.

Daily Schedule

	Meet with Mrs. Wright	Library	Reading Center	Writing Center	Reading Games	Listening Center	Magazine Center	Math Center
9:00–9:30	Roberta Rita Mort Paul	Daphne	Betty Joyce Mandy	Alex Mitch Pat	Hilda Jeff Daisy	Chip Carl Steve	Mike Manuel	Butch Horace Larry
9:30–10:00	Mike Mitch Mandy	Joyce Larry Pat	Horace Roberta Rita	Daphne Hilda Betty	Carl Alex Mort	Jeff Daisy Manuel	Chip Butch	Paul Steve
10:15–10:45	Manuel Steve Larry Pat	Carl Betty Horace	Daphne Hilda	Roberta Mandy	Butch Mitch	Alex Joyce Mort Paul	Jeff Daisy	Chip Rita Mike

I also have a box of objects in the center for the children to pick any three objects from and write a story which includes them all. There is also a new supply of pictures about which they might want to write and the flannel board with Valentine cutouts. They also have paper, crayons, and colored pencils so that they can illustrate their stories. This is a very popular center but because of space limitations I limit the number of children to four at a time.

I also have a new reading games center. Here I have put several games I made as well as some I bought. I taught Larry and Mitch to play these games and they are teaching the other children. These games are designed to give the children practice and review with the most common words and to help strengthen their knowledge of letter-sound relationships.

Of course, I still have the listening, math, and magazine centers in which I constantly change the material. Now when the children come in each morning, they choose the centers in which they wish to work. We have a chart on the bulletin board with spaces for each center and each activity. We first decide which children are meeting with me and these children tack one of their three name cards in that block. They then get first choice on the other two blocks. The rest of the children then choose their three blocks for that morning's work. We set the timer for twenty-five minutes and when it rings, the children have five minutes to get finished up and move on to the next center. We follow this kind of schedule on Tuesday, Wednesday, and Thursday. Our schedule for last Thursday appears on the opposite page.

Many children have begun reading the primers this month. I have made a chart for the stories similar to the one I made them for the pre-primers. Next month, I will put some 1^2 books out and also some 2^1 books. When the children start reading those books, they will be able to make their own charts to record the stories. Joyce finally wrote a whole story last week. She had pantomined a story about a witch and a frog during a creative dramatics session, and the next day I got her to verbalize her pantomine. She is very imaginative, a trait I hope I can continue to build on.

Mandy told the strangest story last week. She always sees things from a different point of view. Her story illustrates that.

THE REAL STORY OF THE THREE BILLY GOATS GRUFF

Once upon a time there lived a troll under a brand new bridge that he had just finished building.

He had worked hard to make it a very nice bridge.

You might be wondering why a troll would need a bridge. Well, I'll tell you.

Trolls live under bridges just like we live in houses.

That's just the way they are.

He was just sitting under the bridge minding his own business when he heard this little noise up on top.

He went up on top and said very politely, "Excuse me. I think you must have the wrong bridge. This is where I live."

He couldn't help but notice the muddy footprints the little goat had made on his nice clean bridge.

The little goat was real smart-alecky and said, "Naaa! This bridge takes me across to the meadow and I'm going to go over and eat some grass. So there!"

That made the troll very unhappy—so unhappy that he said something he later was sorry for. He said, "Yeah! Well, get off my bridge or I'll eat you for dinner!"

That scared the little goat so much that he ran off the bridge and said, "Oh, please don't eat me. Eat up my brother. He's much bigger."

The troll said that he would do that, but he only said it to scare the goats away from his bridge.

Later on, the middle-size Billy Goat Gruff came onto the bridge. The troll again went up and asked the goat to leave, for this was his bridge.

The goat laughed in his face and spit on his freshly cleaned bridge.

That made the troll so mad that he said, "If you don't get off of here right now, I'm going to eat you up!"

The scared goat started crying and said, "Oh, don't eat me. Eat up my big brother. He'll fill you up much faster."

The troll patted him on his head and said, "OK, I won't eat you. But stay off my bridge."

The troll cleaned his bridge again and then went down under for a nap. He was sound asleep when he heard an awful clumping on his bridge.

He was grumpy from being awakened, so he roared, "Who's walking on my bridge?"

The big Billy Goat Gruff said, "It's me! What are you going to do about it, Shrimp?"

Boy, the troll got so mad that he went up to yell some more at the goat, but the goat, who was *so* big, just knocked him into the water. The troll decided he couldn't stay there any longer, so he just moved away and built a new bridge where there weren't any goats.

by Mandy

This was parent conference month. All the children had someone come in except Paul and Jeff. The most amazing thing I learned was that Alex does have an aunt who is a witch and she did come to visit them for Halloween! His mother and I were talking about his vivid imagination and I used his witch story for an example. She hesitated and said, "Well, some people have skeletons in their closets, we have witches! My sister-in-law believes that she is a witch. I don't know what kind of an effect this is having on Alex. But, she is family, so, what can we do?" For starters, I will start to listen to Alex with a more open mind!

Manuel's parents both work, so I met them here one evening. They were very nice and were so pleased that their only son is doing well. "I tell him all the time how important it is to have a good education," said Mr. Tomás. Chip's mother also came at night. I told her that Chip was a hard worker and was making progress. I wanted to broach the subjects of nutrition and food stamps, but she was so proud, I was afraid to insult her. Perhaps I will talk with Miss Grant about Chip.

Mort's mother said he is as bored at home as he is in class and she doesn't know what to do about it. Daisy's mother, on the other hand, said that her little darling had lots of energy at home and never fought with the neighborhood children. Now, that I just can't believe!

Daphne's grandmother came. I can see now why Daphne is so sedate and proper. In behavior, she and Betty could be twins! Roberta and Betty's mother is very pleased with the way they are both doing and wants them kept together in the same room next year. I'm not so sure that is a good idea but she is their mother.

I tried to explain to Mike's mother how his constant movement has inhibited his learning this year. She agreed that he is a handful. I suggested that she take him to the doctor for a complete physical examination and she told me that she had done that when Mike was in kindergarten and the doctor had said he was borderline hyperactive. She wasn't sure what that meant and neither am I. I hate to put labels on kids but he certainly is at least the active half of hyperactive.

Mitch's mother informed me that he felt out-of-place because he is so much bigger than the other children. I never realized that bothered him. He is the biggest boy in the class and a little clumsy, but he is also almost a year older than the others due to his November birth date. I did suggest that Mitch is a bit overweight and that added to his size problem. She said she would watch his eating habits, and I said I would try to make him feel good about his ample size.

I also gained some insight into Butch's behavior. His father came in—I guess there is no mother in the home. Butch is the oldest of four children and it is his job to look out for the younger ones. Butch's father is very proud of his son's toughness and bragged that Butch was "all boy!"

MARCH

This month our big project has been to make dictionaries from our word banks. The children are doing so much independent writing now that they needed to have their words organized in order to find them when needed. I made a booklet for each child in which I had stapled dittoed sheets with one letter in upper- and lower-case form and two or three familiar words beginning with that letter on each sheet. Each child went through all the words in his or her bank and wrote them on the appropriate pages. Once they had all the words written in their dictionaries, they came to me individually to read each word aloud. I put a check next to those they knew. Almost all the children knew most of the words and a few knew them all.

During math class, we counted the words on each page in their booklets and wrote the number at the bottom of the page. I helped the children add the numbers and get a grand total. Roberta had 456 words and she knew every one; Betty had 389 and she, too, knew them all. Everyone was surprised that Larry didn't have the most words, but I guess he is just too busy reading and writing to be bothered.

All this took several weeks to complete and the children needed a separate box in which to store the words that they had already recorded in their dictionary. From now on, they will add new words to their dictionaries as they learn them. I will periodically check to see that they know these words. Several children have not yet completed theirs. Mike just can't sit still long enough to get very much done, and Mort finds the job too tedious. Daisy was unhappy because she didn't have more words, so one day when Roberta was absent, she copied from Roberta's dictionary. Roberta was furious when she found out. "Those words belonged to me," she protested. "I thought them all up!"

The children find all kinds of uses for these dictionaries. The other day during the phonics lesson I wrote the word *trumpet* on the board. I then divided the word into parts (*trum pet*) and asked the children to think of rhyming words for each part. Several children observed that *pet* ended like *get* and *wet,* but *trum* had them stumped for a minute. Suddenly Pat said, "I don't have a word like that in my head, but I must have one in my dictionary." All the children then began to look through their dictionaries. Pat found the word *plum* and Mike found *drum.* We wrote these words under *trum* and then discussed the whole word, noting that that was the instrument Carl's father played in the band.

During phonics this month we have worked with the initial blends and have continued our substitution and context exercises. We have also extended our "think-of-the-word-that-looks-like-this-one" exercise to two-syllable words. I choose words for which I know the children have some matches and then I divide the word for them. In this way they learn to see familiar parts in an unfamiliar word.

For the reader to do

Think of words you know which look like the parts of these words:

crack/er	ban/dit
re/treat	pil/low
pan/ther	prob/lem

● ● ●

Of course, as with the one-syllable words, some words have more than one possible match. In those cases, we see which of the matches results in a word we recognize. Also, in dealing with polysyllabic words, there are some parts that never occur in one syllable words but occur regularly in polysyllabic words. These include *–tion, –sion, –al, –le,* and *–el.* To learn these parts, we first learn as sight words some two-syllable words which contain these parts (*motion, action, animal, little*). We then use these two-syllable words to match polysyllabic words which end as these do. We also build on their spoken language abilities and try to transfer this to written language. Children know that if a chair is *able* to be *moved*, we say it is mov*able*. If a dog is *able* to be *loved*, he is lov*able*. We do some exercises like this and then generalize about the sound change in *–able* when it occurs at the end of a big word.

This month, I have tried to individualize the children's activities more when they are in the centers. Some of my best readers (Rita, Mandy, Alex, and Joyce) are not very good at math. They have specific assignments in the math center each week.

In the magazine center, instead of working on large whole class charts, many children are working on individual assignments. Paul and Daisy are cutting out pictures of objects and placing them in a book I made for them. Each picture is pasted on a page labeled with the letter the object begins with. The children bring the book to me periodically, and I write the names they tell me under these pictures. They are developing some facility with consonant letter-sound associations, but it is slow!

Steve is making a nature book. He cuts pictures of woodsy scenes from magazines and lists the wildlife he thinks he would find there. Chip, Butch, and Jeff look for words they already know and then put these words together to form sentences. Roberta and Horace are making riddle cards—they cut out a picture, paste it on a card, and then write a clue on the back of the card, such as, "This is something you use to clean the house and it begins with *M*." They love to share these riddles with the other children.

Many children now use the magazine center to browse for pictures to inspire stories or to find new words for their dictionaries. As a result many of the dictionaries now include such immediately recognizable words as *McDonald's, Fritos,* and *Holiday Inn.*

Mike is having a very difficult time with the morning block of time now that it is less structured. Almost every other day I revoke his game center privileges because he won't follow the rules. I always give him another chance after a suspension, because if I don't he will never learn to play by the rules. I try to make allowances for Mike's extra energy, but sometimes the other children resent the extra freedom they think he enjoys. I guess they will just have to learn that treating everyone fairly does not necessarily mean treating everyone the same.

I now have the whole range of books out. The children, for the most part, select those they can read and which interest them. Roberta, Rita,

Mandy, Larry, and Pat are reading second-grade books and lots of library books. Daisy, Paul, Butch, and Chip are still reading in the pre-primers (*when* they read!). The rest go back and forth between the primers, the 1² books, and library books. I have found that first-graders enjoy the basals when they can easily read them and often read them on their own or with a friend.

APRIL

April has been much like March, only warmer. The children are continuing to make great strides in their independent reading and writing skills. We are now up to twelve minutes of SQUIRT time daily. I am still worried about Paul and Daisy. They are reading a little in the pre-primers now, but don't seem to be making much progress. Daisy will not do anything constructive unless I am sitting with her, but I can't be with her all the time. Paul is still in a daze. He doesn't cry as much now and he will talk to me if I ask him a direct question. He has no friends, however, and seems to be constantly preoccupied. Miss Grant tells me that his mother is probably alcoholic and no one knows what that boy endures at home. It doesn't seem right that there is no one who can do anything about such an obviously intolerable situation.

This month, I have been particularly concerned with helping the children extend their meaning vocabularies. When their primary reading source was the stories they had written themselves, they automatically understood all of what they read. Now, however, as they branch out into books written by others, a new meaning vocabulary must be learned.

Of course, many of our activities are geared toward enriching their background of experiences and thus their meaning vocabulary. Experiencing things, talking about them, and writing about them are the natural ways to enlarge vocabularies. The stories they hear in the listening comprehension center help, as does my daily reading to them.

One strategy that I have used occasionally to foster vocabulary and categorization development during science or social studies time is a "List, Group, and Label" lesson. This strategy was originated by Hilda Taba for use in the social studies curricula. The "List, Group, and Label" lesson is started by asking a question which will elicit many responses. This question may be used to focus interest on a particular topic to be studied or may be of a more general nature. Last week, in science, we were to begin a unit on nutrition. I asked the children to think of foods, and I listed these foods on the board. From time to time, I stopped to read what was already listed on the board and encouraged them to think of more foods. Finally, when we had filled almost the whole board, I said, "Let's just have Mike, Roberta, and Horace tell me their foods since they have their hands up. We will then have the whole board full of food." I then reread the whole list letting the children read along with me if they desired. I then left the list on the board for the next day.

On the following afternoon, I pointed to our list of foods and told the children that I was going to read the list again and that this time they should listen and think, "Are there any foods on the list which seem to go together in some way?" I then read the entire list and asked if anyone had a group of foods which seemed to go together.

Categorizing

Mitch said that cake, cookies, chocolate pie, ice cream and gingerbread went together. I wrote these five on a sheet of chart paper and asked him why he had put these foods together. He said, "Because you eat them all after the meal." I then asked him if he could think of a name or label for his group. He hesitated a moment and then said, "Desserts."

Steve put mushrooms, grapes, berries, rhubarb, and nuts together. I listed these five foods on the chart paper and asked him why he had put those particular foods together. He said it was because they all grew wild. I then asked him if he could give a name or label to that group. After some hesitation, he said, "Things that Grow Wild."

Chip put peanuts, chocolate candy, hamburgers, potato chips, soda, oranges, and tomatoes together. I listed them and in response to my "why" question, he said, "Because they are my favorite things to eat." When I asked him to give a name or label to this group, he couldn't. I said that that was fine, that we couldn't always think of names for groups, and went on to the next child.

While doing these lessons, I accept every child's response. During the listing process, everyone usually contributes something, but I call on the children with smaller vocabularies first so that they have a chance to contribute. I usually save the grouping and labeling steps for the next day so that the lessons don't take more than twenty-five minutes. When we form groups, each child who wants to organize a group tells me why those particular things are grouped together and then attempts to give a label to that group. This labeling step is difficult for many of my children and if they can't do it, I simply accept that and go on to the next volunteer.

As you can see, the children have different categories and different reasons for grouping things together. Therefore, no child is allowed to add anything to another child's group. I also write the name of the child who labeled a group under that group. Objects from the list can be used over and over again as different children make groups. The children enjoy these lessons and I can see that they have had an effect on their vocabulary and categorization skills.

For the reader to do

Write down three questions you could use to elicit a list of objects for a "List, Group, and Label" lesson.

● ● ●

For readers to do together

Make a list of all the things you read that are not books, magazines or newspapers. Use this list to group; tell why you grouped and label. Discuss why reading is a survival skill in our society.

● ● ●

MAY

Well, the year is almost over. Just one more week of half-days of school for the children and lots of report-writing for me. I always feel sad during this last week of school—so much yet undone. It has, all in all, been an exceptionally good year. During this last month, we had SQUIRT time for fourteen minutes each day. The children were so proud that they could sustain their reading almost as long as the third-, fourth-, and fifth-graders do. During SQUIRT, I always read something of real interest to me. This is part of the modeling process. Children should see adults reading for pleasure and information. This month, however, I found something I was captivated by and which I could share with the children. I read *Watership Down* and each day at the end of SQUIRT, I would tell the children what was happening to Fiver, Silver, and the other rabbits. Finally, I got so involved I took the book home over the weekend to finish. When I sat down for SQUIRT on Monday with a new book, the children were dismayed. How could I finish the book without them? We talked about how we sometimes get so involved with a book that it is hard to stop reading. I then related to them the last 100 pages of *Watership Down* and we went on with SQUIRT time. Reading something which interested me and which I could share with the children was so successful that I shall look for other books like that next year.

Well, we prepared books to take home again as we did at Christmas. This time we did some editing on the stories the children had written themselves. We decided that if people other than the children themselves are to read their books, we want to make the book as readable as possible. Therefore, spelling and punctuation must be correct. I put a sign which said "Editor-in-Chief" near my typewriter and we spent much of our morning time editing and rewriting or typing. The children saw the need to make these changes and cooperated willingly. The stories that went home were far from perfect but they were readable by others and I think quite remarkable for first-graders. We also prepared their word banks and dictionaries to take home. Many children plan to add words to these over the summer and to show them to me in the fall.

We held an auction for the charts we have been making during the year. (I saved several to show at the end-of-year grade level meeting. Miss Kurt, the Chairman has asked me to talk to the other first-grade teachers in the district about Language Experience.) Each child was given twenty tokens (bottle caps) and Larry was the auctioneer. This was a huge success and, of course, just as at any good auction, we were all hungry at the end of it and needed refreshment! The mothers provided this and we had a party.

We also had our annual book fair this month sponsored and run by Ms. Maverick's fourth-grade class. The children bought many books, and we also sold many to parents during our end-of-year conferences. I hired Chip to help me clean up the room each night and paid him with books!

Of course, Miss Launch brought her class to see their new room and new teacher. Gosh, the kindergartners look so tiny. It always makes me stop and reflect on how much the children grow during first grade. Next year's class looked like a good group. I doubt, however, that they will be able to compare with this year's group. Just yesterday I remarked to Mr. Topps about the diversity of this class and how my next group of children couldn't be as interesting as this one. He nodded, smiled, and said, "Mrs. Wright, you say that every year!"

The First Grade Meeting

Mrs. Wright had been secretly pleased when Miss Kurt asked her to explain her reading program to the June meeting of the first-grade teachers. When she had first begun using the language experience approach, she had been very zealous and had tried to convert her fellow teachers to her method; and had been quite taken aback when a veteran teacher informed her that "every year there is some young teacher experimenting on the children with newfangled ideas." Since then she had quietly gone her own way and let the other teachers go theirs! The word had spread, however, that her method worked, and now she had been asked to address their group! Mrs. Wright was indeed pleased, and she was also prepared!

Mrs. Wright brought samples of the whole-class and group stories to the meeting. She had also borrowed some of the individual books, word banks, and dictionaries from the children, promising on her honor to return them promptly, and had also brought the charts showing the schedules her class had followed, and overhead transparencies of the various room arrangements.

She began by explaining how she started the program. She showed some of their first whole-class charts and pointed out she recorded exactly what each child had said and put his or her name next to it. She then explained how she divided the children into four heterogeneous groups and met with them four days a week to write group stories. She showed the Beatles's chart, and explained about the centers and how the children worked independently. Several teachers' eyebrows rose as she said this, and Mrs. Wright elaborated on how she got them working independently.

"In the beginning of the year I had quite structured activities in the centers," she explained. "In the listening center, the children put on headphones, listened to a story and did a simple follow-up activity after the story. One child in each group was responsible for turning on the tape, rewinding it afterwards, and collecting the follow-up papers. In the math center, again the activities were quite structured. There were specific sets of objects to count, patterns of beads to string, objects to measure, or problems to solve. In the magazine center, children looked for specific objects or letters and pasted these on the appropriate charts on the wall. Each group had one person who was responsible for seeing that everything went smoothly in each center. This is another advantage to having the groups heterogeneously formed so that they have both very mature, capable children and some less capable ones. Before the children went to work in the centers, I took a few minutes to point out what their tasks would be, and as the groups changed centers each half-hour, I circulated and made sure that each group had begun their work before I joined the group with which I was writing group stories. At the end of each morning, we discussed the morning's activities and noted new additions to the charts in the magazine centers. When there were problems, we discussed what had caused them and what we could do about them. Of course, some children had a difficult time working independently in the centers, but these same children would have had difficulty completing exercises at their desks. I find I actually have fewer discipline problems now than I did when each child spent the morning sitting at a desk copying the daily story from the board and completing dittoed sheets."

Several of the teachers were nodding their heads and taking notes, so Mrs. Wright continued. She explained how she usually began the individual story writing sometime in October when the children were adjusted to the independent activities. She pointed out that she changed the schedule by not meeting with the groups two days a week to allow her time to meet with children individually. At this point, she digressed to rave about "her" parents and how easy it had been for parents to help her after they had watched her write down the children's stories. She was tempted to tell them about Larry's mother and Mike's shocking story, but decided that might scare some of them. "Later," she thought, "I may tell them."

She then showed them several of the children's word banks which contained the words underlined by the children as known words as well as the picture word cards the children had made from magazine pictures. She told them how she drew on the known words in the banks to help the children build consonant, digraph, and blend letter-sound associations, and how, once they had made these associations, she used substitution and context-plus-consonant exercises to help them apply these associations to the pronunciation of unknown words.

Finally Mrs. Wright talked about getting the children into the basals and handed out copies of the charts she had stapled in the children's folders in order to keep track of the stories the children had read. She emphasized that during the last half of the year many of the children were writing their own stories and that her conferences with each child now varied according to his or her wishes and needs. For some, she continued to write down their stories and help them add known words to their banks all year. For others, the conference became a time for discussing the basal stories and library books they were reading. Other times, she used this individual time to help children edit the stories they had written.

Mrs. Wright ended her talk by showing the teachers the transparencies illustrating the room arrangement at various times during the year. She also related to them how the work centers and the individual conferences were tailored to individual needs as the year went on.

After a break, the teachers got together for a discussion and question period. They seemed enthusiastic, but had many practical concerns. One teacher asked what the children found to write about—she had tried to have the children do some creative writing toward the end of the year and the children complained that there was nothing to write about. Mrs. Wright told them that the experiences the children have all day during science, social studies, and math are story material, and that she constantly pointed this out to the children. In addition to this natural stimulation for writing, Mrs. Wright suggested many "artificial" stimulations for writing—she told them about the flannel board cut-outs, the pictures, the boxes of objects and story starters which she used as motivators in the writing center.

Finally, she pointed out that the notion of "story" is really too limiting. Many experience stories are actually lists of facts or directions. She showed them the story the class had written after Mort's mother talked to them about Hanukkah, the chart of rules which was displayed in the games center, and the chart with the recipe for Christmas cookies. She told them about Steve, who always wrote stories based on facts of life in the wilderness. Finally, she told them about Joyce, who was so imaginative in her creative play but could never "think of anything to write about" and how she often capitalized on this interest.

Another teacher asked about children with dialects. Mrs. Wright, who was originally from another part of the country, pointed out that she thought all the other teachers spoke a dialect, and they admitted that they thought she spoke a dialect. The conclusion was reached that everyone speaks a dialect of English, but some dialects seem to be more generally acceptable. Since Mrs. Wright knew that what they were really asking was, "Do you write down a child's improper grammar?" she shared some of Chip's and Jeff's stories. Several teachers seemed appalled at the notion of actually writing down sentences like "They sure good," and "That bird don't never stop singing." Mrs. Wright tried to explain that the language experience approach is based on the principle that what a child says can be written down and read by that child and others. To violate that principle destroys the very reason for doing the stories in the first place.

She further pointed out that children learn language by hearing it spoken, and that in a language experience classroom, there is a lot of speaking going on. The children who speak language patterns which many consider incorrect will have many opportunities to hear other children and the teacher speak, and may begin to modify some of their speech patterns. The goal of the language experience approach to reading, however, is not to change speech patterns but rather to provide a bridge which will carry a child from facility with oral language to familiarity with written language. Once this familiarity with written language is established, the child can move into reading all kinds of language patterns.

To the question of whether sentences like "They sure good" confused other children, Mrs. Wright responded that they were no more confusing than "They sure are good" looks to Chip. After some laughter, Mrs. Wright went on to explain that the only time this would cause confusion was during the whole-class or small-group stories, and that this was one of the reasons she put the child's name after each sentence. In this way, each child could read his or her own sentence as it had been spoken. "When other children correct a child like Chip, I tell them that that is the way Chip says it."

Several teachers wondered if it didn't take a lot more time and preparation to teach in this way. Mrs. Wright responded that she really didn't think so once the class had been organized and begun. "I used to spend hours each week correcting workbooks and preparing ditto sheets and charts to introduce the basal reader stories. Now I spend that same amount of time getting the centers ready, changing the materials in them often, and thinking of activities for individual children. Initially, I spent a lot of time worrying about the composition of my reading groups. Just at the time I had them set up and had everyone at the same place, one child would begin a growth spurt and another would reach a plateau. I just never was happy with grouping them according to ability. In addition, I used to spend endless hours on the phone explaining to Billy's mother why he wasn't in the top group with Johnny!"

Finally, a teacher asked if there was any research to support the language experience approach to beginning reading instruction. Mrs. Wright reminded them that research consistently rated the teacher as the most important single variable in the classroom and that, according to research, there was no one superior method. She did point out, however, that in most research studies which compared children from a language experience approach with those in a basal reader approach the language experience students equalled or surpassed the achievement of those in the more traditional approaches (Wrightstone, 1951; Hildreth, 1965; Allen, 1962; Hall, 1965; Bond and Dykstra, 1967).

Mrs. Wright then drew on her own years of teaching experience using both the basal reader approach and the language experience approach and gave her reasons for preferring the approach she was currently using. "I like it because it is integrative," she explained. "The children talk and listen. They then write about what they have discussed, and read what they have written. The reading material is pertinent to the child. There are no comprehension, vocabulary, or sentence structure problems when a child is reading what he or she has written or dictated. The language experience approach builds on what all the children are already good at—talking! They have an immediately successful experience with reading and go home after the first week of school thinking 'I can read!' This feeling of achievement is heightened when I decide that most of the children have a large enough sight vocabulary to read the pre-primers independently. Reading their first real books is easy and fun, and they read them again and again to anyone who will listen."

Mrs. Wright ended the meeting by pointing out that although language experience was the core of her program, she actually used a combination approach. The children began with language experience stories, then moved into independent reading in four series of basal readers, and finally into a more individualized library book reading program. Throughout the year word identification skills were continually developed so that her children became independent decoders of words.

Miss Kurt ended the meeting by reminding the teachers that they could use their two professional days for classroom visits and suggested that they might want to visit Mrs. Wright's class. The response was enthusiastic and Mrs. Wright promised to put them to work when they came!

References

Allen, R. V. "More Ways Than One." *Childhood Education* 38 (1961): 108–111.

Bond, Guy L., and Dykstra, Robert. "The Cooperative Program in First Grade Reading Instruction." *Reading Research Quarterly* 2 (1967): 5–142.

Goodspeed, Peter. *Hugh and Fitzhugh.* New York: Platt and Munk, n.d.

Hall, Maryanne. "The Development and Evaluation of a Language Experience Approach to Reading with First Grade Culturally Disadvantaged Children." Unpublished doctoral dissertation, University of Maryland, 1965.

Hildreth, Gertrude. "Experience Related Reading for School Beginners." *Elementary English* 42 (1965): 280–97.

Taba, Hilda. *Teachers' Handbook for Elementary Social Studies.* Palo Alto: Addison-Wesley, 1967.

Wrightstone, J. W., "Research Related to Experience Records and Basal Readers." *The Reading Teacher* 5 (1951): 5–6.

Miss Nouveau

HIGHLIGHTS

Grouping
Listening Potential Test
Informal Reading Inventory
Vocabulary Tests
Diagnosis
SQUIRT
Workbooks
Dittos
Organizational Patterns
Discipline
Behavior Modification
Vocabulary
Games
Parents as Volunteer Aides
Grading
Learning Centers
Bulletin Boards
Individualization
Ring of Words
Motivation
Directed Learning
Poetry
Creative Writing
Basal Reading Levels

from the desk of MR. TOPPS

*Ms. Maverick —
Please note that although Miss Nouveau has some initial difficulties, she does begin to plan an effective program after Christmas. Remember what the first year was like!?!*

Miss Nouveau

The Parent Meeting

Miss Nouveau arrived at the school two hours before her 8 p.m. parent meeting was scheduled to begin. She wanted to be *sure* that she was well-prepared for this one, <u>her very first</u>. She was even more anxious than one might expect because she had not wanted this group of children for her class.

Last spring when she had been hired, Mr. Topps and the other second-grade teacher had told her that two different approaches were being used in the first-grade sections. One class used the basal reader approach; the other class had gone through a language experience approach with Mrs. Wright. Miss Nouveau was not even certain what the language experience approach entailed. Since she was going to teach the basal approach, she was hoping to have Mrs. Allen's class. Of course, as luck would have it, she got Mrs. Wright's class.

Now the parents of these children were coming to find out about the instructional program that she had designed for the children and ask her questions about it! It was going to be a long night! But, at least, she thought, Mr. Topps would be there to help. He had generously offered to come to her meeting and to help her.

She was looking over her new bulletin board when Mr. Topps arrived at 7:45 p.m. He told her that the board was lovely and that the fall theme she had chosen brightened the room. She didn't tell Mr. Topps that she had been working on that bulletin board for two weeks, sometimes until 2 a.m. She wanted him and the parents to think that she was efficient and organized.

Miss Nouveau had made name tags for all of the parents to wear. In that way she could easily identify each parent, and she would know from the leftover name tags who had been unable to attend. When all of the parents had had a cup of coffee and were seated, Mr. Topps, as had been agreed to earlier, introduced her to the group.

"As you all know," he began, "I am Mr. Topps. I especially wanted to come this evening to introduce your child's teacher to you. Miss Nouveau comes to us this year as a first-year teacher. She did exceptionally well both at the university and during her student teaching, so that when this position opened up last spring, I was delighted to have Miss Nouveau among the applicants for the job. I know that you will be as happy with her as we are. If there is anything that you would like for either of us to do, do not hesitate to call. Now, let's hear from Miss Nouveau."

"Thank you, Mr. Topps. This is an exciting moment for me. All my life I have dreamed of being an elementary school teacher.

"I want to explain to you the kind of program that I have planned for this school year. You see here on this table the reading books that your children will be using. It is the *Reading Can Be Fun* series published by Basic Publishing Company. In addition to reading these books, your children will be working with these workbooks. When they are not with me in one of the three reading groups, they will be at their seats doing follow-up skills in workbooks or other assignments that reinforce the basal's skill development program or reading a book from the library shelf over there. My assignment of the children into these three groups has been based on the results of a test which accompanies the reading series called an Informal Reading Inventory (IRI). It measures your child's performance in oral reading and comprehension." Miss Nouveau, relieved that *that* was over, hurried on to a topic she knew more about.

"You know that physical factors are quite important in determining how well your children do in school. You can be most helpful in seeing to it that your children get to bed by 8:30 at night, that they come to school after having had a nutritious breakfast, and that they play out in the fresh air for a while every day after school. I intend to emphasize these basic health habits with the children this year. We will be studying nutrition, the value of recreation, and the importance of adequate rest. Starting on Monday, I am going to ask you to send a snack to school with your child. We will have snack-time every morning in order to help keep the energy level of the children high. The school nurse will test vision and hearing in October, and if there are any problems, I will be in touch with you."

Miss Nouveau looked at her watch and saw that what she had planned to take thirty minutes had only consumed fifteen minutes of time, so she asked Mr. Topps if there was anything he would like to add. There was not. The time had come for the part of the meeting that she had been dreading. She turned back to the parents and asked, "Are there any questions?"

All over the room, hands shot up. She called on Mrs. Moore first.

"You will be using the same set of books for all of the children? How can you do this? Aren't they at different reading levels?"

Miss Nouveau replied, "Yes, they are at three different levels. Some of them are reading below grade level and they are reading in this first reader; most of them are reading right on grade level and they are in this 2^1 book; however, some of them are reading above grade level and they are reading from this 2^2 book." She smiled proudly! "The difference in instruction among the three groups will be not only the book they're using and the pace at which they move through the books, but also the amount and kinds of material covered."

Mrs. Penn raised her hand to ask, "Why are you using *this* particular series?"

Mr. Topps intervened. "If I may, I would like to answer that one, Miss Nouveau, since the decision was made before you were hired. You see, Mrs. Penn, the teachers in this school who use basals met together last spring and selected this series from among the six state-approved adoptions. Most of the teachers at that meeting felt that this series allowed for the most flexibility while still retaining the structure and sequential development of skills which is a strong point of the basal reader approach."

Another hand went up, and Miss Nouveau called upon Mr. Tomás. "When the kids aren't with you, how will they know what to do? Won't they just waste time and not do their work?"

"I take time every morning to explain to the children what they are to do on their work papers. You see, they all do the same ones, so I can give those instructions to everyone. In their reading groups, they have been told what they need to do in their workbooks. They do have instructions, and they know what to do. But sometimes some children don't complete their work. When that happens, they just have more to do the next day."

Mrs. Penn glanced over at Mr. Topps for his reaction. Had he pressed his fingertips to his forehead because of a headache?

With all of the questions answered, Miss Nouveau thanked them for coming. She started to gather up some of her materials when she noticed Mrs. Penn at her elbow.

"Miss Nouveau, I just want to offer to help you in any way that I can. I used to be a teacher, so I think that I might be of some help to you. *Please* feel free to call on me. I really enjoy helping out, and I know what a difficult task you have."

"Oh, thank you, but I'm sure that won't be necessary. I think that I have things pretty much under control now. But I do appreciate your offer. I will call for help if I need it."

"Fine. See that you do. Good evening. It was lovely meeting with you this evening."

Mrs. Penn and Mrs. Middleman left the room together. They were talking quietly, but Miss Nouveau heard some of what was said.

MRS. MIDDLEMAN: Isn't she a dear little thing? So cute! And just look at that lovely bulletin board. My, she certainly is creative.

MRS. PENN: Yes, she is. But, you know, I always rather like to see the children's work up on the bulletin board. It's not as pretty or tidy but there's something wonderful about your own child's work displayed. Mrs. Wright did so much of that last year.

Miss Nouveau was crestfallen. All of that work, and they would rather see things that the children had done! "Maybe I should think about having the children do something to put up. Oh, but it will be so messy!"

Monthly Logs

SEPTEMBER

My major premise is wrong! I thought that all children loved to read or that at the very least they were eager to learn. How wrong! How wrong! I just can't understand it. Butch sits in his seat (sometimes) just waiting out the day. If I ask him to practice the sight vocabulary words with which he is having trouble or to do one of the other assignments, he just looks at me and asks, "Why?"

"So that when you grow up you'll be able to read. You need to be a good reader to get a job."

"Oh, yeah," he replied. "Well, my dad, he don't read so good, but he got a job. He makes a hunnerd bucks a week!" That sounds like a great deal of money to a seven-year-old, but if he only knew!

One of the most frightening aspects of this teaching business is the weight of responsibility one feels. I was so excited to have my own classroom assigned to me and spent a lot of time here this summer getting my room ready for the first days of school. But the full realization of the responsibility didn't hit me until I saw the first children come into the room—my room—*our* room.

I fervently hope that I will never again live through a day like the first day of school. The children were quite well-behaved (I suppose the novelty of returning to school) and I had prepared an excess of material for them, just in case. I had enough for two days—so I thought! By noon, I had used up everything I had planned for the first day. They worked so much more quickly than I ever imagined! By lunch time I was rattled. What to do? As I started to sort the children out for lunch (lunch box children in one line, those going home in another, and those who were to eat in the cafeteria in the third) I pulled out the lesson plans for the second day of school so that I could fill up the afternoon.

The moral of this is, "Never try to do two things at once on the first day of school." The reason: I had the children sorted and sent to the various lunches, and I had just picked up my tray to eat, when Alex's mother walked into the lunchroom with Alex in tow and explained patiently to me that Alex had *paid* for his lunch and I had sent him home!

Another horrible feeling of incompetence came when I realized that I had to put these children into reading groups, and I didn't have the foggiest notion of what criteria to use. How many *is* a group? Grouping had been talked about in my undergraduate reading course, but no one ever explained how to do it, and it never occurred to me to ask.

At least I had the books straight in my mind. There are so many that I found it very confusing to see a huge stack of books in the office with my name on them. I must have looked shocked, because Mrs. Mainstay came over to me and asked if anything were missing. Missing? Good grief! I thought that perhaps they had given me someone else's books as well. I finally admitted to her that I didn't understand all of those markings on the books—PP and P and 1^2 and 2^1, and so on. Because she has done the ordering of textbooks for so many years, she knows them well. She grabbed a pile, motioned for me to do the same, and we went into my classroom where she proceeded to explain the hierarchy in basal reading books. When she had finished, she told me that the fourth- and fifth-grade books would be available whenever I needed them. I thanked her but said I wouldn't need those: "My children are in second grade." She smiled and said, "Well, once you get to know the children, you may see a need for the other books, too."

I went to Mrs. Wise for help. I asked her how she would form reading groups if she were using basal readers. We talked for some time, and afterward I felt much more confident. During our discussion she showed me the IRI which accompanies the series. The criteria on this test were 95 percent accuracy in pronunciation and being able to answer 75 percent of the questions. She said that this would help me form my reading groups, for while some of the children may be able to read the *words* in the passages, their *understanding* of the passage itself might be deficient. The IRI uses comprehension of the material as part of placement criteria.

I must admit that I was puzzled. "But what are all of the other children doing while I am sitting down with each child to administer the IRI? Won't they be running all over the room?"

Mrs. Wise smiled kindly at me, put her arm around my waist, and guided me to a chair where we could sit down. "How about my running through the way that I give them to children! First of all, I explain to the children that it is important for me to check on some of their reading skills. I make my statement as nonthreatening as I can so that they will realize that I am not administering the test in order to grade them. In other words, I try to make them understand that I merely want to find those things which they know so that I can *then* begin to teach them those things that they need to know. I select a corner of the room that is out of the mainstream so that we can work uninterruptedly."

"Yes, I can see that," I replied. "But what about all of the questions that they are bound to have with their work?"

"Generally, it is possible for them to go to one of the other children to get help with unknown words or with directions on some assignment. That has been no problem for me. The important thing is for them to realize what assignments you have planned for them and to know the order in which they must complete them. Be sure that they know what they are permitted to do if they are finished with all of the work. You might even select groups with a mixture of capable and less capable children in them in order to form teams. You can select or have them choose a team captain who would make sure that all in the group completed their various assignments. He or she could read a story to the group or lead them in a language arts game when other work is done. It would be a good idea, too, for you only to do a few IRI's a day. It will take some time for you to complete all of the tests, but it is best if you aren't away from the children for too long. I do all of my testing in the morning, for I know that the children are not as fresh in the afternoon, and I want them to do their best. Does that help you know how to get started?"

I said that I thought that I would be able to handle the job!

"How about a marking system for their oral reading errors? Do you have a system which you can use easily?" she asked me.

I showed Mrs. Wise the marking system that I had learned in college. I told her that if she approved of it, I would prefer using it to the one that the basal series IRI had. She thought that it would be fine. So that weekend, I typed the IRI paragraphs from the basal series test on to file cards as Mrs. Wise suggested. By Monday I was ready to test!

I did the preliminary explanation that Mrs. Wise suggested and then called Horace to go with me to the desk I had set up in a corner of the room. I gave him the first card to read. As it was on the pre-primer level he had no difficulty at all with word identification or with comprehension. As he read aloud, I marked his errors on a sheet of paper that duplicated the passages he was reading. After the reading, I asked the comprehension questions. After completing that, Horace also had to read a passage from the primer silently, and I checked that passage for comprehension as well. The first reader (or 1^2 passage) also presented no problem. He was beginning to make several errors, however, as we began the 2^1 passage, and he finally went below the criteria for instructional level on the 2^2 passage.

I used this marking system because it is so simple:

Reversal	⌢an⌣d
Hesitation (prolonged)	He ✓saw.
Omission	The ⬭big⬭ boy left.
Addition	He went to the ⋀ store. *(grocery)*
Substitution or mispronunciation	He was ~~huge~~ for his age. *(large)*

Awkward phrasing	Fred was / unable to / see her.
Word supplied	Can you <u>advise</u> me?
Repetition	He saw it then.

I remember thinking, while in my college classes, that I would *never* learn this marking system. But one of the professors brought in a tape of children reading and we practiced until we *could* do it. Now it comes very easily and naturally to me. However, now that I am using it to place my real kids, I've wondered a little bit about it. It seems rather strange that one kind of error is as wrong as another. It seems as if "omission" would be more serious than "hesitation."

Another measure of my class's abilities which I have given this month is a listening comprehension test. I used the same IRI, and put the entire test on tape. I made a note of which passage marked the beginning of the reading instructional level for each child, and that is where we began the listening test. After the child had listened and answered questions, I had a listening comprehension level as well. Putting the test on tape freed me to do some of the other work that I've had to do this month, and children could be taking the listening comprehension test while I did other testing. The children used a multiple-choice answer sheet, and I read those choices to them from the tape. This helped to eliminate some of the error resulting from faulty reading of test questions and also to focus on what is being evaluated—listening comprehension. The answers were given at the end of the tape so that the children could check their own work, and I merely reviewed it and evaluated what they had done. Most of the children handled those sessions quite well, although Paul was unable to figure out what to do. I administered the test to him individually.

The score from the listening comprehension test can also be figured in basal reader equivalents (see p. 109). I find the passage for which the child was able to answer questions with 75 percent accuracy. This is the level at which he or she is capable of reading if all conditions are positive—word identification skills, health, good teaching, interest, and so on.

For readers to do together

Divide the class into six groups. Each group will be assigned a grade level, 1–6.

Devise a listening comprehension test in a manner similar to the IRI described later. Duplicate copies for the entire class and include answer sheets.

Administer the test to an elementary school child. Compare the child's score on this with his or her score on the IRI you constructed. Report your results to the class.

● ● ●

By the time of the parent meeting, I did have my groups formed, though that had not been as easy as I felt it would be. Larry gives every indication of being an extremely bright child, yet when I was grading his IRI, I was amazed at the number of errors he made in oral reading. Instead of "He could not get the car to start," Larry read, "He couldn't get the car started." Yet with all of those errors, his comprehension remained high! As a matter of fact, he did amazingly well, answering every question asked of him without error. I put him into the middle group anyway, because the requirements for the IRI include both oral reading and comprehension. I thought Mort would do better, too, but he was so inattentive that he made all kinds of silly mistakes. We can work on improving his oral reading in the low group.

I assigned children to reading groups and let them choose a group name. For some of the groups this took a long time, but eventually all three groups were named. Some things do puzzle me about these groups. Why are the Butterflies all girls and why is there only one girl in the Monsters? I wonder if there's any significance to that?

Monsters	*Astronauts*	*Butterflies*
Mike	Horace	Mandy
Daisy	Daphne	Pat
Paul	Betty	Roberta
Butch	Steve	Rita
Carl	Alex	Hilda
Jeff	Mitch	
Chip	Manuel	
Mort	Joyce	
	Larry	

For readers to do together

Which group is Miss Nouveau's "top" group? Her "middle"? Her "low" group? Do you agree with her groupings on the basis of what you already know about the children? Why or why not?

● ● ●

Mrs. Wise had indicated that I might want to construct my own IRI some day, either as a supplement to, or in place of, the prepared one for the basal. She gave me a sheet outlining the steps involved. I was amazed at how much such a test involves. I don't think I'll be able to work on one until next summer when I have lots of time!

	Instructional Level based on IRI	Listening Comprehension Level
Alex	2^1	2^1
Betty	2^1	3^1
Butch	P	1^2
Carl	1^2	2^1
Chip	P	1^2
Daisy	PP	1^2
Daphne	2^1	2^1
Jeff	PP	2^1
Joyce	2^1	3^1
Hilda	2^2	3^1
Horace	2^1	2^1
Larry	4	went beyond range of test
Mandy	2^2	4
Manuel	2^1	2^1
Mike	1^2	2^2
Mitch	2^1	2^1
Mort	2^1	3^1
Pat	3^2	5
Paul	PP	P
Rita	3^1	3^1
Roberta	2^2	3^2
Steve	2^1	2^1

For readers to do together

Form the class into six groups.

Each group will do part of an IRI for grades 1–6. Duplicate what each group turns in, collate, and make sure that each class member receives a completed copy of the IRI.

How to construct an IRI:

1. Get copies of the basal series being used by the children.
2. Select representative passages of approximately this length from each book:

   Pre-primer: 75 words

   Primer: 150 words for each of two passages—one from first half, one from the second

   First Reader: 150 words for each of two passages—one from first half, one from the second

Second Reader: 150–200 words—one passage from each of the two books for this level

Third Reader: 150–200 words—one passage from each of the two books for this level

Fourth through Sixth: 200–250 words—one passage to be chosen from the middle of each book

3. Prepare questions utilizing both high and low level conceptualization, so that children must answer with more than one word and so that they must draw conclusions, make predictions, etc.

Pre-primer: 3 questions (use pictures)
Primer: 3 questions
First Reader: 3 questions
Second through Fifth: 5 to 7 questions
Above Fifth: 7 to 10 questions

4. Beginning with the first reader, also select a parallel passage for silent reading. Prepare questions as in (3) above.

5. Duplicate passages and questions with answers and assemble into book form. This is the pupil record book in which you will mark errors while the child is reading. Make sure that the grade level is typed in one corner.

6. Type the passages on file cards, using a primary typewriter for the passages from the books for the first three grades. Type a "cover card" that tells the series from which the passages were taken. Sealing the typed side with clear adhesive plastic paper will insure a longer life for the cards. Punch a hole in the upper left-hand corner. Put a single ring binder through the hole, so that the cards will remain together and in the proper sequence. This is the set that the child will read from.

7. This is to be an individually administered test. As a screening device to determine where you might begin the child's reading, prepare a series of word lists. Choose the following number of words from the different books:

Pre-primer: 10 words
Primer: 15 words
First Reader: 15 words
Second and up: 20 words

Choose them randomly from among the "new words" lists in the backs of the books. Have the child read the word lists to you. Stop when the child mispronounces 20 percent of a word list.

● ● ●

One thing that really concerns me is the name of one group. I tried to get them to change the name, but Mike, the leader in the group, convinced the others that they should keep it. I just hope that no one thinks that *I* named them! (They certainly chose a descriptive name!)

When the groups begin to work each morning, they can see the order of their assignments on the chalkboard. The first thing that each child must do is work on the writing lesson which I have placed on the board. Children need this practice in handwriting and it keeps them busy until they come to their reading group. If they finish that and their other work, they are permitted to choose a book from the library shelf to read quietly at their seats. The reading group order changes every week so that I do not always see the Monsters after recess when they are so excited! Here is this week's schedule:

Monsters	*Astronauts*	*Butterflies*
work papers	reading group	workbook
reading group	workbook	work papers
workbook	work papers	reading group

I haven't written a time schedule for them, for I find that I'm never quite sure when I will be done with one reading group and ready to call another, or how long it will take a group of children to finish their workbook assignments.

I've been having trouble with some of the children not finishing their work. At the beginning of the month, they all worked so hard and cooperated with me very well, but as time went by, I found they didn't maintain that attitude. Roberta, for instance, says the workbook is stupid. When she refused to do it, I had no choice but to move her into the middle group where the work is easier. Last week I began keeping those children who didn't complete their work in at recess, so that they could finish what had been assigned. They were not permitted to go out unless all of their work was finished. So on Monday and Tuesday I had Mort, Mitch, Mike, Daisy, Paul, Jeff, Butch, and Roberta stay in and finish work. On Wednesday Daisy, Butch, and Mitch didn't have to stay in, because they had finished their work. I thought my system was working until I checked over their work. I found it had been done very carelessly and that it needed to be done over again. By Wednesday, I noticed that Carl, too, dawdled over his work and seemed delighted when I told him that he would have to stay in. Thursday, the same children were told to stay in to work when I suddenly realized, after looking at my planbook, that I had to go outside since it was my day to supervise the playground! I got chills thinking what this group of children might do if left unsupervised in the classroom, so I did what I thought it best to do—I marched them down to the office and told them to sit on the bench and do their work there. From what Mrs. Mainstay told me later, there was little work accomplished. Mr. Topps came down to talk to me after school, as he does nearly every afternoon, and suggested that I might be able to find another solution for this problem. He reminded me of my own statement at the parent meeting that children require recreation and fresh air. I thought hard about it all night, and decided that any work left undone at the end of the week would be sent home with the children to be completed over the weekend. That should take care of that problem!

For the reader to do

What other solutions might Miss Nouveau have come up with to resolve the situation? How will the parents respond to the "homework" idea?

● ● ●

I've had to send a note home to the parents about our morning snack time. It never occurred to me that there might be problems, but several children bring nothing. I don't know whether Chip, Paul, and Jeff forgot to bring something, but they look hungrily at the other children who do bring snacks. And Daisy! The first day she brought three cupcakes, a bag of potato chips, and a can of cola (warm)! The rest of that first week was just as bad, so I have written to the parents asking them to please send snacks like fruits, vegetables, peanut butter and crackers, cheese, and so on. I also informed the parents that we would be putting all of the food together and letting each child choose something to eat from the accumulation. Maybe now Chip, Paul, and Jeff will have something to keep them going until lunch, although Chip did bring in something this week. He said that they had had a few leftover beans at home and he brought them for snack time. No one chose them of course, so I took them in place of the orange slices I had brought for the food dish.

SQUIRT is such a neat idea! I usually have the children reading for five minutes a day when we do it. At first I read along with them as Mr. Topps told me I must, but I am getting so far behind on grading all of these assignments that I'm sure it won't matter if once in a while I check a few papers while they read. I always make sure that the children do the reading. Sometimes, however, I get so involved with my work that they read for eight or nine minutes. I am usually reminded by my clock watchers that we have gone past the five minute mark. Other days, we only read for three minutes. I figure that makes up for it, and besides there are so many things that we have to get done!

OCTOBER

If only I can survive until January! I student taught during the winter quarter last year, and if we can only get to January I'll know what to do! Why did everything look so easy when my supervising teacher did it? Either I am doing something wrong or else I have a really rough group of children. I always wanted to teach second grade because the children are still so cute and they already know how to read. That seemed like the perfect grade to me, but how different it really is! Some of them can't read and some of them are definitely not in the "cute" category!

This class makes me wonder about the first-grade experience that they had. Whenever I walk by Mrs. Wright's classroom, it *appears* that she has good discipline, but I wonder if she does really. If she had good control of her class, how could a class like this one be giving me so much trouble? I know that Mrs. Wright is an excellent teacher—listening to the reading of Pat and Rita convinces me of that, but perhaps she is just not a disciplinarian. Well, whatever the reason, I've really had to crack down on these kids. I've started putting much longer writing assignments on the chalkboard just to keep the children from running around the room. That should keep them sitting a little longer! The problem with the added material is that they take less time to copy it than it takes me to think it up and carefully write it on the chalkboard.

Another thing we have been having trouble with is going to the bathroom and getting drinks of water. Every morning at 10:10 we go to the rest-rooms and water fountain. The teacher under whom I did student teaching called this "watering" the children. I never understood the real significance of that until Paul came back from the rest-room one day soaking wet. Bit by bit, I got him to tell me that Mike, Butch and Mitch had been dunking him in the toilet. (I hope it had been flushed!) I give the children five minutes in the rest-rooms, which should be adequate time for them without allowing too much extra time for "messing around." Obviously, for some of the children five minutes is several too many!

And the pencil sharpening! At the end of the day I require the children to turn in their pencils that need sharpening. After they leave I sharpen the pencils. Yuk! But what else can I do? They would probably be at the pencil sharpener all day long if I let *them* do it.

The children have also not been conscientious about their workbooks. Every night as I check them, I find that many of the pages are completed incorrectly, if they are completed at all. I think I'm going to have them bring their workbooks to reading group so that we can do them there.

But, gosh, where am I going to find the time! As it is, I am spending thirty to forty-five minutes with each reading group. *They* get tired, and so do I! But how else can I do everything that the lesson plan in the manual outlines? By the time that I have introduced new words, reviewed old words, gone through the phonics lesson, gone over the oral language lesson, had them do all the ditto sheets that accompany the story, read the story out loud and answer their questions (I gave up the silent reading section during the fifth week—just no time for it!), and then do the follow-up activities, the best part of an hour is gone. We haven't had a social studies or science lesson for two weeks because there just is not enough time in the day to do everything. I haven't read stories to the children in so long that I can't even recall the title of the last one. I love to read aloud, but something has to give with a full curriculum like ours.

The oral reading of the children is very poor! I wonder if that could be related to the fact that the first time they see the story is during oral reading? Maybe I should have them practice the story before they come to the reading group. I didn't want to let them take their reading books back to their seats because they might read ahead and spoil the fun of the stories coming up, but I think I'm going to risk it. If nothing else, these children must learn to read!

In addition to everything that has been happening within the room, this was the month for vision and hearing tests for the children. I was convinced that Mort had an auditory problem, for he seems to be tuned out a lot of the time. He doesn't hear me when I call on him, and when he does hear, he doesn't immediately follow through on what I ask him to do. I referred him for a hearing test and was amazed to learn that his hearing is perfectly normal. Why, then, doesn't he do his work, and why doesn't he pay attention?

I referred several children for vision testing because I have been noticing symptoms such as headaches, rubbing the eyes, head close to work, head far from work, and others. I went with the children when Miss Kurad, our school nurse, administered the Snellen eye chart test. According to the test, none of the children had problems, so I went home puzzled. That night I called a former professor of mine and asked if there was an explanation for the difference in my perceptions and observations and what the tests had shown. When I told her that we had used the Snellen chart because the school system doesn't own a telebinocular, she offered to let me borrow the one that the University Reading Laboratory owns. I thanked her profusely, but wondered where I would ever find the time to do that, too! Her advice to me was that I train a mother or father to use the telebinocular just as she had trained us. Since the test is only a screening device, the administrator need not be an expert. The parent who helped would not, after all, be prescribing glasses, but only recommending that the child be taken to an optometrist or ophthalmologist for a thorough eye examination. I was convinced that this was what I needed to do. I'm sure the parents won't think less of me for asking for help—other teachers do it all the time!

Mrs. Penn, when I called her that evening, was delighted that she could help me. We planned for her to come in and do the vision testing. We referred four of the children to eye doctors—Jeff, Mandy, Larry, and Manuel. We also found that Butch is color-blind. No wonder he couldn't do the work paper that required him to color according to the directions given at the top! I am sorry to say, I made him do it over three times before I finally gave up on him in disgust! Oh, Butch! I'm sorry! This experience makes me wonder if, out of ignorance, I have been doing similar things to other children.

Some days I have the children reading twelve minutes for SQUIRT. This is a long time, and Butch and Mitch become even more rambunctious. I am becoming concerned about SQUIRT. I had been told about the plan when I was hired and I had the idea the children loved it. But I keep hearing groans when the bell for SQUIRT begins to ring. Maybe it's not as great as it is cracked up to be for the children, but I can sure get a lot done while they read.

NOVEMBER

Butch, unable to complete his daily work, has been the bane of my existence lately. Two weeks ago he had accumulated so many work papers that by Thursday evening I could see that he would have a lot to do for the coming weekend. That Friday morning he arrived at school with a cast on his left arm, and I'm ashamed to admit that my first reaction was, "Oh, thank goodness it's his left arm. He can still do his work!" He came into the room grinning and showing off his autographed cast. During work time, I noticed that he sat at his desk without working. I told him that he had better do some of his work or he would have even more to take home that evening. He simply looked up at me and said, "I can't. My arm's broke." "Yes, I know it's *broken,* but that's only your left arm. You can still use your right one." He grinned and said, "Yeah, but I'm left-handed!" Oh, no! I had never noticed—I had never thought to notice handedness before. I glanced around the room and saw that Pat, too, was using her left hand. There must be a conspiracy against me!

How is Butch going to do his work? I finally decided to let him do what he could (circling answers, and so forth) and paired him with Larry or Pat to do the rest of his work. He thoroughly enjoys having secretarial help. Sometimes I wonder—is it really broken?

I think I should resign at Christmas. I'm not doing these children any good and they are not doing any good for me. I go home every night at six or six-thirty simply exhausted. Even then I take work home with me so that I don't get to bed until after midnight. I barely can make it to school by 8:00 the next morning; I haven't been to a movie or on a date for weeks. I had no idea that teaching would be so difficult and so depressing. I thought that children were lovable, but I have found I cannot bear to be around some of them. I must be an ogre not to be able to love them all.

I have been talking quite a bit with Mr. Topps recently, and he has been making some very positive suggestions. He tells me that I shouldn't quit, but that instead I should talk with Mrs. Wise or some of the other teachers to get some ideas for control and organization. He helped a lot when he came in after school one day as I was grading workbooks. I marked them as usual—"x" on the wrong ones and a −12 (or whatever for the total incorrect answers) at the top—when he suggested that I might want to emphasize the positive with the children. He told me that when he had taught he always marked those that the children had done correctly with a " $c\!/$ " and wrote +9 (or whatever) at the top. He said that by emphasizing the elements which were correct, I would help the children focus on those elements. They would still see at a glance which ones they had missed, but those were not as obvious or as embarrassing. A lot of children, he said, come to fear the red marks on papers because we only use them negatively. They should learn to see the red marks for what they are—aids to understanding the material. I tried Mr. Topps' idea, and though it took me a while to adjust to the system, I use it all the time now. An interesting comment was made the other day by Chip, whose papers had formerly been bloodbaths of red marks: "Wow! Look how neat my paper is! See all the things I did good, Manuel!"

Two of the children have started wearing eyeglasses this month. Larry came in with his first and all of the children wanted to get them! Mr. Topps told me that Jeff, whom I had referred for further testing, had not yet been to the eye doctor. When I questioned him about it, Mr. Topps indicated that Jeff's family couldn't afford the glasses. I was appalled! A child not able to get the glasses he needs! I remembered something in my notes from college and checked them when I got home that night. One of my professors had indicated that service organizations often provide funds for school children to get glasses or other medical attention. I got the phone number of the local organization from Mr. Topps and called that night to explain the situation. The club president was very helpful and told me that his organization would be glad to help Jeff get his glasses. I also discovered that his organization acted as a collection agency for old pairs of eyeglasses which people didn't use. They take these glasses to eye doctors who are able to re-use the frames and regrind the lenses to provide glasses more cheaply for those who need them. I told him that in return for helping Jeff, I wanted to do something to help his group, so my class and I began canvassing our neighborhoods to collect old pairs of eyeglasses for the service organization. I dittoed a sheet for people whom the children contacted so that the youngsters wouldn't have to remember all the details about why they were asking for glasses. They handed a sheet to whoever answered the door and asked if they had any old eyeglasses to contribute. My kids collected fifteen pairs of eyeglasses! Boy, was I proud of them!

The workbooks are still causing me some problems. They take up so much time in reading group and I have to grade them all at night. Four pages per child is a lot of work for me to correct in addition to all the dittos they do. I sat down one night to try to find a solution, and I thought about it for a long time. Why is it that the workbooks are provided with these basal reading programs? I came to the conclusion that the authors wanted to provide practice for some of the skills they had introduced in the story. Also, the workbook has vocabulary practice. I had already noticed that some of the children didn't need the vocabulary practice, so I can be more selective in which pages they do. In addition, why should I stay with them while they worked through those pages I assigned? Couldn't they work through those pages and check them as a group while I worked with another group? I decided to try it. I've done it for three weeks now and it seems to be working well. I ask one of the children to be responsible for the group—that is, to make sure that they work together, read over the material, and work out the responses cooperatively. When all the pages are finished, the one in charge gets my teacher's copy of the workbook which has all of the answers. The children swap books and the leader then reads the correct responses and everyone checks the workbook which he or she has. They use the new marking system which I use and mark only correct responses. When they are through with this, I come back to the group and we go through the responses they missed and analyze their answers. Sometimes, I found, their reasoning was right even if the answer, according to the key, was wrong. Children made errors because they knew *more* than was being asked for! My only real problem with this new workbook procedure has been that the middle group is too large to work together independently. All sorts of disagreements were occurring that had nothing to do with workbooks, so I just divided the group in half and let them work together in two groups of five.

I have tentatively moved Larry from that middle group into the top group, for I found that he seemed bored with the middle group, and while he still makes oral reading errors, his errors consist of rewording sentences. He *never* makes comprehension errors. Maybe his IRI score wasn't very accurate. I find *myself* making oral reading errors now that I'm more aware of them, and I know that I can read well. Sometimes my mind condenses what is written on the page—it's like my brain is ahead of my voice. Perhaps that's what happens to Larry. Mort has been moved into the middle group; he's just too far ahead of the other Monsters.

Another problem has been that the low group has been unable to work independently on workbooks, so I sit with them and go through the same process that the others are going through. It's amazing how much more time I have now that we are doing this. Also, I am beginning to know the children so much better as we sit and discuss the reasoning behind their answers.

Nevertheless, I am still discouraged about the conflict between what I had hoped to accomplish this year and what I am actually accomplishing. I am rapidly coming to the conclusion that a job at a five-and-dime might not be so bad after all! Or maybe I can try to support myself with my writing. Since I love to write children's stories, I might be able to sell some of them for publication. I will talk with Mrs. Wise and see what she suggests, for I have found her name to be quite descriptive of her ability to analyze a situation.

DECEMBER

The first of this month we stopped SQUIRT. It seemed obvious to me that it was ineffective. But Mr. Topps, who rotates from classroom to classroom during SQUIRT, came in a few days after we had given it up. He walked into the room, book in hand, ready to settle down to a session of reading, but noticed immediately that the children weren't reading. I told them to get out their books and begin reading. "But why?" asked Alex. "You said we wouldn't do it anymore."

Mr. Topps said, "Oh, is there a problem, Miss Nouveau? Maybe I can help. Let's chat after school." Then he sat down in a chair and began to read as if nothing were out of the ordinary. Of course the children and I began to read, too. We read for eight minutes, and Mr. Topps signaled me at that point that we should stop. I told the children to put away their books and return to work.

After school, clutching my keys, I knocked on the open door to Mr. Topps' office. He looked up and said, "You didn't have to come up here, Miss Nouveau. I would have come to your room on my way home later this afternoon."

"Well," I replied, "I would rather get it over with now. I know that I'm a disappointment to you—I am to myself. Would you like me to resign now or wait until Christmas?"

"Who said anything about resigning? Miss Nouveau, I think you have the wrong notion about my role in this school. I see myself as a facilitator and a resource person. I want to help you, because I remember well the agonies of *my* first year as a teacher! Now, what seems to be the problem with SQUIRT?"

"The children are restless and bored with it. Maybe second-graders are just too young, or perhaps this particular group of children are just too undisciplined. Anyway, I can't seem to control them."

"We know they aren't too young, Miss Nouveau. They have been involved in SQUIRT since kindergarten. While I do agree that you have an unusual class, I have seen SQUIRT used with enough classes to know that it will work with your class, too. Let me just run through some of the hazards that one might encounter when using SQUIRT; perhaps being aware of some of these might prove useful to you in organizing the program. First of all, and probably most important, children must know that *we* value reading. They see that we do when they realize that *everyone* in the school begins reading at the same time. Janitors, cooks, parent aides, principal, secretary, teachers—*everyone* must be reading to make this work. ("Oops!" I thought) Also, SQUIRT must be done every day and the sustaining power of the children must be increased gradually. We start at five minutes a day in second grade, permitting those who wish to continue reading longer to do so, of course. When you begin to see them sustaining their reading for five minutes with no difficulty and exhibit eagerness to read longer, then you increase the time to six minutes. In that way you build up their reading time gradually. You only create uncertainty when the children have no notion of how long they are to read. *Never* let them read eight minutes one day, three the next, and twelve the next. ("Oh, no," I cringed.) Also, some of the children will become clock watchers if you don't cover the face of the clock during SQUIRT. ("Of course!" I nodded.) Most of the teachers have a timer which they can set and face away from the class, but if you don't have one, you simply slip a piece of paper over the clock face so that the children cannot see the passage of time. You want them to focus on reading, not timing. They will know, of course, because you have told them, how long they are to read, but it's much better when they can't watch the clock. ("So that's it!" I thought.) Ask Mrs. Wise for the Lyman Hunt (1971) article which details sustained silent reading. I know that she has it, since she is the one who introduced the idea in our school. Do you have any questions about SQUIRT? I hope that some of the things I've mentioned might be useful. And, Miss Nouveau, please don't make a decision now about resigning. I've been really pleased to note your enthusiasm, sincerity, and dedication. I think that you have worked out some difficult problems for yourself, such as the workbook situation. The longer you teach, the more easily you will be able to make curricular adjustments. I have a great deal of confidence in you, Miss Nouveau!"

Wow! Maybe things will get better for me. I think I had better call Miss Kurt and ask her for some suggestions. And Mrs. Wise has always been most helpful.

I have tried, up to this point, to write in my journal at the end of each week so that I could keep up with what was happening, but since my chat with Mr. Topps, so many things have been happening that the weeks rushed by until the holidays gave me a chance to sit down at home and continue my journal. I am so excited by the changes that I have made and the ones I am going to make! I called Miss Kurt the evening after I had talked with Mr. Topps. She told me that she had been planning to see me that week since she had just come back from a convention where she had been given some sample books from a salesperson. She wanted me to take a look at them, and told me that if I liked them, the budget would permit us to order five more copies of the series. Not much, she admitted, but at least it would be a start.

She brought them to school and showed them to me. They seem to be just what I need for two of my groups. The series is a total language arts program which integrates reading, writing, speaking, and listening. I asked her if she thought I could use this same series with both my top group and my low group. She assured me that they should work out very well, since the groups would be at two different levels. The low group needs much more of the integration than our present series provides, and the top group could work independently on many of the activities included in the program. "But what about your middle group? How many are there in it and what will you do with them?" she asked.

I told her that I felt I could use the basal series which we were currently using, but I wanted to divide that group. There were too many for me to work with at one time; in addition, there was such a wide range of abilities. Did she think that I could handle four groups? Miss Kurt assured me that she had always found four or five small groups easier to deal with than three large ones, for she had been better able to provide for individual differences and, therefore, discipline was easier. She thought I would find that to be true, also.

While she began to unpack the new reading materials, I picked up a stack of pencils and began my nightly routine of pencil sharpening. Miss Kurt paid no attention to me until I was working on my eighth pencil, when she turned to me and said, "Good grief, you use a lot of pencils! What do you do—chew off the points?"

"Oh, these aren't mine. I sharpen the children's pencils."

"*You* sharpen? Do they all have broken arms? My dear, your time is more valuable than that! Let the children sharpen their own. I know —you're afraid that they'll stand there all day just sharpening and not have any pencil left. Yes, that will happen at first, especially since you have made it such a high priority. They think it must be something pretty special if you always do it. But they'll soon tire of it, and will only sharpen when they need to. You know, one of the best ways to ward off trouble is to create a routine. If things get bad, just make a routine like having them sign a sheet of paper every time they use the sharpener, or putting a ticket on your desk. Children will soon tire of the extra step and you can see more clearly who is still a problem. Now that we're on the subject of management, how do you handle the bathroom situation?"

I explained to her about the "watering" procedure, and my general dissatisfaction with it, primarily because some of the children claimed they didn't have "to go" when we went! But later, they needed to go by themselves. I also told to her the story of poor Paul's dunking.

"Then why don't you just let them go when they need to? How would you like someone to tell you when to go to the rest-room? Try this. Have a symbol for the boys and one for the girls in the chalkboard tray. Whenever a child wishes to use the rest-room, he or she comes to the front, picks up the symbol, places it on his or her desk, and goes to the rest-room alone. The child returns the symbol to the chalkboard tray when he or she returns. When the symbol is in the tray one child may go to the rest-room; when it is missing, the next child must wait. Now at first, there will be problems for going to the rest-room alone will seem to be a big deal. But again, as with the pencil sharpening, the novelty will wear off if you don't make a fuss."

So far, so good. The children went through the stage that Miss Kurt predicted and are now settled down into this new set of routines. Without her warning of what to expect, however, I think that I would have chucked the whole thing when the negative behavior increased temporarily.

I was quite eager for the holidays to begin! Not, as originally, so that I could get away from this place, but to have the time to reorganize myself, the children, and the materials. I needed the uninterrupted time to examine the new series carefully and to plan my instructional program. For the first time since school began in the fall, I am truly excited about teaching. I think that I *can* do it, and I will!

For readers to do together

Divide the class into groups of five or six. Each group will examine a basal reading series in light of whatever criteria the class established.

Spend approximately one hour examining the assigned series. Each member of the group must know the series well, for during the second hour of class, the groups are redistributed, with one member from each group in a different group.

Each person will share what it is he or she knows about his or her basal reading series with the others in the new group. Plan about ten minutes of sharing. Each person will share what he or she knows, so that by the end of the second hour, everyone in each group will know about the other basal reading series being examined (jigsaw technique based on article by Aronson, *et al.*, 1975).

● ● ●

I remember how excited I was as a child to receive the weekly newspaper that was published for children. Every Friday we got our copies and read the paper as a whole group. I was not then aware of the problems that my teachers must have faced! First and foremost, how in the world did they ever keep up with all of them? I swear, some weeks I am sure that they send us three sets of newspapers. They seem to multiply like rabbits. And then, when we get busy I forget to have the class read them. By Christmas vacation, I had five weeks' worth of papers. So, I just rolled them up, put some holiday wrapping around them, and distributed them to the children as they walked out the door that last day. They were delighted, and I was grateful to be rid of them. Maybe some of the children will read the papers over the vacation, so that when they come back they won't have forgotten how to read! Please don't let that happen to me! But when the kids return, we are no longer going to do the paper as a whole group. I am going to have good readers paired with less able ones and let them read the paper together. Then, perhaps on Friday afternoon, we will have a discussion of any things in the paper which the children especially enjoyed or were curious about. I hope the children enjoy it, for it certainly sounds more appealing to me, at this point. Happy Holidays!

JANUARY

Throughout the fall I anticipated this month because I was certain that once I got here I would know what to do. But for some reason that is not the case. I don't know if my supervising teacher did not give me good instruction or if it's just that I cannot carry out what she did. Maybe it's that children differ so much that no instructional program can ever be repeated exactly with the same success. Whatever the reason, I find that Mrs. Wise, Mr. Topps, and Miss Kurt, busy as they are, are more help to me than my student teaching experience was.

With Mrs. Wise and Miss Kurt's help, I have reorganized the reading groups. I now have four groups instead of three. The low group works in the reading-language arts series as does the top group. There are two middle groups working in the series we have used all year. Mort, though bright, has such poor work habits that he is assigned to two groups so that he can get the skills which he needs with the one group and do the reading that he is capable of with the other.

Again I permitted the children to name their groups. So that they would not be influenced by any other child, I had them vote by secret ballot within their groups. Mike was furious, since he wanted to rename the group Monsters. Daisy told him to "shut up"—she said that if everyone else got a new name, then she wanted one, too.

The Friendlies	Help, Inc.	Streakers	Fantastic Five
Carl	Mandy	Mike	Horace
Manuel	Pat	Daisy	Daphne
Mitch	Larry	Paul	Joyce
Alex	Rita	Butch	Hilda
Steve	Betty	Jeff	Mort
Mort	Roberta	Chip	

For the reader to do

Which groups will be using the new series? Which groups will be using the old series? Do you agree or disagree with Miss Nouveau's new group assignments?

● ● ●

The Help, Inc. children decided on their name after I had asked them to be classroom helpers. If any of the children have trouble with their work or reading, they will go to one of the members of that top group and ask for assistance. That system has freed me amazingly. Now there aren't twelve hands up all over the room waiting for me to come to them, nor is there a constant line beside my desk. Members of this group also sit with the Streakers and help them work through their workbook pages just like the other groups do. Later, I meet with the Streakers to discuss their answers. The Streakers feel that they have gained some autonomy by this plan. They had resented being the only group with whom I worked through the workbook in its entirety. Now they have developed some group spirit as the others have, and they are very pleased when I tell them that I think they have been good workers. Occasionally, I ask children from the Fantastic Five to be helpers as well. It is my goal to find tasks for children from all of the groups so that they can experience the satisfaction of making a classroom contribution.

Vocabulary presentation has been very difficult to deal with. At the beginning of the year, I presented the new vocabulary to everyone in the group and then let them do the workbook pages which gave practice with those words. Later on I stopped doing the workbook pages with them in order to save time, but I discovered that some of the children needed more practice with the words than they were receiving. During Christmas vacation, I decided that what was needed was to teach the words only to children who didn't know them. I tested their knowledge of the words and then during vacation put the upcoming basal reader words as vocabulary tests on ditto masters. I made a test for the beginning of each unit in the reading books. Each child has a copy of the tests, and I ask each one to read these words to me. Any words which the child doesn't know are circled. Those words are the ones which the child must be taught during the course of reading that unit. Each word is written twice—once beginning with the lower-case letter and once with the upper-case letter. I use the backside of discarded computer paper to write the words on, cutting the paper so that the holes are on the left. I cut these into individual word cards and then place them in a loose binder ring, one for each child. Now all of Chip's words (ones which he has to learn to read) are together on one ring. He brings the ring of words to me every day and I check them. If he reads a word correctly, I make a star on that word card. If he doesn't know the word, no star is made. After three days of his saying the word correctly, I rip the word off the binder ring and let him take it home.

For the reader to do

The children are taking home words they have learned from the ring of words. Write a letter to the parents outlining five games/activities for further use of these words.

● ● ●

After the unit in the reading book is finished, the test is administered again. Words still unknown go back on the ring of words for further work. I try to check the words every morning and put new ones on every afternoon. I also ask the children to tell me any other words they would like to have on their rings in addition to the ones which I put on. I am usually given one or two to add to the rings.

The children are encouraged to practice their words at their seats and to teach them to the other children. Larry, Pat, and Mandy came to me one day and asked if each of them could have a ring, too. When I commented that they always know their words, they said they knew that, but wanted to learn some new ones. Needless to say, they got rings! By the way, I now have mothers and fathers coming in on a rotating schedule to help check the words for me. A tremendous help!

For the reader to do

Form a basal reader used in the school where you are teaching; make a vocabulary test similar to the one Miss Nouveau described. Make a ring of words for the child with words he or she missed. After the child has finished the unit, give the vocabulary test again.

Describe to your classmates the results of this procedure and any observations which you made.

● ● ●

I have really saved time by omitting some of the work papers that I had been giving the children and by letting them grade some of the ones they are still doing. I let them grade some of their own work at a table that has an answer key and grading pencils. They leave the paper on the table when they are through marking. One afternoon, Miss Kurt bustled into the room and asked how things were going. I told her that I was quite pleased with the four groups except that it still took so long to go through all of the work with a group. She said, "Well, at least you haven't made the mistake that so many first-year teachers make—they think that they have to do *everything* in the manual. As you well know, *that* is an impossibility." I nodded, realizing she was quite right and resolved then and there to quit trying to do the impossible. Of course, it made sense that the series would provide more material than I could use so that I could pick and choose for the children. And that is precisely what I intend to do!

I made a SQUIRT chart, too. In front of the room is a long sheet of paper marked off by days and months. Along the side the minutes are marked off in five- to fifteen-minute segments. Our bar graph lets us see our increasing SQUIRT time.

When we began SQUIRT all over again, we started with five minutes and increased the time only when I knew that I could do so. Following the rules of SQUIRT has made it so much more enjoyable both for the children and for me. By the end of this month, we had achieved eight minutes of sustained silent reading and the children are nearly ready to move ahead to nine minutes. I am so pleased. They beg to read more, for they love to see the bar graph grow. I am going to increase the time very gradually, though, so that we don't have any of the trouble we had before.

Though my classroom control techniques are improving, and it is so much easier to accomplish our work, there are still many problems. I hate to sound like a fishwife yelling at the children, but sometimes that seems to be the only way to deal with a situation. In extreme cases, I send a child from the room to stand in the hallway until he or she is in control. At other times I send a child to stand facing the chalkboard for a period of time. Unfortunately, the last child I had do that was Mike. He was to stand there quietly until I told him he could return to his seat. I sat down with a reading group, my back to Mike, and worked with them until I noticed children giggling and pointing to the spot behind me where I had positioned Mike. I turned around and saw that he was imitating a monkey for the benefit of the other children, so I drew a circle on the board and told him to keep his face toward that circle. He did, but as soon as I got my group back to work again, there were more snickers around the room. Knowing it must be Mike I turned to find he had drawn a caricature of me on the board, using the circle I had drawn for my head. Not a bad job for a little kid, I remember thinking, right before it hit me that he had defied me again. After school I went to Mrs. Wise and asked her if she knew anything about behavior modification. During Christmas vacation I had read an article about it which made it seem the answer to my problems. Mrs. Wise offered me a cup of tea and invited me to sit down and talk with her.

I asked her if she could tell me about behavior modification—if it works, and how and why. She chuckled and said, "Oh, my dear! That's a rather large order and may take a considerable amount of time to go into. Let me gather my thoughts, for there are so many aspects to consider in the 'if, how, and why' of something as complex as behavior modification. Would it be possible for you to come for dinner tomorrow evening? We could discuss this in much greater detail then."

Of course I accepted and she gave me directions to her house. We had a lovely, relaxed dinner during which she steered me away from school topics whenever I brought them up. As we were stacking the dishes, she told me that she knew I wanted to discuss school, but that her own philosophy of life prevented her from doing so. "We live with school so much of our lives as it is, that I force myself to forget it, or at least not discuss it, during dinner. There are so many disturbing things about school that they can ruin your digestion!"

Why, I could hardly believe that this woman with more than twenty years of teaching experience could still have troubles in school! That made me feel better.

We talked for a long time about the behavior modification techniques that were in current use. She said that her own personal bias prevented her from planning the conscious manipulation of children. She objected to that procedure because it would, in her mind, create automatons— unthinking, unfeeling actors who respond to the cues they are given. She asked if I had ever read Sleator's *House of Stairs* which showed an extreme, though not unreasonable, example of what she meant. When I admitted that I had never heard of the book, she took it from her bookshelf and advised me to take it home and read it. (I began it that night and stayed up until 4 a.m. because I was unable to stop reading!) We also talked about some of the constructive aspects of behavior modification: being positive rather than negative with children, "catching them being good" rather than always noticing them when they aren't, making an effort to respond to children, having a small number of rules, and being consistent.

"But," said Mrs. Wise, "don't think that these aspects are limited to behavior modification techniques. These notions have been around for years and the behavior modifiers just adopted them and used them as part of their system. Good teachers have known these rules all along. I was surprised one day to read an article in one of my journals that extolled the virtues of behavior modification and the techniques that were being used—many of the same things I had done since my first year of teaching! One day, Mrs. O'Reer (she taught in your room last year) told me that she was pleased to see that I, too, was a behavior modification person! I told her that in no way could I be considered a 'behavior mod' person."

I asked Mrs. Wise where she read the information she had gathered. She told me that she belongs to several professional organizations that publish journals. She gave me copies of *Language Arts, Childhood Education,* and *The Reading Teacher.* She told me to take the journals home and look them over. I did and have definitely decided that I'll join them as soon as I get my next paycheck. (See Appendix A for a list of relevant professional organizations and publications.) There are also state and local councils for each of these associations, and she offered to take me to their next meetings.

The doorbell rang, and Mrs. Wise went to answer it. Preparing to leave, I began to gather my things when she returned with her neighbor, a doctoral student at the University. She introduced me to Mr. Horatio Flame, who said, "Just call me Red." We chatted for a while before I left. He seems like a really nice fellow.

FEBRUARY

It has become more apparent as the year progresses that the children in the top group need reading experiences beyond those provided in their series. I now use the basal series as only part of their program. I find the language arts integration exercises really quite good and interesting but these students need more extended reading. I allow them to go to the library regularly where Miss Page helps them choose materials. They also find things to read in the classroom library although there are very few books in my room. We have added to the supply this year with children's paperbacks. The children and I receive brochures every month from two companies which publish inexpensive, high-quality children's books. The children take their individual brochures home and bring back the completed order forms with the necessary money. I mail these and add the bonus books, one of which we get for each ten books the children order. Then we all eagerly await the arrival of our new books. In this way, I have added about twenty-five new books to our shelf this year.

I have also increased my own supply of children's books by placing orders right along with those of the kids, and I have begun to read aloud to the children again. Mrs. Wise convinced me that that is one activity I should never neglect, for children begin to desire to read by learning to love literature. If the motivation is established while they are young, they will face fewer reading problems as they grow older.

Two more devices which are now part of the classroom schedule are the "Fun to Do for One" and "Fun to Do for Some" buckets. I have collected large plastic containers from a fast-food place near my house. Each container is labeled so that when children finish their other work, they may choose something to do from one of the buckets. If the child wants to work alone, he or she selects from the first bucket; if two or more children decide to work together, they choose from the second bucket. Here are sample activities from the buckets:

> You are walking down the road and suddenly a space ship lands in front of you. Space people get out of the ship and take you inside with them. They tell you that they are going to take you home with them. After you have been with them for one week, they will let you mail a letter to anyone you want to. Whom will you write to? What will you tell that person? Write your letter now.

> You and your friend(s) have been working very hard today. Choose a game from the game shelf and play it together. Remember to follow the rules so that you will have a good time.

Another device I use to get feedback from the kids is called "Tell it to Tillie Turtle." While in an undergraduate children's literature course, I constructed a project with papier-mâché characters from *Over in the Meadow*. I kept the characters, renaming the mother turtle, Tillie. So far Tillie Turtle has been a valuable aid. I told the children to write a letter to Tillie whenever they had a suggestion to make or were unhappy with a routine in the classroom. Every day Tillie receives at least one letter and sometimes more. Some letters relate personal problems and some are fan letters to Tillie because the children like her so much. Tillie answers every letter she receives, and the children find this an added incentive to write to her.

Mrs. Wise has encouraged me to go through the materials located in the school storeroom. I didn't even know where it was, so she took me there and showed me the stacks of outdated textbooks and old readers. I got Mr. Topps' permission to take two copies of each book I wanted and cut them into little books for the children like the ones I had seen in Mrs. Wright's classroom. Some children had seemed so frustrated by the length of the books on our library shelf. Mitch and Butch reacted especially well to these little books. They were very glad to find short books to read at their respective levels.

This month we began using the skill kit I found in the back of my own storage closet. The kit consists of a series of graded short stories, each with accompanying skill exercises and comprehension questions. Each passage, set of comprehension questions, and set of exercises is printed on a single sheet of paper. The reading passages range from first-grade through fifth-grade level. I asked Mrs. Wright about them and she said they could be effectively used to supplement the basal program. After explaining the kit to me, she also suggested that the children score their own papers and keep their own records. Since I now fully understood the kit, I went off eagerly to use it with the children. Everyone was to choose one selection to do for reading every day. When they finished that item I told them to choose another. After two weeks, Tillie started getting letters! At first there were one or two complaints, but after a few more days, Tillie's mailbox was overflowing and she was finding it extremely difficult to answer all the letters! To judge from their letters, the children hated doing the skill cards, but I loved them, for each child was working at his or her own level, reinforcing skills, and doing extra reading. I decided that a compromise was what was needed so I wrote a letter to the entire class from Tillie which I left posted on the chalkboard for them to find the next morning.

Hello, Children!

I'm so sorry that you are all so unhappy with your nice new box for reading. I have sent a letter to Miss Nouveau which explains how upset you are. She wrote back to me and said that she would be changing things soon.

Please let me know how you like her new ideas.

Love,

Tillie Turtle

"Now," I told them, "you may choose to do passages whenever you want to, but no one is permitted to choose over five passages a week. You may do them all in one day or one a day or however you wish. You don't have to do any, or you may do any number up to five, but under no circumstances can you do more than five per week." The strategy worked! When I no longer assigned the skill cards, the kids frequently chose to do them. Some even came and asked me to let them do more, but I was adamant! If I let them think that I valued the cards (as I had evidently done with the pencil sharpening) then they would be eager to do them. Of course, not every child responded in that fashion. At first, Mike, delighted at not having to do them any longer, never even went to the corner of the room where I kept the box. But later on, I noticed that he would do a card occasionally—maybe he just wanted to see what the attraction was for all of the children who did them regularly.

I have stopped putting writing lessons on the chalkboard and now I let the children create their own writing papers. About the time we started the ring of words plan for vocabulary, I made a book for each child in which he or she was to write the words I had included on the ring. In that way, we had an accurate record of all his or her words, even after the word was removed from the ring. So, as part of their writing assignment, the children go through their rings every day and write in their word books any new words they have on their rings. The second part of the assignment is to choose six words and write at least three sentences (with at least two words from their word books per sentence). In trying to create sentences for the use of these words, the children come up to me and say, "I need a 'would' sentence. Can you put a 'would' in my book?" I can and I do. In addition, I make a new word card which goes on the ring of words. In this way, the children are finding a need for words which they never would have chosen to learn for fun, and they are often dealing with words which give them much trouble in reading. By developing their own need for it, they learn the word more readily.

In the past few months I have been able to plan a much better schedule. In looking back over what I had done last fall, I was appalled! I really resented keeping the journal last fall when I was so harried, but now I see the benefit of it. *I* have probably learned as much about my teaching as Mr. Topps has. Having to commit to paper the things I am learning, planning, and doing has been important in my own professional development. I was *so* sure of myself at times! And the things I had the children do won't bear repeating. But now I see that I have only begun to learn to teach. I go home only a little later than the rest of the staff now that I am better organized and not trying to do too much. I have taken Mrs. Wise's advice and do not think about school until after dinner so that I can relax and unwind from the day. The children are engaged in more meaningful activities now and are obviously much happier with the new improved me!

I still write the children's weekly schedules by groups on the chalkboard for them, but there are several changes from my original schedules! Here is last week's schedule. They all start with their writing lesson, reading over their reading lesson, and practicing their ring of words.

Help, Inc.		*The Friendlies*
9:00	Check ring of words	Reading group
9:30	Workbooks, papers	Check ring of words
10:00	Individual reading conferences	Free time
10:30	Free time	Workbooks, papers

Streakers		*Fantastic Five*
9:00	Workbooks, papers	Free time
9:30	Check ring of words	Workbooks, papers
10:00	Reading group	Check ring of words
10:30	Free time	Reading group

This schedule seems to indicate that I am in several places at once, but I have found that I need not meet with Help, Inc. every day since they are such independent workers. I can fit two conferences in a day with individual children from that group while the group I am working with is doing some independent work. I give them something to do, turn to the child I must work with for about five minutes and then turn back to my group. It seems so much more efficient to use the time that they are working to get other things done. During the free time they have scheduled, they can work with the skill kits, read, play reading games, catch up on other work, write to Tillie, choose from the "Fun to Do" buckets. I always try to plan for the Streakers to have free time when the Help, Inc. group or the Fantastic Five do, so the more capable children are available to help the Streakers play games or do other activities. I check rings of words in the morning and find that now I am able even to add new words to the children's rings at that time. They enjoy the schedule because they like—and need—some structure. However, by permitting choices within the schedules (such as "free time") they feel that they have helped to plan their own day.

This busy month was also parent conference time. I am ashamed to admit that I am only now beginning to really know the children. Up to this point I have been so concerned with establishing routines and working out discipline problems, that I have been very self-centered. I did learn quite a few things from the conferences, however. I discovered that Mike will be moving to the western portion of the state (Oh, I hope he gets a teacher who understands him!). I remember wishing that all of the children could be like Betty, but now I realize how boring that would be. Children like Mort, Roberta, Mitch, and Mike, though difficult to deal with, add spice to a class. I even *like* them now—I never thought this would happen.

The children's parents were very positive toward me, though Mrs. Smith said that she had had grave concerns early in the school year. Now she and other parents with whom she has spoken are very pleased. I told Joyce's parents that I worried about her, for, though bright, she rarely made contributions to her group. She prefers working alone. Paul's mother again failed to come to the conference and she didn't respond to the note I sent. With their phone disconnected again, I don't see how I can get in touch with her. Chip's father told me that he thought Chip was "doin' real good." Rita's parents were pleased at the amount of independent reading she's doing. Jeff's mother (father?), too, did not respond to my note. I would like to know more about his home life, but he won't talk about it at all.

These conferences were much more productive than the ones last fall. I will keep parents' comments in mind as I plan the instructional program for the rest of the year.

Deer Tilie,

I dont like when we do werkboks. Sume kids laff at me when I do bad. Can we pleez do sume uthr way?

Chip

Dear Chip,

I am sorry to hear that you are unhappy. I didn't know about your problem. I sent a note to Miss Nouveau, and she will probably talk to your group today.

Love,

Tillie Turtle

For the reader to do

How will Miss Nouveau handle this situation? Write three possible solutions to the problem and compare them to what she did.

● ● ●

The grouping system we have been using for some time now seems to have developed some wrinkles. I thought about Chip's letter and decided to try two solutions to the problem.

I have paired a good reader with a less capable one to work on the workbooks. In this way the directions get read, work gets done and checked. One person from each of the four groups is responsible for making sure that the work has been done. They check with the others in their groups and collect the completed workbooks for me. The responsibility for this job rotates from week to week so that everyone should have a couple of turns before the end of the year.

Another thing I have decided to do is to make more frequent requests of mothers and fathers to come and help out in the room. They can be a big help with workbooks, playing games, checking rings of words, and supervising the two centers I have created for the classroom. Several of the parents have volunteered to come in for an hour to help out. Each of them will come for an hour on a different day of the week. They have volunteered to come again or to find other parents to come in their place after two weeks.

I have gathered all of the math materials—manipulatives, games, papers, and so on, and put them all in one corner of the room called the Math Center. Children may go there in their free time, or I assign them there when we do math in the afternoon. The other center is called Stories. It includes books, pictures to stimulate creative-story writing, paper, crayons, magic markers, flannel-board stories, filmstrip stories, and anything else I can find that might pertain to creating and/or enjoying stories. The two centers also have activity cards which direct the children in some specific activities.* Here is one of these cards:

> Watch the filmstrip of the fairy tale "Rumpelstiltskin."
> Write down three important ideas in the filmstrip.

The Math Center is color-coded blue and Stories is green. Each child is given ten tickets made of colored construction paper. Five are green, five are blue. If a child wishes to go to either of the centers, he or she must use one of the tickets. The tickets are put in a slot in a sealed box at the entrance to the center area. In that way, the children decide when and to which centers they will go during their free time. A periodic quick check assures me that children are not illegally using centers. They also must learn to plan ahead: the first week we had the centers and tickets, Mike ran out of tickets by Tuesday afternoon. He asked me for some more for the rest of the week and I had to remind him that ten tickets was the limit for the week. The following week, he spent longer periods in the centers and managed to get through Thursday morning. After that, he could plan well enough so that he at least would get through Friday morning before running out of tickets.

Butch took some of Paul's tickets when he had exhausted his own supply. When I discovered that, I began having the children write their names on each of their ten tickets. I like this system not only because of the help in stopping "borrowing," but also because I have a good check at the end of the day as to where the children spent free time.

could I have done it before

For readers to do together

Divide the class into groups of five and six. Each group must plan a different language arts learning center, including a diagram of the center, descriptions of activities, activity-card ideas, and games. Indicate the grade level.

Duplicate these ideas so that everyone in the class has several learning center plans to use later.

● ● ●

---

* The various skills dealt with on these cards have been explained and demonstrated to children prior to their use in centers. For example, children work with me in small groups to identify main ideas in filmstrips before attempting the task alone.

The Streakers are still having so many problems with sight vocabulary that I have decided to do something further for word practice. I have made cards like Bingo, but with words on the squares rather than numerals. We called ours Wordo. Spaces for twenty-five words allow me the opportunity to practice some of their old words as well as to add new ones. I made different sets of cards for the pre-primers and primers which they were working on. Each set was made from a different color of construction paper so that I could sort the sets easily. I sealed them with clear adhesive plastic for durability. The caller, a child from another group, would call from a list containing the words. Having played Bingo before during math practice, the children knew they had to have five words covered horizontally, diagonally, or vertically to win.

For the reader to do

Make a game like the one described above. You can use the words in the back of the basal reader for any grade level. Play the game with a small group of children.

● ● ●

SQUIRT is working so well now! The children and I enjoy the reading immensely and we love to watch our progress on the bar graph. We are now up to eleven minutes daily, which is still too short for some of the children. They continue reading after the majority of the class goes back to other activities. I am so glad that Mr. Topps straightened me out on this.

I have been so concerned about some of the children that I thought about sending some activities home for them to do—not, however, like those stupid work papers which I deluged them with earlier this year! To make the activities more attractive, I would not require that they bring the exercises back to me. The only thing I would insist on is that they bring the box back to me when they want a refill of materials. The "Homebox" notion had been in my mind for some time, and it has been most successful. I do not put any ditto papers in the box—they see enough of those at school! The materials included are activity-oriented ones which require participation rather than passive marking by the child. Chip's box, for instance, includes materials that strengthen his oral language skills. There are small finger puppets to tell a story with, pictures to stimulate language, circular pages stapled for him to make into a circular book, a word-picture game, and an inexpensive storybook I bought at the grocery store. I try to require as little parental aid as possible with Homeboxes so that parents who don't work with their child won't ruin the intent of the box.

For the reader to do

Make a Homebox for one of the other children in the Streakers or The Friendlies group. Include four or five activities to help reinforce an area of weakness you have determined that child to have. Share your box with the class and have them evaluate what you have planned.

● ● ●

Red, who is working to put himself through his doctoral program, has offered to come to school early next month to show the children the musical instruments that he plays. He is the leader of a rock band that he calls "Red and the Flamers." I know that Mike and many of the others will be enthralled with his presentation as well as with his personality, which matches his gorgeous, curly, auburn hair. I realize how busy he is—and am delighted he is willing to talk to the class.

APRIL

Red's appearance was enormously successful! We discussed rock bands, and I was amazed at how knowledgeable these young children are about rock groups. Mike was fascinated with the drums. Red had brought an amplifier along as well, and we just caught Butch in time; he had plugged in the electric guitar and was ready to strum—full blast!

After Red left, I had the children tell me about his visit and I wrote what they told me on chart paper. We read it over together, cut apart some of the sentences, and relocated them in the correct order of occurrence. Here is what they came up with. (Hilda reminded me that Mrs. Wright always put their names after their own sentences.)

Mr. Flame of "Red and the Flamers" came to our class. (Alex)
It was really cool, man! (Mike)
He showed a variety of instruments. (Larry)
Some of us danced when he played. (Rita)
I almost played the electric guitar. (Butch)
It sound good. (Paul)
He asked Miss Nouveau for an aspirin before he left. (Mandy)

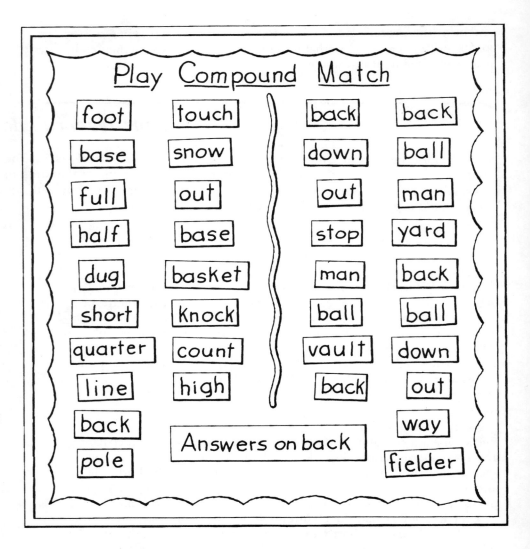

Play Compound Match

foot	touch	back	back
base	snow	down	ball
full	out	out	man
half	base	stop	yard
dug	basket	man	back
short	knock	ball	ball
quarter	count	vault	down
line	high	back	out
back			way
pole			fielder

Answers on back

The children move the cards around on the board to form compound words. When they have made all that they can, they check their words against the answer key on the bulletin board. Any words they form which are not on the paper, they check with me to see if they've found one I missed.

I am so tired of making beautiful bulletin boards that the children never seem to notice! I can spend days constructing one, and they don't notice that it's even there! Well, no more! From now on, beginning with the ones I just put up, the children will notice! One bulletin board has some of the pictures they did in art class. The other is a game board for practicing a reading skill. I looked over some of the upcoming lessons and noticed there were several compound words, which seemed like a useful theme for an otherwise strictly decorative bulletin board. The class chose compound words to write on cards, and then we put them up on the game board (see opposite page).

The children really notice their own work, and they love to play the game on the bulletin board. Even children from the top group like to play the bulletin board game. I'm going to plan some more bulletin board games over the summer so that I can put up several next year.

For the reader to do

Construct a teaching/learning bulletin board game. Place it on the wall of your classroom or in the schoolroom where you are working.

● ● ●

One day last week when Mrs. Penn was helping, she played the Wordo game with children in the Streakers and The Friendlies. After she finished, she asked if she could take some of their reading books home and make a new game for them to play. She said she had a game in mind that had been very successful in her classes when she taught school. I was delighted and gave her the poster board and reading books she wanted. At the end of the week, she sent Pat to school with many bundles of 2" circles in groups of twelve and a checkerboard. She included this note to me:

Dear Miss Nouveau,

This is the checker game I used for further sight word practice. You will notice a numeral on the back of each checker. All twelve checkers in a set have the same numeral. That way, you can sort them out quickly. The two children playing will place their own checker sets word-up and on the right squares. They then play just like checkers, except that every time they move, they have to say the word on the checker being moved. I always allow other children to help with pronunciation if the word is not known, but I do insist that the child receiving help repeat the word.

To keep track of who should use which set, I made a chart listing all of the children's names along the side and all of the numerals for the different checker sets along the top. When a child came to me and read all twelve words in a set, that set was marked with a check beside the child's name. They could see at a glance, then, which set they were allowed to play with next.

I hope that your children will enjoy this game. My own four girls have had fun with it, because children of different abilities can play together. Carol, with her difficult words, likes to play with Jan, who is learning the names of the alphabet letters with her sets. Have fun.

Mrs. Penn

For the reader to do

Make a checker game like the one Mrs. Penn constructed. Play the game with children.

● ● ●

Though there are still discipline problems, I find myself much better able to handle my class and the instruction now, and I must confess that a large portion of my troubles were related to poor classroom organization. Some children were frustrated because the work was too hard, and some were bored because it was too easy. All of them thought the work uninteresting (which it was). Now that I have thought through what I hope to accomplish with the children, I can relax and enjoy my job. I was so tense earlier this year that I never took the time to enjoy my class. Now I do. I think that I must have the greatest second-grade in the world! What terrific kids! They are unique individuals who have taught me more this year than I have taught them, I'm sure. In addition, we're up to thirteen minutes of SQUIRT time—not bad for having to start all over again!

I went back to the storeroom this week and brought out some more of the old books for our classroom. One concern I have had is trying to have the children working with me on their instructional levels. When we do that, there are so many things that have to be taught (vocabulary, phonics skills, and more) that I don't spend as much time on comprehension skills as I would like. So, I thought, why not bring in some different readers at each child's independent reading level and then set purposes for their reading from those. Now, two days a week, each group (except the Help, Inc. children, who are already at the independent level with their series) has independent reading from the other series and three days a week they continue working in their regular series. I decided that for independent reading, the children should read in books one level below their instructional level. Paul will continue to work in pre-primers for his independent work and Manuel will read from 2¹ books. Now on Monday, Wednesday and Friday I work with the groups at their instructional levels in their regular basal series. On Tuesday and Thursday we work on independent level reading from other series. On a Tuesday or Thursday, I meet with each group briefly before we begin the day's work. At that time I give them the readers and set the purpose for reading. Then, when we meet during their reading group time, we discuss the story in light of the direction that I have given them. I have found that they are more able to focus on comprehension when reading on an independent level, for they do not need to be concerned with decoding the words at the same time. Horace, especially, has shown growth with this system. I only wish I had started it earlier.

MAY

The Three-Toed Sloth

"Horrible! Horrible!" cried the three-toed sloth,
"That I have to sip this banana broth
And stay in bed with this cast on my knee.
I wish I were hanging in my tree!"

"Hush up!" said the nurse and took his pulse.
"You'd better be quiet or you'll convulse.
Cut out that squirming and twisting around;
In here nobody sleeps upside down."

The three-toed sloth told the nurse to leave;
"I've got an ace up my pajama sleeve,"
He mumbled, and put the phone to his ear.
"I'll call up Phlebas the engineer."

He talked to Phlebas and Phlebas said, "Right.
I'll be down there about ten tonight.
Since there's no doctor to ease your pain
I'll bring along my giant crane."

He hooked the crane to the hospital wall
And pulled, but nothing happened at all.
He said, "I'll try once more for my old friend,"
And stood the hospital on its end.

The other patients slid all over the floor
And two of them rolled up against the door;
But the three-toed sloth, who was strapped to his bed,
Spent a happy night asleep on his head.

Recently, while checking through the poetry section of the library, I discovered *Friends of Yours, Friends of Mine,* a delightful book of poetry by Dabney Stuart. I had gone to the library to find some interesting poems to read when I spotted an unusual book jacket. Intrigued, I sat down in the aisle to read a few poems. It took only a few to convince me that this was one book I wanted to share with my class. I read many of the poems to them, but one they asked for again and again was the one entitled "The Three-Toed Sloth."

The children did everything imaginable with this poem. They made pictures of the different sections, they acted it out, they rewrote the poem into a story, and they added other adventures for the three-toed sloth to have.

For the reader to do

Compile an anthology of twenty-five poems that could be used with children in the primary grades. Plan follow-up activities for at least five of them.

● ● ●

We had to add on to our SQUIRT chart, for we have reached sixteen minutes of SQUIRT time! I never thought last fall that I would be here in May, and I probably wouldn't have been if Mr. Topps and the others hadn't helped me isolate my problems and correct them. I certainly never thought that I would see my class sitting still and reading attentively for sixteen straight minutes and liking it!

In some ways it has been a long year, but in others it has been too short. How I wish I could have begun my independent reading program earlier!

Anticipating next year and the first day of school (it just has to be better!), I asked the children to think back over the year and all of the things we have done. I wrote their comments on the chalkboard and we filled it in no time! I had no idea that we had done so many things or that the children could remember them.

The next instructions that I gave them were to pretend that they were their own desks. As the desk, they were to write a letter to whoever would be sitting in that seat next year. They were to give the new second-graders an idea about what to expect during the new school year.

We would leave the letters in the desks and surprise the new children with them when they opened the top to put in their supplies. The children seemed excited about the project and eagerly began to write. Here is a copy of the letter that Roberta wrote:

Hi, Kid,

You're pretty lucky to be starting second-grade already. And, boy, will you have fun. Especially sitting at this desk. This is where Roberta Marie Smith sat last year, and she had fun.

This year you will learn to read harder books and you'll have a ring of words and you'll do your workbook (if you're better than Roberta).

Have a good time, kid, 'cause it won't last long. Soon you'll have to go to third grade where they really have hard work to do! Maybe I can ask Roberta's desk in third grade to write to you, too.

Love,

Clarence, your desk

"Mutter reading" has taken over the classroom. I have been noticing for some time that the children vocalize during their so-called silent reading. I have been concerned about it, so I called Miss Kurt and asked her if she would stop in the next time she was in the school. Two days later, Miss Kurt walked in during my lunch break and asked what I was worried about. I told her that the children rarely, if ever, read silently. She told me that most of us don't. It seems that everyone tends to vocalize to some degree or another. Well, that surprised me!

"What do you suggest that I do? Ignore it?" I asked.

"Oh, heavens, no! I suggest that you capitalize on it! Don't you find yourself reading something *sotto voce* when you are having a hard time understanding it? The auditory cue seems to be an important one for many of us."

"But, Miss Kurt, I don't understand. What do you mean by 'capitalize on it'?"

Miss Kurt leaned back in her chair and began to elucidate the joys of "mutter reading" to me. She said that I should encourage children to read aloud, but quietly when they were reading for comprehension exercises or for oral reading practice. Throughout the room would then be heard "mutter reading." The light began to dawn. Miss Kurt went on to say that she had first discovered "mutter reading" when she was doing an in-service workshop for teachers. She had placed a story written in code on the chalkboard for the teachers to figure out. She told them to read silently, but soon, around the room, were the soft voices of teachers trying to figure out the story. One teacher would say something, and another, from across the room, would say, "No. That's not quite it. How about . . ." She pointed out to the teachers what they were doing and asked them what they would have done if their students had done the muttering. They shamefacedly admitted that they would have silenced the children. They had never realized the supportive value of oral "silent" reading.

So, "mutter reading" is the order of the day. I don't find it as distracting as I thought I might, for it is the sound of children learning. I find that I like it very much!

I have the children in two different basal series this month. The primary basal is the one we use on Monday, Wednesday, and Friday. This basal is at each child's instructional level and is the same one that he or she has been using this year. By means of a second IRI which I gave this month, I have placed children in a secondary basal which is on the child's independent level. These are used on Tuesday and Thursday and are entirely self-paced. I call children to see me individually during the time that they are reading, so that I can check on their progress and help them with any difficulties. I am able to see half of the children on Tuesday and the other half on Thursday. The children have responded very well to this system. Even Mike wants to know if we can have easy reading—as I call it—on more than two days a week!

Another achievement this month is that I finally figured out what to do with my spelling program. I asked Mr. Topps if there were any reason why we had to use the spelling series that had been ordered for my room this year. When he asked what I would use instead, I told him that I wanted to try to develop my spelling program around the words the children were learning in their instructional level basals. He became as excited as I was, and began to offer many positive suggestions for me to incorporate. He showed me how I could individualize such a program by giving a pretest on the words to determine those which the children needed to study. The children could pair up to administer their final tests to one another, since they would have so many different lists to study. By having the children test one another, I would be free to supervise or to work with other children while the class would be gaining independence. I tried it and it works so well that I am going to spend the summer preparing games, tests, word lists and other aids for my new spelling program so that I can start at the beginning of the year.

This has turned out to be such a good year after all! I never would have thought that I would be saying that six months ago! Have a good summer, Merritt Elementary School! I certainly will!

The Student Teaching Seminar

Miss Nouveau, veteran of one year in the classroom, had been asked by Dr. Link to talk with her student teachers at their weekly seminar. At first, she had protested that she was the last person who should be asked to lecture. After all, she was still learning herself, and she didn't think she had anything of significance to contribute.

Dr. Link explained that several students in the class had asked her to find a first-year teacher who would talk to them. They wanted to know what it was *really* like when one started teaching. While teachers like Mrs. Wise could contribute a great deal to the seminar, they had been teaching too long to focus honestly on the first year of teaching. And, she added, she had been observing Miss Nouveau's progress throughout the year, and was pleased with the growth that had been taking place. Miss Nouveau finally consented to address the class. "But," she cautioned, "I'm not promising that it will be any good."

"If you just tell them what you have lived through this past year," Dr. Link replied, "they will be more than satisfied."

And that, she resolved, was precisely what she would do. These students would find out the real truth from her before they had to live through it themselves! She requested that they meet in her room.

The afternoon of the seminar, Miss Nouveau stood at the back of her room while Dr. Link greeted the carefree students. After Dr. Link had introduced her, she began her talk by saying, "To paraphrase an old television program, 'I Led One Life.' For me, that life was school." She then related her inaccurate judgments, errors in placement, discipline problems, and poor assignments she had made. As she spoke, she noted looks of disbelief turning to looks of pity and fear as she related anecdote after anecdote. Not wanting to discourage them, however, Miss Nouveau then began to relate the positive things that had happened to her and the consequent changes she had made in her program since Christmas. When she finished, several hands went up for questions.

"If you knew you weren't doing very well in October, how come you kept right on doing things wrong? I mean, if *I* were doing something I knew was wrong, I wouldn't just keep on!"

"Well," answered Miss Nouveau, with a smile, "maybe you would and maybe you wouldn't. I would have thought that same way a year ago, but it's so different when you're actually there day after day with the children and you know you're totally responsible for their instruction. There's neither the opportunity nor the knowledge to do it any other way! I was fortunate, though, to be in a school with a principal who cared, other teachers who helped me, and an elementary supervisor who showed me alternatives. Though they were all busier than I was, they gave freely of their time and advice. If it hadn't been for them, I know I would have resigned at Christmas."

"What would have helped you, though, before you got to your first year of teaching?" another student asked.

"If only I had been given more experience in classrooms prior to my student teaching, then I could have spent student teaching time learning more about classroom management. The better prepared you are when you enter your student teaching, the better you will be at the end of it. Also, if my reading-language arts course had been more activity-oriented, I would have been better prepared to evaluate and teach the children."

Another student raised his hand to ask, "Could you just summarize for us a few of the most important things that you learned this year?"

Miss Nouveau thought for a moment before replying, "I suppose that one of the most important things I learned was how to get kids to the bathroom." The class exploded into laughter. "You laugh! But when it happens to you, it won't be so funny!" She smiled at them and began again. "Another thing was locating the school storeroom. It's often a goldmine of books and materials just lying there, gathering dust. Also, I learned that I must have some time for myself. One reason I was so depressed last fall, I'm sure, was that I had no time to do things that I had always done and that I enjoyed doing. I regret very much some of the things I did this year, and if I could be granted one wish it would be that I could repeat this school year knowing at the beginning what I know now!"

"How are you going to start next year, since obviously you won't repeat what has been done?"

"Well, for one thing, every child is going to learn the names of the characers in all of the basal series. That way, I will be able to move the children from group to group with more ease. That was one reason that I didn't have more mobility among my groups, for it was just too difficult to go through all of the introductions to characters every time I felt that a child should work at a higher or lower level. By the way, that is one habit that I am going to break myself of over the summer—no more 'high' group or 'low' group labels. It bothered me that I referred to the children that way in my mind. Soon I found that I actually thought of them as 'high' or 'low' children. I want to try to get away from that. While some are more capable than others, certainly, it is not right that I pigeonhole them as I have done this year.

"Furthermore, I am going to be aware of the hazards inherent in informal reading inventories so that I won't misplace children like Larry again. I am going to plan more learning centers over the summer and develop some teaching/learning bulletin boards like the one you see here. Also, I plan to begin the independent reading level activities much earlier in the year. I think with that kind of system, my next year should go fairly smoothly."

"What I don't understand is why you are using basal readers again. In my reading-language arts course we discussed some of the problems with basals. Why don't you use some of the new materials that are available, or individualize your program?"

"I know that there are other methods of teaching reading. In fact, this school has several different approaches being used. Mrs. Wright teaches reading through language experience, and Mrs. Wise—who was *so* helpful to me this year—individualizes instruction with children's literature. I do incorporate some of these techniques into my basal program, and I hope to do more next year. But basals are organized, sequential, systematic methods of teaching reading that can show the beginning teacher a lot about the reading process. I still have much to learn, which is one reason that I want to continue using basal readers next year. However, I know better now than to make basal readers my entire reading program. I think that I will be able to use them much more intelligently than I did this past year. For example, next year I will know from the beginning how to group the children without some of the problems that I had this year. I know, now, how to give and interpret IRI's. That should help me to form four or five groups rather well. In addition, I will feel much more confident about having children participate in more than one group at a time after my experience with Mort, which I mentioned earlier. I am going to go through the school storeroom and look for another series or two to use next year. I just don't feel that any one series is adequate for the needs of all children, no matter how good it is.

"The group which gave me the most problems (the Streakers) is the one for which I must find more material. I feel that I must supply a variety of materials to provide for their different levels, interests, and needs, for they are not as capable as the others of searching out their own. I intend to bring in all of the pre-primers from all of the series which we have in our school. I will have children read these in order to build a broader base. Then I will bring in all of the primers that I can find, and so on. The first-grade teacher in our school does this and it seems to be an effective technique. I will keep one basal series for skill instruction and the others for vocabulary and concept development.

"I will never again make the mistake of having the children read round robin style in their reading groups. They need experience in reading aloud, however, so I will set up one period a week during which the children will choose their favorite story and let them read aloud to one another in small groups. They will get practice reading and the experience will be so much more meaningful to hear and read an entire story. They will read the stories silently before coming to the reading group, but I will tell them what to read for on that particular day—sequence, main ideas, or details. Knowing what the purpose (or purposes) will be for each day, the children can read the passage for that purpose and be prepared for the questions. In fact, I think I'm going to give them the questions in advance sometimes; that will be *real* directed reading.

"Pairing up the children for reading and working on workbooks is another approach that I am going to incorporate early next year. They learn from one another, do not tend to resent the suggestions of another child, and they gain independence. They can help one another to do the exercises and to check the work. That saves me time and gives them a part in their learning. So often the children never even looked at the pages which *I* had marked errors on. They forgot the page because it was old stuff—yesterday's stuff. When they mark their *own* errors, I have found that they are much more eager to discover where they went wrong. Also, I will circle the numeral at the bottom of each page that the child is assigned to do—if there is no circle, he or she will know that the page need not be done. In this way, I can individualize their work much more. Even within the same group, the workbook pages assigned can be different.

"Not only will I be bringing extra basals in for the children who are less able, but I also intend to bring in some for the others. I think that they will be able to read them as supplementary reading and to reinforce vocabulary better than I did with flash card drills! Besides, children enjoy reading stories that they can read with ease. There's real satisfaction in that. These books will be one level below the child's current instructional reading level.

"I will permit the children who are the most capable to read in their basals without my intervention. They will meet with me periodically to discuss the stories and to work on specific skills, but for the most part I will be encouraging them to read beyond the basals in the books in our room library or in the school library. Most of their skill instruction will be geared toward the basal to which I have assigned them, for I want to make certain that there are no gaps in their learning. So most of their reading will be done independently and we will meet occasionally for skill group instruction.

"One mistake which I will not repeat is trying to do everything suggested in the basal manuals. I know now that this is impossible. The series are provided with more material and suggestions than any two teachers could use! So from now on I will pick and choose what my group needs.

"I will continue to give sight vocabulary tests of words in the basals to determine those words which the children need to learn, and I will continue to make rings of words for the children. Though it is time-consuming, I have found that this system of vocabulary presentation works best for me and the children."

She paused to catch her breath before going on to say, "Perhaps you would like an opportunity to look over the materials that I used this past year. This series is the one the middle groups in my room were using. The series is graded and has grade level designations—1^1, 2^1, 2^2, etc.—to indicate the various books. This other series is a total language arts series which I used with the low and top groups—oops!—I've got to stop calling them that. As you can see, even though the series is graded, that company uses levels to designate the gradations of their books. That way the children who have to read at the first-grade level don't have to see a big number one printed on the front of the book. There happen to be five levels in what is traditionally considered first-grade work so that when Chip saw 'level four' on his book, he felt pretty good about it. One needs to have a system for classifying books according to increasing levels of difficulty, and I prefer this level system to the one with grade designations."

Dr. Link interrupted to say that the time was up, but that the students could stay for a few minutes longer to talk privately with Miss Nouveau. Several did, and they all thanked her for sharing her experiences with them. She thought to herself later if she had helped one of those students to have a better first year, it was all worth it!

References

Aronson, Elliot, *et al.* "The Jigsaw Route to Learning and Liking." *Psychology Today* 8 (1975): 43–50.

Hunt, Lyman. "Six Steps to the Individualized Reading Program (IRP)." *Elementary English* 48 (1971): 27–32.

Stuart, Dabney. *Friends of Yours, Friends of Mine.* Richmond, Va.: Rainmaker Press, 1974.

Mrs. Wise

HIGHLIGHTS

Parents as Volunteer Aides

Reading to Children

Children's Literature

Record Keeping

Organizational Patterns

Making Reading Games

ARRF

Work Folders and Assignment Cards

Children Planning Their Own
   Schedules

Learning Centers

Use of the Tape Recorder

Comprehension

Flexible Skill Groups and Skill Cards

Differentiated Assignments

Child-created Dittos

Story Writing Activities

Anecdotal Records

Book Reports—Innovative Ways

Dramatization

Word Books

Student Aides

Making Books in the Classroom

Making a Card Catalog

Making a Dictionary

Poetry

Self-corrective Materials

Learning Activity Packets (LAPs)

Mrs. Wise

The Parent Meeting

Mrs. Wise walked around the room, carefully placing materials for the parents to examine when they arrived for the meeting later that evening. She went about the task methodically, for she had been having parent meetings for most of her twenty-five years as a teacher, long before they became an "in" thing to do. As a matter of fact, she was the one who had suggested to Mr. Topps, some ten years before, that these meetings become a regular part of the school routine. She had also initiated the parent conferences which everyone now held twice yearly. There were those who called her an innovator and those who said it was amazing that a woman of her years could be so up-to-date! Mrs. Wise always chuckled over that one! She told them all that it had nothing to do with innovation or age—she simply knew what her children needed and how *she* could best teach them.

She was always exhilarated by these meetings, as she was by the parent conferences. It was astonishing how much one could learn about a child in half-hour conferences with the parents. She made the parents feel relaxed by sitting in a chair beside them rather than in the more formal position behind the desk. She had acquired a knack for knowing what to say and how to say it that helped put parents at their ease and yet elicited from them the maximum amount of information about the child. To-night, however, she was to meet the parents *en masse*. She enjoyed explaining what she and their children were going to be doing, for she loved teaching. She was not looking forward to the day in the near future when she would be retiring.

Shortly before 8 P.M., the parents began to arrive. Mrs. Wise didn't begin the meeting until 8:15, however, for long years of experience had taught her that many parents would arrive late no matter when the meeting was to begin. At least most of them would be there by the time she started.

"Hello. Some of you I know quite well as I have had other children of yours. Some of you are new to me as I am to you. I certainly hope that we will become well-acquainted this year. I want to urge *all*, mothers *and* fathers, to come visit the classroom. I have only two requirements: (1) that you let me know in advance when you want to come so that I can let you know whether or not it is convenient, and (2) that you plan to stay at least an hour so that the children will settle down and forget that you are there so that you can really see the program. I warn you! You may be put to work, though. Any extra hands in my class can and probably will be used. Just ask Mr. Topps! I'm sure that is why he has been avoiding my classroom for the last couple of years!"

She paused for breath and to let the laughter die down. "We, at this school, decided many years ago that we felt strongly enough about the place of children's literature in the curriculum that we would make a concerted effort to include it. To this end, I read daily to the children. In addition, I have built my entire reading program around children's literature. You are aware, I'm sure, that many critics feel that some of the finest writing being done these days is in the area of children's literature. In order to make the reading situation as natural as possible, I have implemented an individualized reading program. Let me explain to you how it works.

"I have hundreds of books in this room; many of them belong to the room, many belong to me, and quite a few belong to your children. I classify the books into three large groupings: below average for *my* students, average for *my* students, and above average for *my* students. The books are color-coded for these three groupings, so that children will know which groups of books they may choose from to read. Your children are on a five-day cycle: one day they read on the tape recorder allowing me to evaluate oral reading skills, another day they confer with me so that I can work on specific individual problems and check on comprehension, and for three days they read intensively. When your child finishes a book, he or she writes the title in a booklet. After five books have been read, the child chooses one of the five to report on. Few children choose the traditional, formal, written book report, for there are so many other ways they can indicate that they have understood and enjoyed a book.

"Children's reading assignments are recorded on a card like this file card. It lists the date, the assignment, and the evaluation of the assignment. Each child has a file folder which has a stapled sheet inside on which I record language arts assignments, the date completed, and the evaluation of those assignments.

"Your children will be studying poetry this year as well. I'm afraid that it is sadly neglected in our curriculum, and I'm doing my part to see that children have some exposure to it.

"We will be cooperating with other classes in the school. We will help the kindergarteners write their letters to Santa, we will produce books and reading games for other classes, and dramatize stories for the enjoyment of other grade levels. We also will be developing a classroom dictionary."

She looked at the parents sitting before her and said, "I think that's enough talking for me. Why don't we get some refreshments and come back here for a question-and-answer period in five minutes. I don't know about you, but I could use a cup of tea right now."

The parents drifted out into the hall where Mrs. Wise had set up the coffee pot and hot water for tea. As soon as the five minutes were up,

Mrs. Wise resumed the meeting by asking if there were any questions, comments, or concerns.

MR. PESKINS: Mrs. Wise, this all sounds so, so busy! How are you going to be able to do all of these things at once? Won't children be running wildly around the room while you're in conferences? And I don't just mean my Butch, either.

MRS. WISE: It is my contention that if we give children meaningful tasks at their individual levels of ability, we reduce the possibility of that occurring. Besides, they have assignments to be working on while I work with individuals or groups. They might be working at their seats, at learning centers, in the hall, or in the library. I have never yet had a child run "wildly around the room."

MRS. MOORE: But what about the other part of the question? How can you meet with all of these children one-to-one? Isn't that what individualizing instruction means?

MRS. WISE: To me, individualizing instruction means providing children with what they need, when they need it. Therefore, some instruction will be one-to-one, some will be one-to-five, and some will be one-to-twenty-one.

MRS. FIELD: Daphne came home and told me that she didn't have to write about books when she finished. I thought that she was just telling me a story! I always had to write book reports in school. How else will you know if they've read their books?

MRS. WISE: But didn't you dread doing those written book reports? I know that I did, even though I always did rather well on them. I remember how sorry I felt for a friend of mine who was not quite as good at writing as I was. There are other ways: dramatizing the most important ideas, selling the book to friends by convincing them that this is the greatest book ever written, or painting a picture that expresses a mood upon completion of the book. These techniques require children to evaluate a work of literature, not merely regurgitate it.

MRS. SMITH: But how will you keep track of all these children? They are doing so many different things.

MRS. WISE: The children will keep many of their own records, which is a big help to me. In addition, I have the assignment cards and sheets which tell me exactly who is doing what. Also, I have skill cards that show me at a glance what skills the children have learned and which they still need to be taught.

MRS. PENN: Well, I for one have every confidence in you, Mrs. Wise. I am convinced that Pat and every other child in this room will come to love reading.

MRS. WISE: Are there any more questions? If not, thank you and good night. I hope you'll visit us soon.

Monthly Logs

Now that this busy summer is over, climaxed by Miss Nouveau's marriage in August, I'm ready to begin my last year of teaching. I've been around for a long time—I've seen fads come and go in education, and I have observed the cyclical nature of these fads—the whole-word approach, phonics, altered alphabets, and others. I am, I suppose, reluctant to change, but the program that I have developed for my students is one that I am comfortable with and one that has proven itself to me. I don't need to constantly search and try out new methods. Years ago I read about individualizing instruction through children's literature, and this is the technique I have continued to use.

Quite a lot of time was spent during this past month assessing both children and materials. Also, because we will be working so closely on some projects, I felt that it was important that they and I become better acquainted. To this end, I had the children go through an exercise that I picked up at a Right-to-Read meeting recently. I wrote the following words on sheets of typing paper in print large enough to be seen from across the room. The words remained in the four columns which you see here.

firelight	starlight	sunlight	moonlight
cinnamon	pepper	sugar	oregano
Chevrolet	Cadillac	Jeep	MG convertible
deer	bear	lion	eagle

I placed the sets together so that only the first word in each group could be seen, and then I arranged them at four different points in the room. Children were instructed to choose which one of the four they felt they were most like, to go to that word, to discuss why they had chosen that particular one, and to select a leader to report to the entire class a summary of the reasons. After the top card had been discussed, the second was revealed, the children made new choices and moved to the chosen spot, and the process continued. At the end, the children and I knew one another better. While I tried not to be intrusive, I did join in, for I think they should also know something about me. The very nature of my reading program demands that the relationship between student and teacher be a close one, one of trust and mutual understanding. This particular group of children seems to need more of that than any other that I have taught.

I always assess the children before I begin instruction. So many teachers have indicated to me that they could not carry through with the individualization plans which they had established. With further questioning, I often discover that they have either not tested the children to see what they know and what they need to know so that they can plan intelligently, or they have simply taken the same old material and put the children through it at different rates. Both of these are contrary to the nature and spirit of individualization.

In general, individualization refers to self-paced, self-selected instruction. However, there are as many systems as there are teachers who individualize. The system that I have used for years with my students is one that allows me more control. And, in the beginning of the year, there is more control than there is at the end. When children first come into my room, they have often been through a basal reading program that is highly structured and sequenced. One of the most difficult tasks I face, therefore, is weaning them away from an overdependence upon the teacher for instruction.

These children have had fewer problems adapting to my program than some classes because Miss Nouveau, or rather Mrs. Flame, did an excellent job with them toward the end of the year. Still, they did not know how to go about selecting a book which would not be too easy or too difficult. Also, the children don't yet have the reading stamina that it takes to have a full-fledged individualized program going. They don't know how to prepare for a reading conference, and to many of them, their individual work folders are still somewhat baffling. I noticed many of these things immediately.

On the first day of school, I gave each child a file folder in which to keep assignments. Initially, all the children are given the same work papers so that I can assess skills and work habits. This information, in conjunction with that obtained from an Informal Reading Inventory, gives me an indication of the child's general level of functioning. I give IRI's in September and again in May as a means of measuring reading growth.

As part of my initial testing, I like to give the children an interest inventory as well. As a matter of fact, that is one of the work papers which they find in the folders on the first day. I walk around the room while they are working on it so that I can identify those children who are unable to read the inventory and therefore need to have someone read it to them. I soon discovered that children like Larry, Pat, Hilda, and Roberta were quite willing to be amanuenses for children such as Butch, Chip, and Paul. They were a great help. Questions such as "You are going to be living all alone on the moon for one year. You can take only a few things with you. What three things will you take?" and "I sometimes feel _____." produce many clues to the needs, perceptions, and values of children. With some of this information in mind, I can help the children to find reading materials and work assignments that will be both interesting and informative. I do, however, use the information with caution, for years ago, after assessing a certain child's interest inventory, I gleefully brought several books to the child about things which he had indicated an interest in. After looking through the stack before him, the child pushed them all aside. "Why, Clarence," I remonstrated, "these are all about cars and football which you said that you liked. Why don't you want to read one of them?" He glanced up at me and told me, "Well, 'cause I likes to play 'em, don't mean I likes to read 'em. Does you have any scary stories? I likes 'em!"

Another time, I searched for reading materials in another child's interest area of the Civil War. He *wanted* to read about it, but I could find very few materials written on his low reading level. These experiences have tended to make me somewhat cautious in use of an interest inventory, though I still feel that it can yield much information that will prove helpful.

For the reader to do

Construct an interest inventory that you think will survey children's current interests. Duplicate it and share it with your class. Have the class evaluate your efforts.

● ● ●

This month we have been working toward independence. That is, the first part of the month was highly structured by me—"Do this." "Tape now." "See me at _____." In this way, I helped the children to learn the routines. They soon knew that they would have to tape record once a week, confer with me once a week, read intensively for three days, work on their folders, and meet for skill group instruction. At the beginning of the third week, I gave each child a ditto paper that had the five days marked off with time slots. On Monday of that week, we spent time filling in the day's plan. I reminded them that they would have to sign up on the chalkboard for a conference as well, since I could only meet with a certain number of them each day. At this time, too, I assigned each of them a day of the week for taping their oral reading, and thereafter each student knew on which day he or she was to tape.

On the day that the child chooses to have a conference, he or she comes to see me early in the morning. I indicate the purpose for which he or she is to read during the morning reading time. I indicate whether to read for main ideas, details, or sequence. In that way the child has a structure around which to build the given work time. Being able to choose a book and read it silently was one of the major accomplishments for many children during this month, though there are still some who cannot accomplish this. Children tend to browse too long or select too quickly so that they find the book they selected too hard or not appealing. One morning we just had "browse time" so that they could peruse some books for future selection. That really did seem to help. Also children suggest books to their friends. ARRF (Average Reader Readability Formula) has helped, too. The books in my classroom have been arranged in three major categories—too easy for my average third-grader, just right, and too hard—by means of ARRF. Dr. Cunningham (1976) developed ARRF as an alternative to the readability formulas currently available. Her plan is that you choose an average reader from your class, 100 books, and two hours of time. Horace Middleman was willing to be my guinea pig when I told him that I needed the help of someone just like *him* to assist me with a job that I couldn't do myself. Well, that intrigued him, for many children get the idea—perhaps from teachers themselves—that teachers are omnipotent. I explained that his job would be to go through the books and choose a page near the middle of each book. He was then to read some of it aloud and with my help we would determine if the book were too easy, just right, or too hard for third-graders and then place it in the appropriate pile. Once the piles were finished, Horace helped me to color-code them by placing one of three different colors of tape on the binding: blue was "easy," green was "average," and orange was "hard." Now my books are codified for this year; of course one must go through the same process every year to tailor the book groupings to an individual class.

Larry (whom the children are beginning to call "Ace") and Pat may choose from any books in the classroom. Paul, Mort, Daisy, Jeff, and Chip will find greatest success with the "easy" books. The others will be reading the "average" books, though sometimes they may dip into the "easy" or "hard" ones. These are not inflexible categories, for sometimes interest will carry children through materials that are too hard by standard criteria. One child I taught was fascinated with tales about the knights of the Round Table. Unfortunately for him, there were not many of these tales written on his second-grade reading level. We did get the easiest ones that we could, though, and he and I struggled through them. He used the dictionary and me constantly, but refused my offer of finding him simpler, though less interesting, reading. He taught me a great lesson.

For readers to do together

Who are the other children not mentioned above in relation to the ARRF books being read? What level books are they reading from? Why do you think so?

●   ●   ●

The children have had some difficulty adjusting to being responsible for their own time. They see that they have a folder of work to do, but they also notice that there is no set time for them to work on it. Butch came to me the third day of school and asked me when he was to do the work because, "I don't see it nowhere on the chalkboard." I explained to him (again—for I had gone over this with the entire class) that he could plan when to complete the assignments written there. He must plan around his other responsibilities, such as taping and having a conference, but other than that the time was his to plan. At the end of the week Manuel, Mitch, Butch, Paul, Chip, Daisy, Carl, and Mort had not completed their assignments. Realizing what I should have seen immediately, I told them that they were to be my special helpers for some of the room jobs that needed doing (watering plants, feeding animals, and various other tasks). The only restriction was that they were to complete at least two assignments before doing the job, and that the job must be completed by 9:30 A.M. This plan helped to get them organized so that they had some sort of goal that they could aim for. Carl, however, did not do well with this system. We sat down and talked about his problems during the third week of school, and he told me that he just couldn't seem to get going on a task. I asked him if he would like to try an experiment. When he agreed, I told him that when he got his folder every day, he should select one assignment and come to tell me how long he thought it might take him to do the task. I then set my timer for that period of time and he raced against the clock to complete the job. Sometimes he became careless when he knew that time was nearly up, but a little talk about the importance of doing well the first time, rather than having to redo the assignment took care of this problem for him.

Mitch had a different kind of problem with his work. He was so easily distracted by what the other children were doing and so easily tempted to join in with them or bully them, that I tried the tack of offering him an "office." One corner of the room is relatively quiet, so I moved a desk and chair there. I told Mitch that sometimes I would have some things for him to do that would require privacy and quiet, and I would like him to have such a place available. Immediately after I told him about this and showed him the office, I asked him to correct a few work papers for me with the teacher's key. He felt very important, sitting there with my—his—grading pencil. The next day, I gave him some more work to do for me in his office. After he finished it, he brought the papers over to me and asked what I did with his office when I wasn't having him work there. I told him that it just remained empty, but that if he would ever like to go over there and work on his other things, that would be fine with me. I told him that I realized that sometimes things got to be a little exciting in the room, making it difficult for him to do his own work. Needless to say, for days afterward he took nearly all of his work over to that corner. After the novelty wore off and he no longer went there, I would sometimes drop by his desk and ask if he wanted to go the office to work. He usually agreed to do so, but that is probably because I never ordered him to go there. It was always his choice.

Manuel has taken to coming to sit beside me while I am working with an individual or a group. He brings his work there and sits quietly, doing his assignments. I asked him after this had happened several times why he came when he rarely had any questions. He responded with the wisdom that children have, that he knew he could not work by himself at his seat; he just needed to be closer to me. So, if I didn't mind, he would like to come sit near me whenever he felt that he couldn't get his work done at his seat. I wonder what his response would have been had I suggested that he sit near me?

These children who have been through basals are unaccustomed to sitting and reading for long periods at this time of the year, so rather than the large blocks of reading time which I will have later in the year, I have broken up the time with social studies. After an hour of reading, assignments, centers, taping, and so forth, the children put away their things and we do an activity-oriented social studies lesson. This helps the children to relax from their long periods of concentration, and allows them to talk and release pent-up energy in a constructive way. After the lesson, we go back to our reading-language block for an hour and then to lunch. I intend to increase gradually the time for the first reading period by delaying the start of social studies as I find the children more able to cope with the longer periods. Eventually, the entire two hours will be in one block.

Many children were anxious about the skill groupings. They wondered why they were in a skill group with children who had not been with them in reading group the year before. I relieved their anxiety about this by showing them my card for sorting them into groups (see illustration on p. 166). After that, they were fascinated with the device and would gather around to see whose names came up.

Conferences, too, frightened them, for they had not had to be responsible for an entire story or book before. In second grade they could depend upon some group support and could learn from the group discussions—now they were on their own! I tried to make their first sessions with me as easy as possible, so that they would come to enjoy and look forward to conference time. I wanted them to see that I really did care what they thought about an instance in the book or what they felt about the entire book. Sometimes it is unnecessary to ask a child how he or she feels about a particular story, for facial expressions or the way the book is held tells more than words. Do we really need to ask comprehension questions when a child closes *Sounder,* clutches it in his or her arms, and sheds tears because there is no more to read?

Another part of my plan to aid the children to develop independent work habits is our "game factory." I asked the children if they would like to devise some games for our class and for the children in other classes. The response was affirmative! Children enjoy games so much, and the thought of producing them was exciting. I have always found that games are very good motivators for learning and for drill. They are, or can be, skill builders that children don't mind doing. With a variety of games, I can avoid using mounds of dittoed papers that so often become the backbone of an individualized program. I have also found through the years that the more attractive I make my games, the more likely the children are to respond to them. Also, sealing the game materials with clear adhesive paper insures durability.

I told the children that it is far more difficult than they might imagine to make up games, because first we must determine carefully what we want to teach or reinforce, and then we must come up with a game that will do the job. The children were told that this might be a long-term task; for some of them it might take months. Since Mike moved this past summer (and I have been told to thank my lucky stars for that!), there are only twenty-one children in the class, so I made up a set of twenty-one numeral cards, three each of the numerals 1 through 7. This insures a good mix of children in each group, for the children draw a numeral and that determines the group with whom they are to work. The first group consists of Larry, Daphne, and Paul. They have already completed their game, which they gave to the second grade. It is as follows:

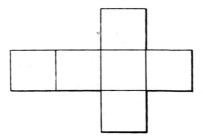

Cut out five cube patterns. Fold the ends and tape them to make cubes.

Each cube has six sides.

Use a thin green marker to write different consonant letters on three of the cubes. Do not write *w, y,* or *z.*

On the last two cubes, write the vowel letters *a, e, i, o,* and *u,* with blue thin line marker. Write the letters *w* and *y* half in green and half in blue, for they can be both consonants and vowels.

Roll all five cubes. How many words can you make from the letters showing on top? Get one point for each letter used in a word. The first to make ten points wins.

The second graders really enjoy it, Mrs. Flame tells me.

OCTOBER

The children are all on their reading cycles now, and things are going more smoothly than they did last month. Other teachers frequently ask me how I can have time to do an individualized program, and I must reply that organization is half the battle. In fact, an individualized program is self-perpetuating, once begun, and I don't think I could return children to the traditional reading groups even if I wanted to. Besides, I enjoy it, and if this is to be my last year of teaching, I want to enjoy it!

As with many teachers, I think, I would rather come to school ill and teach than to have a substitute. I think I can do a better job *sick* than many substitutes can do *well*! And this type of a program is more easily done than explained, so that my lesson plan book, so graciously provided by the school system, is a lovely book for keeping track of social studies, science, and other subjects as well as giving me a place to write down dates for staff meetings and hair appointments. But for the purpose of recording my individualized math and language arts plans, it is totally inadequate. Those assignments are written on file cards and in work folders. You can perhaps anticipate the problems that a substitute—even a good one—might have. One day, Mr. Topps *sent* me home! I had come to school with a sinus headache that increased in intensity as the day wore on, and by lunch I was miserable. He told me that he had already called Mrs. Payne and that she would be arriving soon to take over the class—I was to leave immediately! Imagine speaking to me like that! Why, I'm old enough to be his mother! Anyway, I went back to the room and told the children I would be leaving, and that Mrs. Payne would be coming. Holding my head, I told them to help her figure out the day: "You all know what to do and where your work is."

They all survived the day, but it was rough on Mrs. Payne *and* the children because she wasn't about to trust what the children told *her* to do! She insisted that they all sit in their seats and she passed out copies of the same basal reader (wonder where she found twenty-one copies?) to each child! They had a round robin reading lesson, each child taking a turn reading out loud from the book to the rest of the class. Then she made each one write a summary of what he or she had read and listened to. She graded them before she left that evening—conscientious soul that she is—and left them for me to distribute the next day. I was appalled! The letter grades ranged from *A* to *F*! Paul, Daisy, Jeff, Chip, and Butch all received *F*. She said that she was grading them on their oral reading as well as on their summaries, and that these children had failed miserably in reading the third-grade book and in writing a comprehensible paper on it!

The children are still at the stage where they are planning day by day what their activities are to be, though this month we are working toward two- and three-day plans; I hope that in November they will get to the point where they are planning for the entire week. In their planning, they must allow time for reading, work folders, and skill groups. They are to spend time at various centers created around the room, too. On two days a week, they must allow time for tape recording and for conferences with me. When a book is finished, they must allow time for the completion of a project built around that book. As you can see, even as they achieve the ability to plan for the entire week, they must still be flexible since events occur which alter the schedule.

I have a highly structured individualized program since that is the type of program with which I am most comfortable. I want the children to use the tape recorder at least once a week, and each child is assigned one day for taping, so that I have a sample of oral reading skills. I make notes of the words misread, fluency, and phrasing. I assign them a day so that I never have more than five oral readings a day to check. In addition, if there is any question in my mind after evaluating their tape recordings, I can further check on these skills when they come to me for a conference.

They are to read intensively for three days, but it is up to the children which three days of the week they will do that. In addition, they choose which day they will meet with me and sign up on the sheet by my table. I can only meet with six children a day, so they try to plan ahead. I've noticed some striking individual differences among the children in that respect. Betty, who likes her life organized and balanced whenever possible, reads on Monday; Tuesday, she tapes; Wednesday, she reads; Thursday, she confers with me; and on Friday, she reads. Butch, who likes to delay things as much as possible, likes to read for the first three days, then he wants a conference, and on Friday he finally tapes. And so it goes; within the limits which I have established the children choose a schedule which best fits their individual personalities.

Let me describe a typical morning. The children begin to arrive at about 8:30 A.M. and from then until 8:45 they play games with one another, read, or work in some of the centers. Between 8:45 and 9:00, attendance is taken, the lunch count tallied, and the children listen to me read some poems.

Work actually begins at 9 A.M. Horace got his work folder from the box where I store them, and to which he will return it when he is done for the day. He checked to see if this was a taping day for him and decided if he wanted to sign up for a conference with me. (He did.) He got his reading book from the shelf where we store the ones currently being read and took his materials to his seat to work. During this "settling in" time, I wandered around the room, assisting the children in beginning their work and helping to clarify instructions and to locate materials.

At 9:10, I went to my small desk where I confer with children. I use a child's desk so that I am at their level; this helps keep the atmosphere relaxed. I noted that five children had signed up to meet with me. Rita wanted to see me at 9:15, Horace at 9:45, Steve at 10:00, Carl at 10:15, and Betty at 10:45. Between reading conferences, I scheduled skill groups and wrote on the chalkboard the names of the children for each group with the time that I wanted to see them. Skill groups generally last five to ten minutes, so I saw that I could fit in several today. I noticed, too, that Alex, Pat, Chip, Manuel, and Steve had signed up to record their reading.

While I was having skill groups and conferences, children back at their seats began folder work. Sometimes the work assignments sent the children into the various centers which I had set up in the classroom (see sample assignment sheets for Paul, Hilda, and Larry on p. 164).

For the reader to do

Mrs. Wise has prepared sample assignment sheets for three of her children. Choose a different child and prepare an assignment sheet for a week's work. Keep the characteristics of the child in mind as you make the assignments. Obviously, card assignments are impossible for you, as you do not know what her cards are; so choose other sorts of assignments.

● ● ●

When their work is completed, the children can also *choose* to go to centers, where there is a wide range of materials and activities for them. Every center includes assignment cards which direct the children in some specific activity, or instruct them in other activities, such as games. The cards give varying assignments. For example, Paul must do "listening card #9," which is:

Put the tape of *Sylvester and the Magic Pebble* in the recorder.
Get the book from the shelf.
Listen to the story and turn the pages when you hear the bell.
After the story is over, put the book and tape away.
Make a picture of the part of the story which you liked best.

One of Larry's assignments kept him in his seat for a while, for he had to come up with a crossword puzzle which he put on a ditto master and duplicated for the other children to do if they wished. If they had any questions, I directed them to Larry, since he had been the one to design it. He loved being "teacher." I've been having children make ditto papers for other children to do for a long time, and they enjoy it. In fact, they enjoy it so much that last week even Butch told me he wanted to make a ditto. Although he couldn't yet design a crossword puzzle or anything like that, he devised a train for the class to finish (shown on p. 165).

Have done with children

<table>
<tr><td></td><td></td><td align="right">Paul</td></tr>
</table>

DATE	ASSIGNMENT	EVALUATION
Oct. 4–8	Listening Center—Card 9.	
	Math Center—Cards 4 and 5.	
	Retell story on tape.	
	Alphabet Matching Game.	
	Cut pictures from magazines for *Bb,*	
	Ff, Pp, Ss, Tt (sheets included).	
	Listening Center—6 and 10.	
	Science Box 3—magnets.	
	Read *Hop on Pop* to Daphne.	

<table>
<tr><td></td><td></td><td align="right">Hilda</td></tr>
</table>

DATE	ASSIGNMENT	EVALUATION
Oct. 4–8	"Silly Sentence" game with	
	Horace, Joyce, Steve.	
	Tape a story for Listening	
	Center—make an activity card.	
	Math Center—Card 52.	
	Math Center—Card 54.	
	Math Center—Card 59.	
	Listening Center—Card 16, 19, 21.	
	Create a puppet play for *Charlottes's*	
	Web.	
	Write a mystery story.	

<table>
<tr><td></td><td></td><td align="right">Larry</td></tr>
</table>

DATE	ASSIGNMENT	EVALUATION
Oct. 4–8	Listening Center—Card 32.	
	Math Center—Card 78.	
	Math Center—Card 82.	
	Math Center—Card 87.	
	Make thesaurus entries for these	
	words: *big, little, cute, nice.*	
	Choose a story to read to kinder-	
	garten and make flannel board	
	characters to tell story with.	
	Make a crossword puzzle on autumn.	

Make the rest of the trane and put on a sentense.

by Butch

I approved his plan, and he made it into a ditto. How proud he was when he handed it out to the other children. And how pleased he was to run the ditto machine!

When I meet with individual children for a conference, we discuss the kinds of things that are happening in the book they are reading and why some of those things might be happening. Often, I ask the child to imagine himself or herself as a character in the book and to decide what he or she would do in a particular situation. We also work on phrasing and fluency, and plan what the student's reporting project is to be for the book once it is completed. Conferences are generally five to ten minutes long. During the conference, I check the child's work folder and discuss his or her progress. I don't normally deal with phonics skills or some of the other language arts areas, such as writing, in conferences, for I have small, flexible skills groupings for that purpose. During the conference and during my review of the tape, I make notes on the individual child's file card (which lists the date, the assignment, and my evaluation of the work). I make notes while the child is with me, for it is too easy to forget to write something down later. Because I share my notes with the child, he or she is not worried about what I am writing. As it concerns the child the most, I feel that it is my responsibility to discuss what he or she does well, and what needs to be worked on. One technique I use to help improve the child's questioning ability is to have him or her ask me questions about a reading passage. They enjoy "playing teacher" and are delighted if I seem to have trouble answering their questions. After they finish with a question, I say something like, "Now, if I were you, I would have asked . . ." and employ one of the higher conceptualization levels. In this way, I am providing them with a real model of questioning. I have found that almost all of the children improve their questioning techniques by the end of the year.

The skill groups to which they come are formed by means of cards like the one that I have shown below. The cards have skills written around the outside edges. A hole has been punched above each skill so that a knitting stitch holder can be readily inserted. I form a temporary skill group by inserting my knitting stitch holder (which looks like a giant safety pin) into a stack of the same color skill cards. I lock the holder and shake. The cards that fall off are those of children who have already mastered the skill. Those which remain on the holder indicate the ones to whom I must teach that skill. In this way, I can quickly find which children need to work on a particular skill and I can keep up with their progress. When children master a skill, a second hole is punched, opening the top edge (see *ch, sh, wh*). Note that one corner has been clipped; that is so that the cards for the same skills can be grouped together right side up, and errors in grouping don't result.

I have the skills on the various cards listed by difficulty, so that I can look at an individual child's card and see just where he or she is on the skill ladder. Because there are several different skill cards, I have made each different skill card a different color. Some of the cards look like the illustrated card, except that they don't have skills written in. That is for two reasons: (1) if I want to add to the skill program, I can, and (2) I can deal with skills which I cannot describe in that little space: I can write a numeral in the space and code them to skills indicated on the back.

Another organizational device that I use is the work folder. I bought bright-colored folders, at the office supply store, one for each child. On the inside front cover, I stapled a sheet of paper for their assignments.

Again, I listed the date, assignment, and evaluation of the assignment. I also list each child's work so that both they and I know what things they are to be working on. Their assignments might be work papers, writing assignments, working in centers on specific things ("Do activity card #9 in the Listening Center."), being assigned to play an instructional game with another child, or creating an instructional material, such as a crossword puzzle. Assignments are varied, and I consider the preferred learning modalities of the children when making them.

The second group of game designers finally produced the game that they worked on. Carl, Rita, and Jeff like the dice game that Larry, Daphne, and Paul made last month, so they decided to figure out a variation. They used four different colors of cardboard and traced out six dice—two of green, two of blue, one of red, and one of yellow cardboard. Before assembling the dice, they wrote words on the side sections: the green cubes were to be determiners and pronouns so they wrote *a, an, the, one, his, my,* and other such words on all twelve sides. The blue cubes were nouns, so they wrote nouns on those twelve sides. The red cube had verbs on its six sides, and the yellow was covered with prepositions. They constructed three different sets of these cubes (one set for us to keep in our room) and gave the other two to Ms. Maverick, who said that she had some children who could use work with sentence construction. They enjoy rolling the dice and figuring out a sentence from what comes up, especially if they can make up a silly one such as this: "One frog ate up his car."

NOVEMBER

A new student has arrived—Tanana—and I am afraid that she will have some rather severe adjustment problems. Tanana is an Eskimo child and is so accustomed to wilderness and freedom that she must be finding her new life here rather confining. I have asked two of the girls, Daphne and Betty, to be her special friends until she becomes acclimatized. Those two girls are very outgoing and friendly, and will help Tanana feel at home here.

Tanana, and many of the others, have difficulty writing stories, so I created two story stimulants that I thought might help. One is a deck of cards that is divided into three equal parts. Each part has a colored line drawn along one edge, to distinguish it from the others. All those with a red line are characters; those with blue are situations; and those with green are places. The cards are separated into three piles and then a child draws a card from each pile. He or she must then make up a story using those elements. Alex told a hilarious one when he drew the cards that indicated that his story would be about *a bear, sleeping, in my bed.* Very imaginative child! I must make a note of that on the anecdotal record card which I keep on him and on all of the children. I find that when it comes time for conferences and written reports, I have a much easier time if I have dated records indicating some of the things that I note.

The other device is a golden egg that originally served as a container for nylon hosiery. Inside the egg I have placed many story starters this month. (Later on there will be story middles and story endings.) An example is, "The boy lay quietly, trying not to let the sound of his pounding heart drown out the sounds that he thought were coming from behind his closed bedroom door. Finally, he worked up enough courage to get out of bed, cross the room, and fling open the door. He couldn't believe his eyes! There before him was . . ." That kind of starter can spur children on to writing, for who would not be caught up in the excitement? Well, I must admit that Mort was only mildly interested, though Daisy seemed very excited by some of the story starters, particularly the ones that she thought had violence in them. I'm very concerned about her social and academic growth, and I must make an appointment to speak with her mother soon.

Paul is another one for whom I have grave concern. This child has been virtually sitting out his last three years in school. He has attended regularly, and I know that he has had the best of teaching. So what is the problem? Why is he so unresponsive to stimuli? Why does he go off into some kind of dream world from which it is extremely difficult to recall him? I have filled out a form for the school psychologist, Dr. Case, to see him for testing. If past experience is any kind of indicator, I should get the report from the preliminary testing some time in January! That there should be one psychologist for all of the elementary schools, the middle school, and the high school is absurd! No one person could possibly provide us with the kinds of services which we need. Quite apart from the testing and evaluation which must be done, there are guidance techniques which I would like to have done with Butch, Mitch, and Daisy.

Tanana has been getting a great deal of attention from her classmates, and I suppose that it was just too much for Mitch. One day last week, he went up to her and extended his hands for her to take, which she did, thinking as I did, that they had been extended in friendship. What happened next happened so quickly that even by running I didn't reach them until after Tanana had begun to cry. Mitch, holding tight to her hands so that she couldn't run away, was stamping on her feet! I shouted at him, but it was just so senseless and cruel I couldn't restrain myself. Mitch hung his head and said, "I was just kiddin' with her. I didn't mean to hurt her. How did I know she couldn't take a joke?" Poor Mitch! Disliked himself, he is unable to bear it when he sees someone the other children not only like, but are eager to help and to be near. I hope I can help him to conquer this.

The children are now enjoying many books and I thought it was time to have them think of some other ways to let me know that they had enjoyed their reading other than the ways which I had suggested to them. At first they protested by asking how else they could report on their books, other than the suggestions which I had made. "Fine, I'm glad that you like them, but there are so many other ways to show that you love a book, let's see if we can list them. First, though, tell me the ones I have suggested so that we don't get confused."

My Suggestions

1. Make a painting which shows how you felt when you finished your book.
2. Make up a different story ending.
3. Make a diorama showing the characters or a favorite scene.
4. Make a play of some of the most important scenes.
5. Produce a book jacket which shows some of the best scenes, and write a short version on the front and back flaps.
6. Present a puppet show to the class based on the book.
7. Write a letter to the author, telling him/her what you most enjoyed about the book and why.
8. Create a new character for the book. Why is he/she necessary? What is the result of his/her being added to the book?

Several of the children said, "But with all of those, why do we need to think up more? You've got all the good ones!" I told them I knew they could think of some good ones and put them into groups of five or six and told them that part of their morning work would be to contribute new ideas to our list. I then set the timer and told them that they had only twenty minutes to complete this assignment.

There was instantly a hum of activity in the room. Children formed their groups in various parts of the room to insure the privacy that they felt they needed. When the timer rang, I told the children that they were to select one person from their group to report to the class on what they had discovered. As is usual, the natural leaders in the class were chosen: Horace, Larry, Hilda, and Roberta.

Here is a composite of their ideas as they finally appeared on our chart.

9. Turn the poem you read into a play.
10. Turn the poem you read into a story.
11. Turn the story you read into a play.
12. Turn the story you read into a poem.
13. Turn the play you read into a story.
14. Turn the play you read into a poem.
15. Tell a lap story for the class.
16. Make finger puppets from egg carton dividers. Tell the story.

Children's ideas

17. One of the main characters has asked you to spend the night with him/her. What kinds of things will you do? What will you talk about?
18. Dress up like one of the characters in the book. Why do you wear those clothes?

For the reader to do

Devise five more ways that children could report on books that they have finished reading.

● ● ●

When the list was finished, Joyce asked if there was anything else the class could do. Couldn't *someone, sometime* think up *something* else to do? I assured her that that was exactly what I was hoping would happen, for the whole point of this was just to get them started thinking about ways to help others to enjoy their books.

Mort, Daisy, and Hilda finished their game for Mrs. Wright's class. They made a duplicate set for our classroom, too. Daisy was a tremendous help, for she provided her group with the raw materials—popsicle sticks! They used sixteen sticks, blue and green markers, and a small plastic jar with a lid as a container. They called it "Shake-a-Word" and constructed it like this:

(A   D) one side

(E   B) other side

Write the vowels *a, e, i, o,* and *u* on five sticks like the example, capital and lower-case letters at opposite ends. Use the blue marker.

Turn the sticks over and write the vowel letters on the backs of the sticks also, following the example. Make sure that the letters on front and back are different.

On the fronts and backs of ten sticks write the consonant letters (with the exception of *Ww* and *Yy*) in green. One stick will have a blank side. Using blue *and* green, write the letters *Ww.*

Take one more stick and write with blue and green *Yy* on one side and *Ee* with blue on the other.

Place all of the sticks in the container, shake them up, and drop them from the container. Form words using the letters that show face-up.

This was a busy and exciting month, but we have accomplished many things. One of the things that we did was to add to our list of book reportings. I found an old copy of *Elementary English* which had an article by Arlene Pillar on "Individualizing Book Reviews" (1975). I asked a committee of students to go through the article and select some activities which they thought might be interesting from among the thirty listed in the article. They chose these:

19. You are the interviewer on a television talk show and will have one of the main characters in the book you have just read as your guest. List the questions you would like to ask. For as many of these as possible, write what you think the character might answer.

20. King Kong has just climbed through your bedroom window. He is trying madly to rip apart the book you have just finished reading. You must act very quickly and defend it. Convince him not to destroy it by citing incidents that you enjoyed. Prove to him that this book is worth keeping.

21. Invite one of the characters in your book to dinner. Tell him or her why you have selected them above the others. Then, leave a note for your mother describing the person and including a few "do's and don'ts" for her to follow so that guest will feel right at home.

22. You are a fortune teller and have been asked to predict what each of the characters in your book will be doing ten years after the story ends. Think of what each one is like (his or her personality, talents, likes and dislikes) before you answer the question.

23. You are a television commercial writer and have been asked to write a commercial advertising this book to the American Public. In not more than two paragraphs, since commercial time is expensive, tell why your book should be read.

24. Since you have the power to transform the major characters in your book into animals and choose to do so, decide upon an animal for each based upon personality traits. Write a letter to each telling why he or she is similar to the animal selected.

25. You are a real estate agent and want to sell a family a house in the neighborhood in which your book takes place. As part of the job, you must inform your clients about the community, the kinds of people living there, the existing organizations, the types of jobs available, and the schools. Make your description brief and to the point or else you may lose the interest of your clients.

26. The President of the United States wants you to tell him one thing that the character in your book discovered about life which all Americans should know in order to make this a better world. Write him a *brief* letter about this "lesson of life." Remember, the President is a busy man!

27. You are a famous astronaut flying a secret mission to Mars. Certain that there are Martians on the planet, you must be prepared to convince them that Earth people are friendly. Mission Control wants you to bring along the book you have just finished reading to help you show episodes with helpful and friendly citizens. What would you choose to share?

Betty, who had been on the committee, announced to the class that these additions improved our original list immensely. Others asked me if they could see the article, too, so I suppose that they will be supplementing these twenty-seven on the list with others as the year progresses.

The children in my class decided to go on a hunt for books which had been awarded one of the two major awards in children's literature. I was reading *Island of the Blue Dolphins* to them after they came in from lunch recess when I happened to mention to them that this book was a Newbery winner. "A new berry winner?" asked Carl. "Why? Because of all the fruit she eats?"

I explained then about John Newbery and the award which had been established in his honor for books which are of high literary quality. While I was on the subject, I also told them of the Caldecott Award which was established in Randolph Caldecott's honor to recognize superior illustrations in children's books. As I was doing so I was reminded of something I had read that stated perhaps we ought to have a "Caldebery" or a "Newcott" Award for the books which *children* like, for the other awards are selected by adults who think they can choose books which children will enjoy most. Very often the best books are chosen, but it is also true that many times children prefer the runners-up or even books not nominated more than the winners of the Newbery and Caldecott awards.

The children decided then that they would very much like to see how many award-winning books our school possessed. I told them that I would provide them with a list of all the winners and runners-up since the time that the awards began. With this list in hand, the children decided that it would be easier if they divided into groups that could check the books in the rooms and in the school library. They decided that they would need six groups:

Kindergarten and library: Alex, Betty, Daisy, and Jeff
First grade: Butch, Daphne, and Carl
Second grade: Chip, Hilda, and Horace
Third grade: Joyce, Pat, Tanana, and Manuel
Fourth grade: Larry, Mitch, Roberta, and Paul
Fifth grade: Mandy, Mort, Rita, and Steve

Each group was given a copy of the list and told to make an appointment with the teachers to check their bookshelves when it would be convenient. They asked me if we might bring the books to our room for comparison. I told them that they could do so if they could find a place to store the books from each room *separately* and would label each room's stack of books carefully. Some of the children expressed interest in doing more reading from some of these books—it's an interesting phenomenon that the books from another classroom are more appealing!

A young woman walked into the midst of all this confusion one day as the children were organizing the books that they had gathered. There were books on the floor, on tables, desks, window sills, and in boxes—what a mess! Mr. Topps told me that she had introduced herself to him and that she had asked to meet me. It seems that Miss Young is to be my student teacher next quarter. At least she will be if the mess didn't scare her off! She said that she just wanted to meet me and learn if there were anything that she could do during the holiday break to prepare herself for student teaching in my class. Well, I was flabbergasted! The fact that she took the time to come to see me now gave the impression that this young woman was going to be an exceptional student teacher! I gave her some packets of materials that I had prepared for a substitute after that last awful experience with Mrs. Payne, and explained my goals, policies, and program. I also told her that I hoped she had a strong background in children's literature and suggested some children's books she might read during the Christmas vacation.

Meanwhile, back at the stacks! The children found that the school owned nearly every one of the award books; however, they were so scattered that no teacher knew which of the books was available. As a result, there were several copies of some books throughout the school and none of others. They compiled a list of all these books with an indication of which rooms they were in. They made it on a ditto so that they could duplicate copies for all of the teachers and one for the library.

For readers to do together

Do what Mrs. Wise's third-graders did for their school. Find the award-winning books and their runners-up and compile a list for the teachers. If there are enough students in your class, annotate the list.

● ● ●

After we had finished with that project, some of the children were talking about several of the books that they had discovered. The ones that especially intrigued them were the Caldecott winners. Mandy said, "You know, I always thought that those were just books for little kids. But some of them are so interesting!"

Daphne asked, "Couldn't we make plays out of those and give them to the other classes for a Christmas present?" Cries of "Yeah! Yeah!" rang through the room. Mort was the only dissenter.

"Why not a Hanukkah present?" he inquired.

"Well, let's make it a Happy Holidays present," I mediated. This was accepted and we set to work. The children decided that they would keep their original groupings and each group would devise a play for the grade level with which they had worked before. They became as excited about this as they were about the approaching holiday season, so that December became a little harried!

Another helpful holiday deed was sending volunteers from my class to Miss Launch's kindergarten room to write down the children's dictated letters to Santa. I don't know if it's just the thought of Santa's coming or if there really is a change occurring, but both Butch and Mitch have been extremely helpful and kind this month. I *fervently* hope that it will last!

I've also had to add pages to some of the children's word books this month. Each child has a book divided into the sections for the twenty-six alphabet letters. In each section, they have been writing all of the new words that they have been learning this year, either through their reading or by asking me to spell some word that holds special appeal, like "vampire" or "groovy." The words are then available to the children later for writing purposes, or, if they encounter them in their reading but cannot remember what a particular word is, the position of the word on the page often triggers their memories. They go through their books often, showing their words to others and getting ideas for new words by seeing what their friends have collected.

Even with all of this confusion, Betty, Butch, Tanana, and Horace produced a game which they presented to the class as our very own "Happy Holidays" present. They had borrowed from me the Dolch Basic Sight Word List (see Appendix C), for they had told me that they needed "a lot of words." Their game, when finished, was somewhat like tic-tac-toe. They made several 6″ × 6″ squares which they then ruled off into nine 2″ × 2″ squares. They found five different colors of poster board (for the five divisions of the list—pre-primer to third grade). They cut forty green squares, the color for the words on the pre-primer list, and wrote one of the words on each, keeping the words in the order in which they appeared on the list. They then divided the word squares into eight piles of five words. Then, beginning with the words from the top of the list, they wrote the numeral *one* on the backs of all five cards in that pile, *two* on the backs of the next group, *three* on the backs of the next group, *four* on the backs of the next, and so on until all green squares had a numeral (1–8) on the back. Then, with red poster board, they went through the same procedure on the primer list, with nine piles of five and one pile of six. After all five lists were completed they had all 220 of the Dolch words written on squares. Their rules to the other children as well as their record-keeping chart appear on p. 175.

	Green								Red																			Yellow																	Blue																	Orange							
	1	2	3	4	5	6	7	8	1	2	3	4	5	6	7	8	9	10	1	2	3	4	5	6	7	8	1	2	3	4	5	6	7	8	9	1	2	3	4	5	6	7	8	1	2	3	4	5	6	7	8	9	1	2	3	4	5	6	7	8	1	2	3	4	5	6	7	8
Steve	√	√	√	√	√	√	√	√	√	√	√	√	√	√	√	√	√	√	√	√	√	√	√	√	√	√	√	√	√	√	√	√	√	√	√	√	√	√	√	√	√	√	√	√	√	√	√	√	√	√	√	√	√	√	√	√	√				√	√	√	√	√			
Rita	√	√	√	√	√	√	√	√	√	√	√	√	√	√	√	√	√	√	√	√	√	√	√	√	√	√	√	√	√	√	√	√	√	√	√	√	√	√	√	√	√	√	√	√	√	√	√	√	√	√	√	√	√	√	√	√	√				√	√	√	√	√	√	√	√
Daphne	√	√	√	√	√	√	√	√	√	√	√	√	√	√	√	√	√	√	√	√	√	√	√	√	√	√	√	√	√	√	√	√	√	√																																			
Roberta	√	√	√	√	√	√	√	√	√	√	√	√	√	√	√	√	√	√	√	√	√	√	√	√	√	√	√	√	√	√	√	√	√	√	√	√	√	√	√	√	√	√	√	√	√	√	√	√	√	√	√	√	√	√	√						√	√	√	√	√	√	√	√
Paul	√	√	√	√	√	√																																																															
Larry	√	√	√	√	√	√	√	√	√	√	√	√	√	√	√	√	√	√	√	√	√	√	√	√	√	√	√	√	√	√	√	√	√	√	√	√	√	√	√	√	√	√	√	√	√	√	√	√	√	√	√	√	√	√	√	√	√				√	√	√	√	√	√	√	√
Alex	√	√	√	√	√	√	√	√	√	√	√	√	√	√	√	√	√	√	√	√	√	√	√	√	√	√	√	√	√	√	√	√	√	√	√	√	√	√	√	√	√	√	√	√	√	√	√	√	√	√	√	√	√	√	√						√	√	√					

Check the chart to see which set you may use. Use the next set after the last check mark. [I had also devised a chart to keep track of which sets children could show me that they had mastered. A √ indicated mastery.]

Get a friend who uses a different color to play the game with you.

Keep all of your squares word-side down until you are ready to use them. The shortest person goes first.

Decide where you will play your first square, just like in tic-tac-toe. Place your card word-side up on that space and say the word. If you need help, that's okay. Have your friend tell you, but you must say it, too.

The winner is the one who gets three words in a row, going across, or down or "kitty korner."

rules for game on p. 179

This month I finally received the preliminary report on Paul from Dr. Case. He would like to do further testing, but on the basis of what he has already learned, he wrote that he is certain Paul is severely emotionally disturbed. That was certainly no surprise to me! It was because I knew this that I wanted him evaluated. He told me that it was impossible to get a valid I.Q. score on him or indeed any valid test score, for Paul simply does not "attend" enough to any task to complete it. Well, where do we go from here? I suppose I should let Dr. Case continue the evaluation and try again to get in touch with Paul's mother for a conference. She always puts me off because she is going to be "workin'" or "sleepin'" or "not home."

Well, my expectations about this term's student teacher seem to be supported by her deeds. Miss Young is a most eager young woman, staying late in the afternoon to complete a bulletin board or game that she is making for the children. The children have for the most part become quite attached to her. Her special friend seems to be Joyce. Joyce and Miss Young talk at great length on the playground, and I have noticed that Joyce is beginning to get really involved with her work. She doesn't need to be reminded to do it, and even seeks extra things to do now. Part of the reason might be that Miss Young has discovered Joyce's interest in witchcraft and the supernatural, and that she has been bringing some of Zilpha Keatley Snyder's books for Joyce to read. She especially enjoyed *The Egypt Game* and *The Changeling*. Right now she is reading *Below the Root,* a book which I found fascinating. Joyce is really growing up!

Miss Young also taught the children how to construct hardcover books. The children were enchanted with this opportunity to make "real" books. I am including the instructions here so that I won't lose them.

Bookmaking

1. To make a twelve-page book, fold three sheets of typing paper in half. Fold one more sheet in half and place it behind the others.
2. Sew the pages together on the fold either by hand or by using the longest stitch on a sewing machine.
3. Cut two pieces of cardboard that are 9″ × 6″ each.
4. Cut one piece of colored or printed adhesive paper that is approximately 10½″ × 13″. Peel off the paper backing.
5. Place the cardboard on the sticky side of the adhesive plastic cover, allowing ¼″ between the two pieces of cardboard.
6. Fold the edges of the adhesive plastic over onto the cardboard, snipping corners when necessary in order to make "hospital corners."
7. Lay the pages of the book on the cardboard. Glue the back of the extra sheet to the cardboard on both sides. Allow to dry.

8. The book is now ready to be written and drawn in.

Longer books can be made by using more pages. For each sheet of typing paper used, four book pages are made.

For the reader to do

Make a book for your own story. Follow the directions above. When you have finished it, read the book to a small group of children. Tell them that it is your own original story and that they, too, can produce books. Help them to make their own books.

● ● ●

After the children had mastered the process, they decided to make books for the kindergarten children. They brought in all kinds of brightly colored, plastic adhesive paper which they could use for the covers of the books. Then a delegation took several samples of their completed books to the kindergarten room. They told the children that if they wanted to write really good stories, then, they, the third-graders, would be back to help them make their stories into books! They made the same offer to the first-grades, for they knew that Mrs. Wright had her students writing many stories. I let Miss Young continue to be in charge of the project, and though it took nearly a month to complete, the children—all of them—were pleased with the results. Miss Young also thought that it had gone well; however she did comment, "But the next time I see a roll of adhesive plastic will be *too* soon!"

I have had Miss Young help me plan and teach some of the skill groups, for she will be taking them over very soon. I wanted her to see some of the activities and materials which she might be able to use. One group that she observed was composed of Manuel, Mitch, Alex, Carl, Steve, and Mort. They were working with punctuation marks. For those children who showed mastery of the exclamation point, period, and question mark, Miss Young was to prepare the next day's lesson on quotation marks and commas. I began the lesson by putting the three punctuation marks on my portable chalkboard and asking the pupils if they could tell me what any one of them was and/or what it meant. Steve commented that he knew "the curly one" meant that someone had asked a question and so it was called a question mark. Mitch knew that "the dot" meant that a sentence was over, and that it was called something that he couldn't remember. Manuel and Mort said "Period" together. None of them knew what the next one was called, though several said that they had noticed it sometimes when reading. In response to that, I wrote these three forms of the same sentence on the board:

(1) The house is on fire.
(2) The house is on fire?
(3) The house is on fire!

I asked if anyone could read the sentence for me in three different ways, reminding them that number one would be read in a normal tone, as though they were saying, "Please pass the bread."

Alex decided to try it. He read all three exactly the same way except that he kept his voice lower for the first one. He read them all as if they had an exclamation point. I had turned the tape recorder on when Alex began so that we could play it back and let him hear himself. (Incidentally, I have found this to be very helpful in eliminating many of the errors that children make orally, for they can hear themselves as others hear them.) Alex, after listening to the play-back, admitted that his three readings were not really different. Carl decided to take a chance now. He, too, read them all as if they had exclamation points. I stopped the tape and let the group hear it. They agreed that they had been read alike.

"What is it about that sentence that makes you want to read it as if you were excited?"

Alex said, "Well, it would be dumb to say it like, 'The house is on fire,' because nobody would come help you."

"Right. And the mark of punctuation which we use to show excitement, fear, anger, and other strong emotions is this one—the exclamation point. Listen to me read these sentences now." I taped mine, too, for them to hear.

"When would I say it like number 2?"

Carl replied, "Well, maybe you didn't know if you heard it right." I nodded and Steve asked to read them, and then Manuel did. They read quite well.

"Now, I'm going to read a sentence to you. Write on your magic slates (for this we use plastic coffee can lids and transparency pencils so that they can be easily erased and used again) the punctuation mark which I am using." I proceeded to say several sentences. After saying one, I paused long enough for them to write one of the punctuation marks. After they had written what they considered to be the proper one, they individually showed it to me. If the correct mark had been made, I showed my coffee can lid with the "happy face" drawn on it. If I didn't show the "happy face," the pupil tried again. If the child was still in error, I helped him or her hear what I had said and showed the proper mark on the chalkboard.

"Now I am going to show you a mark, one at a time, and you must think of a sentence for that mark." I marked a blank coffee can lid with one of the three marks. We did this activity for a few minutes and then I sent the boys back to their other work. Miss Young commented, "You did so many different things in just seven minutes—I timed you! How can you get so much done?"

I told her that I try to focus on exactly what needs to be taught so that we don't waste time. The children respond well when they expect the lesson to be interesting (because of the frequent changes of pace) and that it will not be too difficult (for I always review what they already know and build from there). She promised to try to come up with a lesson that would do as well, and she did an admirable job, I must say, for her first effort.

I met with Dr. Link after school a couple of times this month to discuss the progress that Miss Young was making. I told her I had been favorably impressed initially, and that she had indeed lived up to those first impressions. Dr. Link was pleased to hear that Miss Young was so involved in the classroom, for some supervising teachers like to have their student teachers just observe for the first weeks.

"Those people must be better organized than I am, then," I told her, "for I can use every pair of hands I can get, particularly when they are such capable ones."

I admitted that I was giving Miss Young more responsibility than I usually give to student teachers so early in the quarter, but that she seemed to be enjoying it. In addition, she and I share many of the same interests, and she had asked if she could begin planning a poetry project for March as her final large assignment. I am eager to get some new ideas from this one! It's a rare student teacher who hasn't taught me something during his or her tenure in my classroom.

Mitch and Manuel, both car nuts, convinced Joyce that the game they were to work on should be a car race game. The problem was they couldn't think of what to do after that. So I worked with them and we constructed a board with a track with spaces for six cars. They made small paper cars, some very fancy, to use as playing pieces. They used the cube pattern an earlier group had developed to make a die. I suggested they make cards for all 220 words on the Dolch list (Appendix C). Even though we call it their game, they needed a lot of help!

Instructions

1. Roll the die. The person with the lowest number goes first, second lowest number is second, and so on.
2. Choose your car and place it in the starting area.
3. The first player rolls the die and picks up as many word cards as the numeral on the top of the die.
4. He or she must say all of those words before moving his or her car. Sometimes he or she might need help, so a friend can help as long as he or she repeats the words.
5. After all of the words are said correctly, the player moves his or her car that number of spaces around the track.
6. Continue playing, placing words already said on the bottom of the deck, until someone reaches the finish line. (You might want to keep playing until all the players reach the finish line.)

I asked the children why so many of their games allowed friends to tell them the words, and Joyce replied, "We think that the important thing is saying the words *right,* and kids shouldn't lose just 'cause they don't know the words. I like to play with Mandy, but she would always win if I could only move when I knew the words. That's no fun!"

FEBRUARY

Complaints! Complaints! Several of the children are upset because in order to find a book dealing with a particular interest of theirs, they must search through all of the books in the room. "Why can't it be like the library?" is the cry heard more and more frequently. So this month I challenged them: "Why can't it be?" We discussed how to find books in the library and what kind of a system is used. I said I was tired of searching, too, and if they could come up with a plan, we would try it. Several days later, the children asked if we could get the entire class together for a discussion. When the entire class had assembled, Larry and Mandy took over. They told the group that they had been asking questions of the librarian and had learned from her that books are divided into categories like history and science. Then within those categories, the authors' names are arranged alphabetically. That is the system, basically, that our school library uses, but Miss Page had told them that she didn't think that they wanted their system to be so complex. "Just divide the books into categories and they will be much easier to locate," she told them, "and the addition of new books will be much simpler."

"What's the first step, Ace?" asked Hilda, who always likes to be prepared.

"Well, the first step, Miss Page explained, is to make sure that somebody has read all of the books in the room." Groans from the children as they looked over the bookshelves loaded with at least 200 books.

"But how can we do *that*?" Carl asked.

"My guess is that we nearly *have* done that. Wouldn't you agree, Mrs. Wise?" asked Larry. At my nod of agreement, he continued, "The first thing to do is find out which books have been read and which ones still need to be read. Mandy and I got some file cards from Mrs. Wise. You are to go to the shelves, find some of the books that you have read, and write the name of the book and the author on the top line. Later, when they are all done, we'll sit down and decide in which categories they belong. We'll all work at the same time so that we don't get several copies of cards on the same book."

"You know what I wish we could do?" asked Tanana. "I wish that we could know what the book is going to be about before we choose it. I know that Mrs. Wise lets us choose another one if we don't like what we get, but sometimes I waste a lot of time trying to find one I like."

"How about this, you guys?" Roberta spoke up. "Why don't we leave the card in the book when we finish, sticking up out of the top like this?

Then when we're all done, those who have read a book get together and think up one or two sentences telling what the book is about."

Remarks of "Yeah!" and "Neat!" were heard around the group, though I could see Mitch and Butch grimacing at the idea of the extra work that this would mean.

"How are you going to show what kind of book it is?" I asked. "How will people know that it is an animal book when they get it off the shelf?"

"Well, we could write on the outside like they do in the library," said Pat. "We could use numerals, like all the books with the numeral *one* would be animal stories. Something like that."

"Good idea, Pat. I think that would work very well. Then we could have a chart in the room in case anyone forgets what a numeral stands for. And we could put all of the *ones* together, all of the *twos* together, and like that," replied Larry.

And so we did. It took the children weeks to get the system organized, materials read, cards made and filed, but they have produced a system that will be used by scores of other children in this room, whoever their teacher might be. I regret that I will not be around next year to reap the benefits of all this work.

This is a most unusual class; in fact, it is *the* most unusual blend of children that I have encountered in my years of teaching. However, they seem to have a great deal of group cooperative spirit (the result, no doubt, of all the team effort that previous teachers have encouraged), so I suggested to them that it might be a good time to make a classroom dictionary. We would include all the words in their word books in the same way that they are listed in the regular dictionary. Butch, foreseeing more work ahead, asked why we needed to do this since we already had five different dictionaries in the room already. Pat, Daphne, Betty, and Tanana hushed him up with an "It'll be fun!" His look said that he was *not* convinced.

"You're right, of course, Butch. It will be a great deal of work, but I'm hoping that you will all learn more about a dictionary and how to use it by actually constructing one. I think that it will be fun, too!"

How did we begin? First, the children formed four groups of five or six children. Each child brought his or her word book to the group. Next they went through all of the *Aa* words and listed them alphabetically. There was one bad moment when Daisy didn't want anyone to use her word *apple* because it was *her* word and she liked it! She actually *hit* three of the children who insisted that they had to include the word. I noticed the first blow and got across the room to her group by the time she had struck the third child. When the children explained the problem to me, I took Daisy over to the shelf where we kept the other dictionaries and turned to the word *apple* in each of them. I showed her that while she may have a special feeling for the word, it indeed was not only her word. It belonged to all of us, but because she liked it so much, she could think up a nice sentence using the word to go into the dictionary.

The next thing that they did after they had gone through all of the words in their books and had alphabetized them was to send one representative from each large group with the list to make a master list for the class. They eliminated duplicates and came up with a final copy with the hundreds of words that the children had learned throughout the year. Needless to say, when the children saw this mammoth list, they were astonished. They had no idea that they had learned so many new words since September. They retained another aspect from their original group word lists; beside each word that they wrote on the list, they put the initials of the first three children who had learned that word. Those three children were to be responsible for the definition, any illustrations they might feel necessary, and a sentence to illustrate the meaning of that particular word. I was somewhat hesitant to allow them to do this, for I thought of children like Paul and Chip who never learn a word first! But I was wrong. The dictionary, being a list of the words learned by the children, included the words that Chip and Paul were learning to read, and since most of the others had learned the word *farm* long ago, it was a word that Chip and Paul could work on this year. When the children completed this task, they asked Mrs. Mainstay in the office to type it for them in dictionary format, and being the dear lady that she is, she readily complied. The children then selected a bookbinding committee to do the various steps involved in making a hardbound copy of their book. They were quite proud of it, especially when Mr. Topps, showing visitors around the school, pointed it out and told them how long and hard the children had worked on it. Butch took special pride in the book and was always first at the door when visitors arrived so that he could bring it to them as soon as Mr. Topps mentioned it. He would always say, "Well, it took us a long time, but it was fun."

For the reader to do

Help a child start a book of words to learn. When he or she has 100 words, help form them into a dictionary. If several children are involved, the dictionary can be made more quickly.

● ● ●

Pat, Chip, and Alex have come up with a really complicated game this month, but one that they claim the fifth-graders will love. Pat and the others have had a lot of fun with it already. The game consists of a game board, playing pieces, letter cards, and a die. First they made their "Letter Worm" game board (shown on p. 183). Then they constructed little worm playing pieces in six colors so that six children could play.

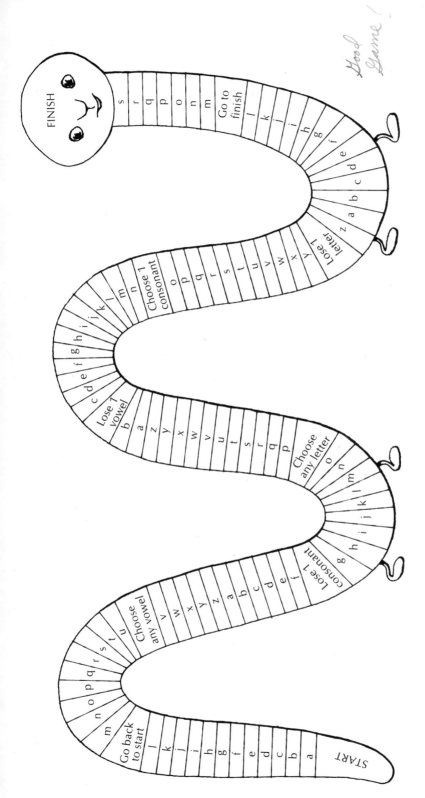

Good Game!

1. Roll the die. The person with the high number goes first, next highest is second, and so on.
2. Roll the die and move that number of spaces. You get one of whatever letter you land on. If you land on a "Choose any vowel," "Choose any consonant," or "Choose any letter" space then you get to select what you want.
3. If you land on a "Lose one vowel," "Lose one consonant," or "Lose one letter," you must return one letter to the letter stack.
4. If you land on "Go back to start," be happy! But if you land on "Go to finish," be sad because you want to collect as many letters as you can. Every time that you have to start over, you get more letters.
5. After everybody gets to the finish space, start to make words from all of the letters which you have collected along the letter worm. You get one point for each letter used in a real word.

Next they wrote letter cards, upper-case letter forms on one side and lower-case on the other. They made them in these quantities:

Vowels (including *y* and *w*): 20 each

Consonant letters *b, c, d,*
  f, l, m, n, p, r, s, t :   10 each

Consonant letters *g, h, j,*
  k, q, v, x, z :   5 each

Blank letter cards: 20 each

MARCH

Miss Young has become invaluable to me, and I told Dr. Link that I was not going to let her go! She laughed at me, of course, and said that if I felt that strongly, perhaps I would be willing to recommend her for my position which would become vacant with my retirement this June. I assured her that I would certainly do that, for Miss Young has been the *best* student teacher I have ever had. It is rather nice to think that someone who spends so many hours with the children working on their classroom catalogue system might be able to benefit from it next year. She is so creative, willing, and sympathetic to the students! And yet she doesn't let that sympathy interfere with providing them with the best possible instruction: she feels quite sad about Chip's home situation, but it is one that we can do nothing about, since his family is too proud to accept welfare. But, we can't let that interfere with doing what we can for him: providing him with the best possible education.

Miss Young has become a real expert at managing her time so that she can confer with five children and meet with six skill groups within a one-and-one-half-hour reading period. With both of us working, team-teaching style, we can accomplish even more, so I was reluctant to give her the experience that she needed in handling the entire day by herself. But, I did allow her two weeks, of course, so that she had a small taste of what it would be like to be totally responsible for a class.

During those two weeks—her last two weeks with us—she had the children making "shape books." Chip made a "hand book" in the shape of a large hand. The illustrations were photos made with an inexpensive Polaroid camera as well as others cut out from magazines. All were pictures of hands doing various things. The illustrations were labeled with descriptions of the hands' actions. One picture had a man's hands playing a piano, and the sentence said, "Hands can make music." Another showed a lady cuddling a baby, and was entitled "Hands can love you, too." Horace made a "foot book" using the same technique. Several other children found shape books to be an entertaining exercise.

Another project of Miss Young's was the long-awaited poetry unit. I knew that these children had had quite a lot of exposure to poetry. They had had much poetry read to them, and they had, in turn, created many poems of their own. I knew that they were ripe for the kinds of activities that Miss Young had in mind for them.

She began the poetry unit by reading to the children from Mary O'Neill's beautiful *Hailstones and Halibut Bones,* a collection of poems about colors. After reading a couple of her favorites and one of mine ("What is Purple?"), she discussed with them the fact that Mary O'Neill is saying that colors are not only things, but also feelings, moods, smells, and sounds. Then she took a stack of colored construction paper from her table and asked the children to form groups of five or six and told them that each group would receive one color sheet. They were then to list all the things that the color could be, feel like, smell like, sound like, or make them feel like within the five minutes that the timer would be set for. They began to discuss furiously and to list all of these qualities while she sat calmly reading more of the book (presenting all the while a good model for the children). When the timer rang, there were some groans of "Oh, no! Not yet! Let us put down some more." She asked each group to choose someone who could read the completed list to the rest of the class. One which I thought was particularly good was this one by Rita, Jeff, Manuel, Mort, Pat, and Steve. Their color was white:

lacy snowflakes	glaring light	refrigerator door
frosty window pane	anger	fear
unfriendly	coldness	sweet apple inside
crunchy ice cube	fluffy whipped cream	winter morning breath
hot mashed potatoes	a story before it's written	clouds above

She told the children that poetry creates images and that those images do not need to be done with rhymes. She said that she was sure that the children could create a poem from what they had listed. She said, "Let me see if *I* can try to make one." And this is it:

> Lacy snowflakes
> Against my window pane.
> Fluffy whipped cream
> Coldness from clouds above.

The children were enthralled, as was I, with this creation. Immediately, each group set to work to create a poem. Miss Young had explained to me that she wanted the children to have many experiences in writing group poems before they attempted to write individual ones. She told me that she had come to love poetry only within the last few years, that she had dreaded and hated it before. She was sure that that was because of the way in which her teachers had dealt with it—not as something to be loved, treasured, and enjoyed, but rather as something to be analyzed, dissected, and criticized. She had vowed that she would do her best to help her students learn to enjoy poetry at an early age. A format which she used with them involved the "diamante" form that Iris Tiedt (1970) had developed. It is as follows:

noun
adjective, adjective
participle, participle, participle
noun,   noun,   noun,   noun
participle, participle, participle
adjective, adjective
noun

The first and last words are to be opposites, and images build on the first noun through the two nouns in the middle. The transition is made here to building images for the last noun. The poem below is one written by the class.

Father
Strong, kind
Working, resting, loving
Bed, baby boy, Mamma
Working, working, working,
Tired, busy
Mother.

Miss Young also had the children complete the following phrases, and with the unifying factor of "The year" repeated at the end of the poem, she found that even the less capable children could produce a poem of worth.

The year. . .
The fall. . .
The winter. . .
The spring. . .
The summer. . .
The year. . .

I knew that the poetry unit had been successful when I noticed that the previously untouched poetry books in the class library became the most demanded ones and when scraps of poetry began to appear in the margins of work papers. The children recited poetry to one another at the playground! If only they keep this enthusiasm!

Roberta, Mandy, and Steve have created their game, the final group of the year to do so. They collected approximately twenty-five pairs of homonyms. They cut poster board into $2'' \times 4''$ cards and wrote the homonym pairs on each of two cards, one word at each end. Then they shuffled the cards and invited the children to play the game in a fashion similar to "Go Fish," only instead of giving that response, the one who does not have the card asked for must reply, "Have a Homonym." Other children have added additional homonym pairs as they have encountered them in reading.

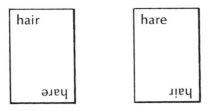

Instructions

1. Deal five cards to each player. The one to the left of the dealer begins. Everyone lays down all homonym pairs.
2. The first player asks someone if he or she has a certain homonym that the player needs to make a pair.
3. If the person has the card that is asked for, then the player may ask someone else for another homonym. He or she continues until he or she can get no more cards and someone says, "Have a homonym." Then he or she chooses from the leftover cards which are in the middle.
4. If the player gets what he or she asked for from the pile, he or she can keep on asking people until he or she no longer can make a match.
5. Then the next player does the same thing.
6. The winner is the one who gets rid of all of his or her cards first.

APRIL

My, how the time is passing now. With April over, only one more full month of school remains. I always begin to panic at this time of the year, wondering if I will accomplish all that needs to be done. Oh, well, done or not, the year *will* end! I've started to go through my file cabinets so that I won't be here all summer, trying to move out of this room. One accumulates a lot in twenty-five years.

While cleaning, I came upon the file folder for individualization I compiled the year that I first began to become discontented with what I had been doing, and was searching for something more satisfying for myself and the children. I had read a lot of articles in my professional journals, attended workshops, and taken courses at the university. I tried, then, to put all of the information together in a way that I could deal with it. I thought that I was ready after we returned from our Easter break (in March of that year). There was still enough time to work out some of the problems and to give it a fair try, realizing that if it didn't work, I wouldn't have wasted an entire year of the children's time. I began with my "top" reading group. I suppose that was because they had already completed the traditional third-grade curriculum and were actually just marking time. I called them together and told them that I wanted to begin an experiment with them. I told them that I had been looking into different ways to teach reading, and I wondered if they would like to help me try it out. I implemented, essentially, the same plan that I have explained in this journal.

I was most eager for them to tell me what they thought of it after we had been at it for a month, so I called the original group together and asked them for comments and suggestions. One suggestion was that they be allowed to work in groups, for I had them all working independently, so that there was little interaction among them. I agreed, and some of the group activities described in this journal are the results of their suggestions. They also wanted more entertaining things to do, for I, in my eagerness to provide them with a good skills reinforcement program, had given them stacks of ditto papers to do every day and very little for pleasure. They were interacting with the material in only a limited way—read the book, answer questions about the book, do a ditto on parts of speech. I promised that I would find some other ways to teach and provide practice. This whole thing became more complex than I had ever anticipated. I changed many of my ideas about teaching reading that spring, and began to be, I felt, a much better teacher. After years of teaching I was finally beginning to be concerned about the children and *how* they learned as well as *what* they learned.

With the children's suggestions implemented, I decided to individualize the middle group of readers as well. Since I had the first ten children going strong, I was sure that I could handle eight more. Well, I did it, but for a week or so I thought I would go crazy! All of those assignments to check every night and then more to make up for the next day! Finally one evening I asked myself why I continued to punish myself that way. Unless this "treadmill to oblivion" was to be my entire life—correcting work and assigning more so that I would have something to do the next night—I had to find an alternative. But what was it? The work had to be checked, but *why* did it have to be checked? The answer: so that the children would have reinforcement for the things that they knew and so that they could see through their errors what they didn't know. It suddenly became apparent that it would be more useful to them if the children corrected their own work. So that is what I let them do. I made self-corrective as many of the materials in the learning centers as I could. When the children did some work papers, the key was made available to them, and they did the correcting. I still saw some of these papers, for I did need to evaluate their work, but it was not necessary to mark a paper in order to evaluate it. Besides, the unit tests that I gave and the skill tests that I devised gave me information about the children's progress so that I did, indeed, know their respective strengths and weaknesses. With things running smoothly, I was able to individualize the "low" group, also, so that I had twenty-four children working more or less independently—and happily.

How I wish that Miss Young had been around that year to help me. If she had been available, I could have been using "LAP's" all these years. She introduced me to the concept and produced a few of them during her quarter in the room. A LAP is a "Learning Activity Packet" that includes a pretest over material in the packet, activities to teach and reinforce, and a posttest to determine how well each child has mastered the materials. She did an excellent unit on "Nyms"—synonyms, antonyms, and homonyms. The pretest had a page with exercises like the following:

Choose the homonym pairs in each row:

her	hair	hare	chair
sore	chore	soak	soar
flour	shower	flower	floor

Match antonym pairs:

hot	ugly
beautiful	laugh
cry	cold

Write two synomyms for the following words:

pretty
said
good

After she evaluated the child's strengths and weaknesses, she assigned certain of the activities within the packet. After those were checked by the child and after he or she felt that the concepts had been mastered, he or she asked to take the posttest. If the child did well, another packet was assigned. If, however, he or she still had areas of weakness, Miss Young had prepared alternative activities to review an area without going over the same work. Some of her packets included a tape which the children could drop into a recorder and then listen to the instructions. These were especially helpful for those with inadequate reading skills, but I think that all of the children benefitted from the ones they used, for it was one more valuable listening exercise for them.

For the reader to do

Choose an area (such as contractions or punctuation) and devise a LAP. Have your class evaluate it.

● ● ●

Before I was introduced to LAP's I had another system which worked rather well for me. I went through all of the old workbooks in the school storeroom, tore the pages out of their covers, and sorted them according to skills. In addition, I had a lot of sample workbooks and activity cards that publishers' salespeople had given me. Those materials also went into skill piles. When I had gathered everything available to me (ditto masters, directions for games, etc.) I labeled file folders and stored the materials in the appropriate folders. Then when I wanted to teach the suffix -ly, I went to that particular folder and got the materials that I needed. They were all there together and ready for use. I think that if I were going to teach another year, I would use a combination of my file folders and those LAP's.

The final report on Paul has come through. Dr. Case is certain that the child is so emotionally disturbed that he should be removed from his home and institutionalized. He thinks that the County Children's Services Board will be able to do so and should place him in the Children's Home. I disagree, but I don't quite know what to do now. This report will, of course, go in the child's permanent record folder, and it is an action that the school will have to initiate if it so desires. Poor Paul! I fear that he will withdraw more and more if placed in an institution and will probably be exploited by those who are stronger than he.

MAY

More drawer and file and cabinet sorting this month. I came across an old cardboard folder in which I found pictures, stories, poems, plays, and other nice things done by my students over the past twenty-five years. Here is the picture that Cathy drew after her mother died and she had such a hard time adjusting to it. And here's the story that David wrote to give me for my birthday. All of these reminders of all the wonderful children who have taught me as much as I ever taught them. I should throw them away, for I can't possibly keep all of these remembrances of years gone by—and yet, how can I possibly discard the souvenirs of so many years of my life?

In this last busy month, I called for parental help to administer the IRI's to the children again. I do this as a further gauge on what they have accomplished. I also have a mother help me by administering the Dolch Basic Sight Word List to the children. They all should have this list mastered by the end of third grade, but, unfortunately, many do not. In the file that is passed on to the next teacher, I will include with the written evaluation each child's skill cards and the Dolch test so that the teacher will know which skills and words still need to be worked on. I also have the children read over the eighty-two words from the Kucera-Francis List which are not on the Dolch list (see Appendix D, Johnson, 1971).

The children have been helping me sort out things in the room to decide which things should be kept (such as the games they made) for the next class. The games that they seemed to have benefitted most from this year were those created by the children or by Miss Young or me. I suspect that this is because "homemade" games can be directed specifically at a skill or area that we know the children need work on. Commercial games do not have this advantage.

For the reader to do

Using the complete Dolch Word List in the appendix, make a test to administer to children. Type the words with a primary typewriter on two 12″ × 18″ sheets of white paper that have been glued to oaktag. Use triple spacing between the lines of words. Seal this with clear adhesive plastic to protect it, for this is what the child will be reading from. Prepare typed papers for yourself, typed in the same order as the child's copy, with room for the child's name and the date. Administer the test to a child and score it according to the directions in Appendix C.

For readers to do together

Make at least five of the games described in this chapter, and test them with elementary school children in a local school. Make a present of them to the teachers with whom you cooperate on this venture. What changes will you need to make in the games for the children with whom you tested them? Remember, the grade levels for which Mrs. Wise's class designed the games are flexible. You may find a particular game works equally well with several different grade levels, or you may find that the games don't work at the grade level the game was designed for.

● ● ●

To help the children become even more independent, I have taught them to use Jeannette Veatch's "rule of thumb" (1967). They can determine if a book is too difficult for them by turning to a full page somewhere near the middle of the book and choosing a paragraph of about 100 words. As they read, they may encounter words they do not know, so when the first one is met, the thumb of one hand is extended from a closed fist; when the second one is encountered, the next finger is extended, and so on. If all five fingers are extended by the end of the paragraph, that book is probably too difficult. They are instructed to make another selection. Most of the children find that this system works quite well for them, but for some few it's not a good system. Mitch finds it difficult to admit, even to himself, that a book that he has chosen from a shelf may be too hard. He "fudges" by starting over if he runs out of fingers. Daisy doesn't know that she has made any errors, so consequently, she ends up with books that she is unable to read. She substitutes words, but since she has extreme difficulty with even literal comprehension, she is unaware that what she says does not make sense.

One of my last tasks for this school system is to write the reports that will inform parents and next year's teachers how well the children have done this year. I administered a pre- and post-IRI to the children to gauge reading growth this year. Even though I don't use basals, I like this measurement device. Maybe I'm getting sentimental in my dotage, but I think that they did remarkably well with my system. I can't imagine myself trying to teach these children, varied as they are, within the confines of a reading group.

ALEX: Alex entered third grade reading at 3^1 level and now is at the book four level. The Dolch test indicated that he was reading sight words at the third-grade level. He has been a diligent worker during skill groups and has shown a lot of interest in reading.

BETTY: Betty thoroughly enjoyed her readings in children's literature this year. She entered reading at the 3^2 level and made so many gains that she is now reading at the fifth-grade level. The Dolch word list has been mastered. She was a willing group participant and worked very well independently. A very responsible child.

BUTCH: Butch's behavior problems have interfered with his learning this year. He finds it extremely difficult to work independently. He can now identify 200 of the Dolch list. He entered third grade reading at the 2^1 level and is now at the 2^2 level. If Butch could exhibit more self-control, he could be a good student.

CARL: Carl has made good progress this year, entering with a reading level of 2^2 and finishing the year with a level of 3^2. He enjoys the reading process and works well independently most of the time, though he does sometimes daydream. He now knows all of the Dolch words.

CHIP: Chip has little energy or enthusiasm, the result, I suspect, of an inadequate diet. He is capable of far better work than he has been doing. He is a hard worker, and he strives to make contributions to the group. He has mastered 165 of the Dolch words. He entered school this fall reading at the 1^2 level and now reads materials with a difficulty of 2^2.

DAISY: Daisy has not made the gains that I had hoped she might make this year. She is quite a capable child, but so self-indulgent and self-centered that she is unable to use her intelligence. She entered the room reading in the primer level and is now at the 1^2 level. She has not found this approach an easy one, for it requires more self-discipline than she has at this point. She has mastered only 115 words on the Dolch list.

DAPHNE: Daphne has made excellent progress this year, for she entered with a 2^2 reading level and she now reads materials for the end of third grade. She has a special interest in fantasy that we should be building on. She has worked diligently and has mastered all 220 of the Dolch words. She does her work well and efficiently. She should manage quite well in school now.

JEFF: Jeff has had some problems this year. He is responsible enough that he should have had no difficulty with independent work, but a combination of low interest and low reading level contributed to his lack of success. He entered with a reading level at the 2^1 level and now tests at the 3^1 level. He knows 199 of the Dolch words.

JOYCE: Joyce has so enjoyed this year, particularly after her interests were revealed and we could find books she liked. She has mastered all of the Dolch words and improved her reading from the 3^1 level she entered with to the fourth-grade reading level she now has. She much prefers working independently to working in a group, though she makes many positive contributions when she does work with a group.

HILDEGARD: Hilda has some difficulty disciplining herself enough to do the routine tasks which must be done. She much prefers to dramatize the ordinary and make a "big deal" out of a small one. She entered with a 3^1 level and is now reading at the fifth-grade level. She has mastered all of the words from the Dolch list.

HORACE: Horace is a very responsible child. He wants to do his best work always, though sometimes he has trouble seeing it through. He contributes greatly to class discussions and works well independently. He was at the 3^1 level this fall and is now reading at the fourth-grade level. He has mastered all of the Dolch words.

LARRY: Larry (I am tempted to call him "Ace" as the children do) has a remarkable mind. He is a brilliant, deductive, logical child who never flaunts his knowledge. He is well-liked by the others and sought after for advice and help. He works as well with a group as he does independently. He entered third grade with a reading level of seventh grade. He is now capable of reading just about anything he wants to read.

MANDY: Mandy entered this class with a beginning fourth-grade reading level. She now reads at the sixth-grade level. She is a practical child with a special interest in science and math. She is logical and well-organized and makes many contributions to groups. She works best independently, however. She has mastered the entire Dolch list and has helped others in the class with them, too.

MANUEL: Manuel has had a good year. He works well with a group and works hard independently. He is responsible and likeable. He knows all of the Dolch list. He was reading at the 3^1 level in the fall and now reads at the fourth-grade level. Manuel makes many valuable contributions to whatever group he is a part of.

MITCH: Mitch now knows all of the Dolch words, and he is reading at fourth-grade level, after beginning this year at the 3^1 level. He must learn to deal with his personal and social problems. He has much difficulty working independently, for his mind wanders and he has trouble finishing tasks. His one real interest is horses, and he read every horse book which we have at and below his level.

MORT: Mort seems so bored with everything. It is difficult to draw him into group work, and, while he does work independently, he doesn't become really involved with any of it. He entered at the 3^1 level and has achieved a fourth-grade level by the end of the year. He knows 207 of the Dolch list, though he should know them all. Mort must find something which interests him, or he will only be "putting in time" at school without taking full advantage of his opportunities.

PAT: Pat has made remarkable progress this year. She entered reading at the end of fourth-grade level and she now reads at the sixth-grade level. She devours books and loves to write down her experiences and fantasies. She mastered all of the Dolch list. Pat prefers to work independently, and does her best work that way.

PAUL: Paul needs to relax and accept his environment. He is fearful of many unnamed things. He is a kind, considerate child. This year he was evaluated by the school psychologist. His reading level has not increased at all. He entered reading below the primer level, and is now reading at the 1^2 level. He knows 170 of the Dolch list, though some days he knows more. Paul makes few contributions to group work and is unable to carry out an assignment independently. I suggest that a closer relationship be established between his home and the school.

RITA: Rita is a delightful child who is eager to learn all she can. She loves reading and has read many, many books this year. She was reading at the fourth-grade level this fall and is now at the fifth-grade level. She mastered the Dolch words with no difficulty. She works well no matter what the task and is self-reliant and dependable.

ROBERTA: Roberta has her problems, but she rarely means to cause the trouble that she does. She is a bright, active child who likes to be in on everything in the class. She is so gregarious that she would rather work with a group than independently, and thus does not always accomplish her work. She entered last fall with an end-of-third-grade reading level and is now at the end-of-fourth-grade in reading ability. She has mastered all of the Dolch list. She has greatly enjoyed this year's reading.

STEVE: Steve thoroughly enjoyed the opportunity that he had to read books dealing with science. He read everything in the room either by himself or by asking someone to read them to him. He entered third grade reading at the 3^1 level and is now reading at the fourth-grade level. He works very well independently, and he prefers to do his work that way. He now knows all of the Dolch words.

TANANA: Tanana has been a delightful addition to the classroom this year. I know that the adjustment has been a difficult one for her—new customs and new people—but she has made some good friends. Cultural and language problems account for the 2^2 reading level that she now has, for she is quite bright and should become an excellent student. She is a rather solitary child with a great sense of responsibility. When she is given a task, either independently or in a group, she carries it out well and efficiently.

The Third Grade Meeting

Mrs. Wise smiled as Miss Kurt departed. There were many teachers who felt considerable fear of that small but dynamic Miss Kurt whenever she entered their classrooms. Not Mrs. Wise! She remembered when Miss Kurt has been *her* student teacher some fourteen or fifteen years ago. It was on Mrs. Wise's recommendation that the school system had hired Miss Kurt and had later promoted her to the position of Elementary Supervisor. Now Mrs. Wise was smiling, for she had just been asked if she would present the program for the final meeting of the third-grade teachers. "My valedictory," she thought. "Oh, well. I suppose they had to ask me now, since I won't be here next year. I was hoping, though, that I could get away without even attending, let alone being the program!"

After twenty-five years of these meetings, she was *ready* to retire; she had often said that the meetings were things she would never miss about school!

But now to plan what to do! She began by going through some of the materials which she had selected for this final meeting, dragging out samples of cards and charts that she had used during this past year. She had asked to have the meeting in her own room so that she would not have to transport all of her paraphernalia across town to the room in the Administration Building, where these meetings were usually held. Here she would show the other teachers the learning centers which occupy the children's time, as well as the card catalogue system that the children had devised. She sat down to plan the meeting for the following week.

One week later, Mrs. Wise was completely organized and ready for the meeting. She greeted the teachers who entered her room and then began the meeting by expressing her pleasure at seeing all her old friends and acknowledging her sincere delight at the interest they had shown in her program. She told them that she was eager to share with them the kind of program that she had been using for many years. Some of those present had visited her classroom in the past and she invited them to make any comments which they felt were pertinent.

"First of all, it is important to emphasize that individualized reading instruction is not a *method* of teaching. Rather, it incorporates the best of all methods. Furthermore, individualization does not necessarily mean instruction on a one-to-one basis. This is a common fallacy. Individualization means *providing children with what they need, when they need it.* Therefore, it can mean teaching one-to-one or one-to-five or one-to-thirty. The point is that the *children* are central to what is being taught, not a curriculum.

"Another factor to keep in mind is that, for most of us, it is better to begin gradually when initiating my kind of program. Until I had worked out many of the details, I only had my "top" reading group involved in the individualized program. It was only after I felt more confident that I included the rest of the children in the program.

"Another fact that I have learned and that I wish to pass on to you is that you *must* provide group activities for the children. It is so easy, really, to isolate the children, to make them so independent of the others that they don't develop the cooperative spirit that is so necessary if they are to make their contributions to society. We tend to give children their work folders and books, send them off to do their own work, and be sadly unaware of the social damage that we may be inflicting upon them. We are, after all, social creatures, and it is just as much our responsibility as teachers to consider that aspect of children's education as it is to provide for the basic academics."

Mrs. Wise then showed the assembled teachers her skill cards ("they operate on the same system as computer key-sort cards"), samples of work folders and assignments, the reading cards on which she kept notes on a child's progress, and the other materials that she used in her daily teaching. She described the conferences and the skill group meetings, the learning centers, the testing, and the games. She then told them that long ago she had given up correcting every one of the assignments *herself*. That statement caused several sidelong glances, and one of the teachers challenged her.

"Maydelle Wise! Do you mean to tell us that you let the *children* mark their papers? I wouldn't dare to try that! Why I'd have children cheating all over the place."

"Yes, you probably would, if you think of it in those terms. Children respond as they are expected to respond. I had few instances of cheating, though there were many instances in which the children, feeling frustrated and concerned, forgot to mark errors. Those instances fortunately occurred early in my experimentation. I discovered that what was actually causing the tension was that the work that I had assigned was too difficult. Once I had planned an instructional program for each child that fit his or her special needs, there was no longer a problem. Letting children know that you trust them and expect them to accept some of the responsibility for their own learning is a most important step. They respond well to this, at least in *my* experience, which, as you all know, has been considerable!"

Mrs. Wise went on to tell them that in order to help children choose books which they might enjoy, she had administered an "interest inventory." It was not complex, and she had devised it after examining several that she had found in journals and books. She had also found that she needed to organize herself, and so she had devised a materials-skills checklist that enabled her to sort out her various materials. This had taken a lot of time, but it had been easily augmented once the initial work had been completed. One of the teachers asked her how it was done, and she drew a diagram on the board to illustrate. The top of the paper was divided into skill areas; the left side listed all the materials she had available for use, either from her own supplies or from those of a cooperative teacher in another grade. Then she marked all of the skills that a particular material would deal with. This had a twofold purpose: first, she could see at a glance all of the materials which she had available for a specific skill, and second, she could see those areas for which she needed to find or develop materials. She had found, she said, that her teaching materials were inadequate in the areas of listening and study skills. If she had not made the checklist, she might not have realized this fact and might have gone on to this day wondering why her students had weaknesses in these areas. Since she had known her for many years, Mrs. Wise was not at all surprised when an older teacher, Agatha Nostic, declared, "It seems to me that you spent far too much time testing your class. How could you get any teaching done?"

"But my dear, how can you teach children until you know what it is that you *must* teach them? What a waste of your time and theirs to go over material which is already known, and how frustrating for you and them to try to deal with material that is too hard. Surely you see the absurdity of it? After careful assessment, I have a notion of what they know and what they need to learn. From there on, it's relatively easy."

"But didn't you repeat yourself a lot? I mean, it seems to me that it is more economical to introduce a new concept to everyone at the same time."

"But, Agatha," Mrs. Wise replied, "don't *you* repeat yourself? Do all of the children master a concept when it is introduced? I found out many years ago that if I introduced something to the entire class that they were not all ready for, I then had to spend the next few months going over and over the same thing for some of the children, trying to drive it into their heads. However, if I waited until they were ready to learn the concept, then the teaching and the learning were less difficult."

"Well, I think that you wasted a good bit of time just playing! Those games! Why weren't the children doing their workbooks and work papers? Nobody learns anything by playing."

"There does seem to some evidence to the contrary (Daniels, 1971), for it would seem that some children learn better through playing games than through traditional approaches. We have talked all year at these meetings about the fact that children are individuals with different learning styles. But I wonder how many of us truly believe it? If we did, wouldn't we be providing children with some of the experiences that they need? Games teach much more, by the way, than simple skills exercises. They help children learn to make decisions, to plan ahead, to work cooperatively, and to enjoy learning. What more could one ask of a simple teacher- or child-made game?"

"One thing that I didn't understand was how you could get through with a conference in just five to ten minutes. I take thirty minutes for a reading group and I *still* feel that I haven't accomplished much."

"Agatha, if your reading groups are anything like the ones I have had, my guess is that you spend a lot of the time in noninstructional roles. 'Eyes on the book, Johnny.' 'Sue, do you know where we are?' 'No voices, please. Mary is reading.' 'Hands on the table and out of your desk, Jake.' Does that all sound familiar? Of course it does! I had a student teacher make a chart of my teaching behaviors on a certain day, and I was appalled at how much time I was spending disciplining or trying to gain the attention of bored and/or frustrated children. That was another thing that led me to try individualization. With only two of us, the child and myself, who is there to show off *for*? If attention begins to wander, I am immediately aware of it. Five minutes of good, solid instruction is worth more than thirty minutes of interrupted and incomplete instruction."

Mrs. Wise paused to notice the nods of agreement around the room. She had had the feeling when she began that some of these teachers were not very sympathetic to what she was doing, but now there was a noticeable change. Several of the teachers wanted to know how to begin her program. She showed them some of the materials that had helped her in the program she had evolved, and recommended that they might find much helpful information in these, for they were practical and realistic.

One important aid was *Helping Children Read: A Practical Approach to Individualized Reading* by Peggy Brogan and Lorene Fox. Another was the IRA Conference Proceeding for 1966, *The Individualized Reading Program: A Guide for Classroom Teaching*. Margaret La Pray (1972) and Robert Aukerman (1971) had also had an important influence upon her. She told them that Jeannette Veatch had written many things about individualizing instruction, and that her writings were very readable. Mrs. Wise told the teachers that she would be glad to have any of them come to her room before school closed and that she hoped some of them would try individualization.

She began to gather up her materials, preparatory to leaving the meeting, when Miss Kurt, with a grin on her face, told her to sit down, for the best part of the meeting was yet to come. And through the door, borne by two of her oldest friends, came a cake of mammoth proportions. The inscription read "Good-by, Mrs. Wise. We will miss you." She was stunned and unable to speak for a moment, but one of her friends thought she heard her mutter under her breath, "I'd rather have a martini!"

References

Aukerman, Robert. *Approaches to Beginning Reading Instruction.* New York: John Wiley and Sons, 1971.

Brogan, Peggy, and Fox, Lorene. *Helping Children Read: A Practical Approach to Individualized Reading.* New York: Holt, Rinehart, and Winston, 1961.

Cunningham, Patricia. "ARRF! A Book That Fits!" *The Reading Teacher* 30 (1976): 206–207.

Daniels, Steven. *How 2 Gerbils, 20 Goldfish, 200 Games, 2000 Books and I Taught Them to Read.* Philadelphia: The Westminster Press, 1971.

"The Individualized Reading Program: A Guide for Classroom Teaching." In *Conference Proceedings of the International Reading Association, 1966,* vol. 11, part 3. 1967.

Johnson, Dale. "The Dolch List Re-examined." *The Reading Teacher,* 24, 1971.

La Pray, Margaret. *Teaching Children to Become Independent Readers.* New York: The Center for Applied Research in Education, 1972.

O'Neill, Mary. *Hailstones and Halibut Bones.* New York: Doubleday, 1961.

Pillar, Arlene. "Individualizing Book Reviews." *Elementary English* 52 (1975): 467–69.

Tiedt, Iris. "Exploring Poetry Patterns." *Elementary English* 47 (1970): 1083–84.

Ms. Maverick

HIGHLIGHTS

Reading in the Real World

SQUIRT

Integrated Curriculum Block

Skills

Revised A and P Word List

Rummy

Sociogram

Lifeline

Map of School

Giant State Map

Wall Vocabulary

Spelling

Directed Reading Lesson:
  Unfamiliar concepts and unknown words
  Purposes for reading
  Follow-up activities

Field Trips:
  Newspaper
  Court house and museum
  State capitol

Directed Film-viewing Lesson

Telegram Writing

Relief Map

Time Line

State Book

Historical Mural

Historical Drama

Math Word Problems

Interviewing

Guided Reading Procedure

Translation Writing

Parent Conferences

Listening-reading Transfer Lesson

Reading Pairs

"List, Group, and Label" Lesson

Group Discussions

Guided Listening Procedure

Book Fair

Ms. Maverick

The Parent Meeting

Ms. Maverick greeted most of the parents by name as they entered the door of her fourth-grade classroom. Five years before, she had known no one in this community and had missed the easy familiarity she had established with the residents of the small mountain community where she had taught during her first three years.

"Welcome," she began. "As most of you know from our annual book fairs, I am Ms. Maverick. I am pleased to see so many parents here tonight. Usually, there is a tremendous turnout of parents for the kindergarten and first-grade meetings, but attendance decreases as the grade level of the children increases. You are to be commended for your continuing interest in the education of your children.

"Tonight, rather than talk at you about the reading program we pursue in this room, I am going to engage your participation in a learning activity similar to many of the lessons your children will be participating in. I would like you now to think back on all your activities over the past week and to try to remember all the things you had to read in order to get along in your daily lives. You see, reading is such a constant activity that often we read without realizing it. We are aware that we are cooking or traveling or working without realizing that reading is an integral part of all these activities. Tonight I want you to tell me all the things you have read this week that were not books or magazines, and as you list these things for me, I will write them up here on the board."

At first there was silence as the parents adjusted their expectations to include their active participation in the meeting and began to think about what they had read that was neither a book nor a magazine. Mrs. Penn broke the silence by volunteering that she had read a map to get over to the state capital for a special meeting of a citizen's action group. Ms. Maverick wrote *map* on the board and then waited. Mr. Moore said that he had read the revised criminal rights statutes which had come in the mail to the police department. Mrs. Smith said that she had read the electric bill. Everyone groaned, the group relaxed, and suggestions came faster than Ms. Maverick could record them: *traffic signs, clocks, patterns, exit signs, blueprints, phone books, letters, sales ads, the dials on the stove, directions on the varnish can.* In ten minutes, Ms. Maverick had the board filled and the parents had "experienced" reading as a survival skill.

"You know, I have always been a reader and thought how unfortunate people were who couldn't read," Mrs. Penn volunteered. "But I never realized how downright impossible it would be to get along in the world if I couldn't read."

Daphne's grandmother recounted, "Once I was in the grocery store and a man came up to me with a can of soup in his hand and asked me what kind it was. I just assumed he had left his spectacles at home, but perhaps he couldn't read the label. They don't put pictures on the cans the way they used to, you know." Her husband added, "You can't even be a successful farmer these days if you don't know how to read!"

Ms. Maverick agreed. "That's right, there are very few jobs you could hold these days that don't require some reading ability. So often, wanting the best for our children, we point out to them that they must do well in school if they want to grow up to be lawyers or doctors. Many children, however, aspire to the 'exciting' occupations: they want to be truck drivers, police officers, medical technicians, beauticians. Little do they realize the reading demands of these jobs.

"My most important reading goal for your children is that they experience reading as a survival skill. To accomplish this, I do exercises with them like the one I just did with you tonight. I also provide them with 'real world' reading materials. I have some of these 'real world' materials displayed here on this table and I will be encouraging the children to bring in reading material they find of interest."

The parents looked over to the table and saw displayed there two daily newspapers, several different magazines, a driver's license manual, maps, menus, pamphlets, telephone books, catalogues, games, and directions for constructing various objects.

"For the final part of my 'reading is real' scenario, I plan to invite people engaged in various jobs to come in and talk with my children about what they must read to do well in their jobs. I haven't done this before but I think it will make a more lasting impression if the children hear people explain the reading needs of their jobs. This is one area in which I am seeking your help this year. I won't ask you to volunteer now, but if you could spare a half-hour to come and talk to the children about your job and its reading demands, please stay a minute after the meeting and leave me your name and the best time for you to come."

Ms. Maverick looked at the clock and realized that she had already used most of her meeting time. ("This is a consistent problem in an activity approach to learning," she thought. "It always takes more time.") She then hurried on to explain the other three components of her reading program.

"While the 'Reading is real' component is an important part of our reading program in this room, it is certainly not the total program. In fact, it is only one side of my four-sided reading approach. A second side of the approach is SQUIRT. I am sure most of you know that in this school reading is considered important enough so that we take time out each and every day to do it. Presently in our class we are reading for fifteen minutes, and I hope that we will be up to twenty-five minutes by the end of the year. During SQUIRT time your children have intensive, sustained practice in reading in material of their choice. I believe strongly in the concept of SQUIRT because it just makes so much sense. All of you know that to be good at anything, you have to learn to do it *and* you have to practice doing it. You wouldn't expect anyone to be a good driver if he or she had just taken driving lessons but had never practiced driving. I believe that our daily SQUIRT time insures the practice half of the instruction/practice partnership which is essential for learning anything.

"The third part of my reading approach is what I call my 'integrated curriculum block.' I do not believe in separating all the subjects so that math is taught for forty-five minutes, followed by forty-five minutes of reading, language, science and social studies. That kind of fragmentation has never made very much sense to me. It seems so much more economical to spend the reading, language, and math time engaged in reading, writing, and doing math problems that relate to the real world topics of social studies and science. So each morning from 9:00-11:00 we have our block time. During this time we are practicing our language and math skills as we investigate a topic from the social studies or science curriculum.

"For the next several months, we will be busy finding out about our state, which is the major social studies topic in fourth grade. We will be reading from all kinds of sources to find out more about the history, geography, politics, and economics of our state. During this morning block time, I will be especially concerned with improving your children's comprehension and increasing the number of words in their listening and reading vocabularies.

"The final part of the reading approach is our afternoon skills time. Many fourth-graders have not yet mastered the basic sight words and word identification skills essential to successful reading. Each afternoon from 1:15-2:00 the children work individually or in small groups on those skills they most need to master. During this time we work not only on reading skills but also on the other language skills and basic math skills. I give several informal tests which I have made to determine the skills your children have not yet mastered, and then assign them to complete games, activities, and worksheets to help them master these basic skills. As the children master certain skills, they move on to others. By the time children reach fourth grade, there are great differences among them. During this afternoon skills time, I work with each child to focus on his or her own individual needs."

Ms. Maverick finished her last sentence hurriedly and apologized for going over the allotted thirty minutes. She thanked them for coming and said that she would answer any questions they might have individually if they would stay for a moment after the others left. She reminded them that she really hoped some of them would come and talk with her class about the reading needs of their jobs and also asked for volunteers to drive the class on field trips.

To her surprise, she had six volunteers to come and speak to her class. Mr. Peskins, who was a truck driver, said he had come to five of these meetings over the years and that this was the most interesting one he could remember. He said he would be glad to come and bring all his maps, routing sheets, and delivery orders. Mr. Moore, the chief of police, also volunteered, as did Mr. Smith, who worked for the gas and electric company. Mrs. Tomás said that she and her husband ran a diner and that one of them would come. She apologized for Mr. Tomás's absence.

"Someone has to be there all the time, you know, so we just take turns coming to these meetings. This year it's my turn." Mandy's parents, both of whom were musicians, volunteered to come together. The last to leave was Steve's mother. She said she didn't usually like to talk in front of groups of people but that she had never thought of how important reading was before. Since she was a waitress she could bring the menus and order pads from her restaurant and let the children pretend to be either waitresses or waiters and customers. That way she could help and wouldn't need to talk too much! Ms. Maverick assured her that that would be delightful and signed her up for the following Tuesday!

Monthly Logs

SEPTEMBER

What an unusual class of children this is! I thought that over the seven years I have taught I had seen every possible combination of children but this class disproves that theory. Of course, I expect to find great differences among children by the time they get to fourth grade, but I have never before seen the range represented by the span between Paul and Daisy, who read almost nothing, and Larry who qualitatively reads almost as well as I do, and quantitatively reads more than I do. Then there are the personality differences. Roberta cannot do the right thing no matter how hard she tries, and Betty, her twin sister, can't do anything wrong. Joyce and Hilda are both very capable and intelligent but they are so independent.

I am pleased, however, with the adjustments most of the children have made to my program. I always enjoy getting Mrs. Wise's children because they have had so much experience working together in groups. It is still a shock to me to see someone else teaching in her room next door.

I am especially pleased with Daisy. According to her records, she just never got anything done. She is working now, although I think she is doing it for me rather than for herself. Each time she does anything, she comes to me for approval. I pat her on the head because I want her to establish the habit of sitting down and accomplishing something, but I am trying to help her develop some internal feedback. Yesterday she brought me a picture she had painted. I said, "Yes, it is lovely. Didn't it feel good to do it?" I have a feeling this is going to be a year-long process; however, I have seldom seen a child with so little intrinsic motivation. For the moment, I am thankful that she is working for whatever reason. Her reading and math skills are practically nonexistent.

Paul is the only one who is as deficient in skills as Daisy. I plan to go and see his mother. Everyone says the home situation is hopeless but that taking him away and putting him in the children's home would be worse. When I did the sociogram, not only did no one choose to be in Paul's car but Paul couldn't even make any choices about whom he wanted to go with. He never speaks up during class, and I have never seen him playing on the playground. If I can't get his mother to come to school this year, I will go and visit her.

Mort is a pill! If I hear that child sigh and say, "Well, it doesn't matter. I don't care," one more time I may lose my composure and shake him! Except I know it wouldn't do any good.

Yesterday I said to him, "Mort, what do you do when you go home after school?"

He replied, "Oh, mostly I just sit around and get bored. Sometimes I watch television."

As far as I can tell he has no friends, no interests, and no aspirations! I guess I should think of him as "a real challenge."

I now have each child working on an individual program during the afternoon skills block. Most of the children spend at least some of their time on math facts. Paul and Daisy still have not mastered the addition facts. Butch, Carl, Tanana, and Alex are working on subtraction facts. The rest, with the exception of Steve and Larry, who have mastered them, are working on multiplication facts, the big computational hurdle in fourth grade.

I used a sample of the revised A and P sight word list (Appendix B) to make sure that the children knew immediately these basic words. All but Paul, Daisy, Chip, and Butch knew at least 95 percent of them. I have constructed some rummy games which I think will help them learn these words.

The first rummy game contains thirty-six index cards, three cards for each of twelve different words. These twelve words were the first on the A and P list that any of the four children did not know. The second game contains the next twelve and so on! To get them started, I sat down with them and taught them my version of rummy. For several days, I sat with them and played rummy until I was sure that all four children understood the rules of the game. I then told them that since they knew how to play, they could choose another person from the class to play rummy with them, and that since they would have to teach that other person, we would need a list of rules. The children dictated the rules to me and helped me arrange them in the proper sequence. I wrote these rules on a chart which now hangs on the wall above where the games are stored.

Rummy Rules

1. Only four people can play with one deck.
2. Shuffle the cards.
3. Deal five cards to each player.
4. Turn over the top card.
5. The person on the dealer's left gets to go first.
6. He picks up the turned-over card or the one on top of the deck.
7. He then discards a card from his hand.
8. You can only pick up the card on the top of the discard pile.
9. When you get three cards alike you put them down and say them.
10. You can get help to say them if you don't know the word.
11. The first person who puts all his cards down is the winner.

Now, each afternoon, during part of their skills time Paul, Daisy, Chip, and Butch can each choose anyone they like and play three games of rummy with that person. The only rule is that they must choose a different partner each day of the week. In this way, all the children who want to, get to play at least once a week and no one spends very much of his or her skills time on words he or she already knows. There are presently five sets of rummy cards from which they can choose. I will periodically check them out and, as they learn these words, make rummy games with the next twelve unknown words.

This system is working well, and I am hoping that it will help these four children socially as well as academically. When I did the sociogram, no one chose Paul or Daisy. Mitch was the only child to choose Butch and Chip. The children do volunteer to play rummy with them because they all love to play it. So, perhaps, some friendships will begin to bloom!

For the reader to do

Here are the choices the children made when asked to choose two children whom they would like to have in the car with them for an upcoming field trip. Construct a chart to show their choices. Write all the names along the outside of the chart. Draw lines with arrows to show the choices.

Which boy was chosen most often?
Which girl was chosen most often?
Which three children were never chosen?
Which three girls all chose each other?
Which boys chose girls?
Which girls chose boys?

Sociogram

CHILD	CHOICES	
Steve	Larry	Horace
Rita	Roberta	Tanana
Roberta	Mandy	Rita
Paul		
Mort	Joyce	Alex
Mandy	Pat	Roberta
Mitch	Butch	Jeff
Manuel	Chip	Horace
Larry	Pat	Horace
Tanana	Daphne	Betty
Alex	Horace	Manuel
Pat	Horace	Larry
Betty	Daphne	Tanana
Daisy	Manuel	Tanana
Jeff	Horace	Larry
Butch	Mitch	Steve
Chip	Jeff	Manuel
Carl	Manuel	Horace
Daphne	Betty	Tanana
Hilda	Roberta	Horace
Horace	Manuel	Hilda
Joyce	Roberta	Pat

● ● ●

While we have not actually begun the unit on our state this month, we have done some readiness activities in preparation for this unit. One of the concepts which is very difficult for young children to grasp is the notion of time and sequence. Last year I had my class construct a timeline showing the important events in our state and their corresponding dates. While the children learned from this activity, it was very difficult for them to conceptualize the differences in time. Last year's class never understood that the spaces between the depicted events were proportional to the actual time lapsed between these events.

In order to provide readiness for the state timeline and to help the children relate time passage and sequence to their own lives, I had the children make a timeline depicting the important events in their lives. I began by having the children put their chairs in a circle and asking them to think about all the important things that had happened in their lives. The children were all eager to respond and everyone had something to share since the subject was one they all knew lots about. Rita recalled her first trip to the library when the librarian told her she was too young to have a library card. Tanana remembered moving to our state and how scared she was when she first came to Mrs. Wise's classroom. Larry recalled the first Hardy Boys book he had read. When all the children had contributed something to the discussion, I suggested that we might create some "lifelines" to show all the important events which had already taken place in their lives. I showed them how we could use string and little slips of paper with words and illustrations to depict our individual histories.

The children were most enthusiastic, so we began right then. I gave each child a long sheet of paper and asked him or her to put his or her birthdate in the top left corner and the current date in the bottom left corner. Although many of the children knew the month and day on which they were born, only Larry, Pat, and Hilda knew the year of their birth. I then asked the others how they thought they could figure out the year in which they were born. After some discussion, they worked out the mechanics of subtracting how old they were from the current date and filled in the year on the chart they were making. In the meantime, I demonstrated by making my chart on the board. Next to my birthdate, I wrote "Ms. Maverick was born" and next to the current date, I wrote, "Ms. Maverick is helping her children to make their own lifelines." The children then followed my example and put appropriate entries next to their own names.

They then listed the important events in their lives. I told them not to worry too much at this point about the date or the order but just try to get down about eight to ten events. Most children had no trouble at all listing a dozen events. Paul, however, needed a great deal of help at this and I fear his lifeline represents my thinking more than his. When the children had finished listing the events, I asked them how they thought we could find out the approximate date of each event. Several suggested their parents kept lists of everything and that if they could take the charts home that night, they could fill in many of the dates. The others they could fill in by knowing in what order they happened in relation to the events with known dates.

The next day, they returned with dates and many more events filled in on their charts. We then cut the charts and arranged the events into the proper order. Next began the construction of the actual lifelines. Since all of the children in the class were either eight or nine years old, we decided to cut the strings either nine or ten feet long. In that way, each foot could represent a year. Any events which happened in the same year would be placed close to one another. If there were a year or two in which no events occurred, that would be represented by the unfilled space for that year. We also agreed that since we were going to hang these around the room for others to read, we should try to spell the words correctly and to use readable handwriting. Each child then measured and cut his or her string and marked it off in one-foot lengths. They also cut and measured strips of colored paper to 3″ × 6″ dimensions. While the children were doing this, I acted as editor, helping children correct the spelling and punctuation on their charted events so that they could copy them correctly on their lifeline slips.

Somehow, it all got done! The children illustrated the events and taped the slips to the strings. Those who finished first helped the others. The lifelines now hang below the windows and the chalkboards, and whenever the children have a spare moment, they can be seen reading their own or someone else's life history. This activity, which started out as readiness for our state's timeline, had value in and of itself. The children helped one another and learned more about one another. They learned that we share many common experiences and that other experiences are unique to each individual. They do seem to have a better sense of time sequence and proportion, and they have certainly practiced their math, reading, and writing skills. I will do this again next year!

For the reader to do

Construct your own lifeline. Then help a child or group of children to construct theirs. How does this activity provide for practice in math and reading and writing?

● ● ●

The other readiness activity this month was constructing a map of the school. We will do a lot of work with maps when we begin the actual study of our state next month and for many children this is their first exposure to maps. Again, I wanted them to relate maps to their own lifespace before asking them to generalize on the less tangible world outside. After a discussion about maps and what would be involved in constructing a map of our school, we walked around the whole building to observe what we would include in our map. The children suggested, and I listed on the board, all the things we might want to include in a map of our school. I then grouped the children in pairs and each pair took responsibility for going to a particular classroom or area of the building, measuring that area, and constructing that part of the map. When all the children reassembled with their measurements, we measured the total length and width of the building and then decided what proportion of that length and width the various rooms comprised. For a while, it looked as if we had a lot less total space in what we had measured than what there actually was in the building. Larry was the one who realized we had forgotten to consider the space taken up by the hallways! After measuring these, we were able to decide on a scale. Each pair of children cut from colored paper the model for the room or area they had measured and labeled it appropriately. We then pasted the individual rooms on a piece of appropriately sized poster board and, six days after we started, had our map of the school. Well, actually, we only had it for a day or two before it was commandeered! Mr. Topps noticed it when he came in to read with our class during SQUIRT time and remarked that we had done a first-rate job and that this map was just the thing he needed to hang outside the office so that visitors could find their way around. He asked if he could "borrow" it for a while. The children all autographed it, and it now hangs outside the office.

OCTOBER

We are now off and running on our state unit. Each unit actually has three overlapping phases: at the beginning, I provide the children with a great deal of input from many different sources. During most of this first phase we work together as a whole class, building some interest and motivation for the unit, becoming familiar with new and specialized vocabulary terms, and discovering enough information so that we can begin to raise some questions to which we can seek answers. During the second phase of the unit, while we continue many whole class activities, the children are also doing extensive reading, listening, and viewing, either individually or in small groups. Finally, they engage in several culminating activities which help them to organize and synthesize the information gained during the unit.

My kickoff motivator for this unit was a large white outline map of our state which I had drawn by projecting the image of an overhead transparency map onto the bulletin board at the rear of the room. After tracing the projected image, I cut along the outline and stapled the giant white map to the red-backed bulletin board. I did this all late one night so that the children's attention would be drawn immediately to the giant blank white map against the bright red background. Of course, they noticed it immediately and were intrigued by its size and blankness. Several correctly guessed that it was an outline map of our state. I had the children move their chairs closer to the board and began to lead them in a discussion of our state. Little by little, in response to their comments and questions, I wrote the name of a particular landmark in its proper location. I let the children help me decide where these landmarks should go by consulting several maps which I spread out on the floor as we talked. At the end of this initial motivating session we had (1) located our town, the state capital, several other cities, lakes, and rivers, (2) talked about what went on at the capital and began to use words such as *governor, lieutenant governor, legislators, laws, and taxes,* (3) used directional words such as *north, south, east,* and *west* and noted these directions above, below, and on the appropriate sides of our map, and (4) begun to discuss various places that the children had lived, visited, or had some other connection with.

I told them that as we studied our state we would use again and again many of the words we had used in our talk. They would need to be able to read the words in order to find out more about our state and they would need to be able to spell them in order to be able to write about it. Mitch, Jeff, and Daisy didn't look too happy at the thought of additional work, so I smiled reassuringly as I picked up a black marker and several half-sheets of different colored construction paper and let them help me remember the "special" words we had used that morning. I then let them watch me print these words on the colored slips of paper. As I was doing so, I remarked about the relative length and distinctive features of the words, pronounced the words carefully and had the children pronounce each word after me. I then had Mitch climb on a chair and tape the words to the wall above the bulletin board. I noted that we had eleven words to start with and that we would add more as we continued to study about our state. I then prepared the children for our following morning's activities by showing them a little color-headed pin and a triangular shaped slip of paper. On the triangular slip, I printed in tiny letters

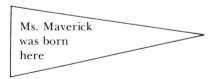

and pinned this slip to our map high in the northwestern corner. Next to the pinned flag I wrote the name of the community in which I was born. The children were fascinated and all wanted to make little flags. I assured them that that was tomorrow's activity and that in the meantime, they should look at the maps and try to figure out places they had been to or knew of to put flags on them. I also suggested that they talk with their parents and perhaps even look at a map with them to determine such family history information as their parents' birthplaces, where aunts and uncles lived, and the names and locations of places they had visited. For the rest of the day, there was always someone at the back of the room looking at our giant map and investigating the smaller ones which I had placed on a table under the bulletin board.

The next day the children came bursting into the room loaded with maps and family histories they had brought from home. We immediately gathered in the back of the room and the children began to spread out their maps, sharing the information they had with one another and trying to locate the places they wanted to flag on our giant map. While still giant, our map was no longer blank. It was covered with place names and flags, all of which the children had some personal affiliation with. We even have a flag marking the city to which Mike had moved. Mrs. Flame would be happy to see that. She still worries about how Mike is doing. We also added the names of several neighboring towns and a few lakes and rivers to our wall vocabulary, which now has eighteen words.

The interest and excitement generated by the giant map motivator has grown throughout this month as have the number of words in our wall vocabulary. We now have thirty-two words up there and as I use these words again and again in different contexts, I try to remember to point to the words and remind the children of the other contexts in which we used them. We also use these words for our daily spelling practice. In addition to learning to spell the most commonly used words we get from the A and P sight word list and which we work on during the afternoon skills time, we take five minutes each morning to practice spelling the words on our wall vocabulary. Each child takes out a sheet of paper and numbers it from one to ten. I then call out ten of the words from the words on the wall. As I call each word, the children are allowed and, indeed, encouraged to look up at the wall and find the word and then write it on their papers. The trick to this technique is that they can't actually copy the words since they must look up and then down at their papers and then up again. In order to do this they have to be trying to take a mental picture of the word and then reproduce this mental picture. When all ten words have been called out, the children check their own papers as I repeat each word and spell it aloud, letter by letter. Most days, all the children get nine or ten right and because they are so successful at it, they love to do it. The other day during recess it rained and when they were trying to decide on an indoor game, Horace suggested that we do the spelling words again! I couldn't believe it, but that's what they "played" with Horace being the teacher and calling out the words. From now on, once the children are very familiar with the words, as they are now, I shall let the children take turns "being teacher" and calling out the words. Strange—I always think I am allowing the children as much participation as is possible and then discover something else that I am doing that the children could do with benefit.

I have done several whole-class directed reading lessons this month. Through these lessons, I help them increase their knowledge about our state and work on increasing their vocabularies and improving their comprehension skills at the same time. To do these, I select part of a newspaper or magazine article or a short selection from a book and type it using Mrs. Wright's primary typewriter. I then run the typed sheet through the machine in the office to make a transparency. Using my overhead projector for group comprehension lessons has several advantages: If the passage I select is unusually difficult to read, I can change a few of the words or omit sections to make it more readable. I don't waste a lot of paper making twenty-five copies of the same story, and I can focus the attention of the children where I want it. I do, however, always show the children the source of the original article so that they know that what they are reading is "something real."

I begin my preparation for the lesson by identifying any words or concepts I think will present difficulty for many of my children. I make a distinction between unknown words and unfamiliar concepts. In the first directed reading lesson, for example, the subject was "things to do in our state." I had taken this article from the magazine section of the Sunday newspaper. Two concepts which I thought would not be familiar to most of my children were *rapids* and *currents*. In both cases, most of my children would probably be able to identify the words but would not have a meaning for those words appropriate to the particular contexts in which they were being used. The word *current* they might associate with the term "current events," and for *rapids*, while they might have the concept of speed, they would probably not readily associate this concept with fast-moving water.

In addition to the two relatively unfamiliar concepts, *current* and *rapids*, I also identified several words for which most of my children would have listening-meaning concepts but which they would not be able to identify in print. These unknown words for the "things to do in our state" selection included *reflection* and *parachute*. In both cases, I was quite sure that the children would have a concept for these words once they were able to identify them but doubted that the "big word decoding skills" of most of my children would allow them to figure out the pronunciation of these familiar concepts but unknown words.

Having identified several unfamiliar concepts and unknown words, I then decided what to do about them. Sometimes, I built meanings for unfamiliar concepts or told them the pronunciation of unknown words before they read the story. More often, however, I alerted the children to the existence of these unfamiliar concepts or unknown words, and challenged them to see if they could figure out what a word was or what the concept meant as they read the selection. This encouraged the children to use the context to figure out the meaning and/or pronunciation of words. This is what I did with *current, rapids, reflection,* and *parachute*. I wrote these four words on the board and asked a volunteer to pronounce *current* and *rapids*. Betty gladly pronounced them. I then asked them if anyone could give me a meaning for *current* or *rapids*. Manuel suggested that current has something to do with electricity and Steve said that it means "like in 'current events.'" For *rapids,* Roberta said that "without the *s* it means fast." I told them that the definitions they had given were right but that, as I hoped they knew, words have many different meanings and that the words *current* and *rapids* in the selection we were about to read had meanings different from the ones they knew. I then told them that, as they were reading the selection, I wanted them to see if they could figure out what these different meanings might be. I hinted to them that the other words and sentences near the words *current* and *rapids* would give them the clues they needed to solve the mystery. To add another element of mystery, I pointed to *reflection* and *parachute* and told the children *not* to pronounce the words. I told them that these two words were different from *current* and *rapids* in that they knew what these second two words meant but hadn't yet learned to identify them in print. I suggested that as with *current* and *rapids,* the words close to *reflection* and *parachute* would allow them to solve the mystery. Once the children had read the selection, they explained what they thought *current* and *rapids* meant in this context, identified the other words which had let them figure that out and compared these meanings for the words with the meanings they already knew. Many of the children had also figured out the unknown words, *reflection* and *parachute,* and explained which other words had led them to solve that mystery.

Having identified and decided what to do about any unknown words or unfamiliar concepts, I then decided for what purpose I was going to have the children read the selection. In a directed reading activity, my goal is always that the children are better at reading for a specific purpose after reading the selection than they were prior to reading the selection. Sometimes, I work on improving their literal comprehension. I may decide that after reading the selection, we will put the events of the selection in order, or that we will read in order to answer the fact questions: Who? What? When? Where? How? For other selections, I may decide that we will work on being able to state main ideas in our own words.

I teach many lessons designed to sharpen the children's inferential comprehension ability. In these lessons, I show them only a portion of the text and ask them to predict what will happen next. I write these predictions on the board and let the children vote to decide which one they consider most likely to occur. I then display enough of the text so that they can check their predictions. Finally, I ask the children who made the correct prediction to read me the words in the passage that allowed them to make the correct prediction. In this way, the children who are not very good at inferring see that inferences are based on something that is directly stated in the text.

The first year I taught, I referred to inferential comprehension as "reading between the lines." One day, I watched one boy squinting at his book and then peering over the shoulder of the boy in front of him who could "read between the lines." It suddenly occurred to me that, from a child's vantage point, it was conceivable that he believed that there was something between the lines that he couldn't see or that was only between the lines of other people's books. Since then I have stopped using that particular phrase. I have begun to ask those who can make inferences to point out the words in the text on which they based their inferences. This allows the children who can't make inferences to begin to observe the way the process works in the minds of those who can.

Finally, I teach some lessons designed to help children become more critical readers. During these lessons, I ask the children to read in order to make judgments or evaluations, and I stress that their judgments are decided on the basis of their own value systems and that there are no right or wrong answers to these "judgment" questions.

For the "things to do in our state" lesson, I decided to focus the children's attention on the main ideas of each paragraph. I displayed only the portion of the text which mentioned a particular place and asked the children to read so that when they finished they could tell me in a sentence what the main attraction was at each place. First, I let the children read silently. When most appeared to have finished, I let a volunteer read the section aloud. In this way, Paul, Daisy, and the others whose reading skills are still very limited could get the content of the selection and participate in the comprehension activity.

After each section was read silently and then orally, I asked a child to tell me in one sentence what the main thing was that most people went there to see. I then made a list on the board which gave each place name and the sentence describing its main attraction. When we had completed reading about the eight places, I read over the list I had made on the board and pointed out to the children that, in addition to being the main attraction, these sentences were also the main ideas of each paragraph. Main ideas, like main attractions, are the most important ideas (attractions); the ideas (attractions) most people would like to remember after reading (visiting) a paragraph (place). While we will continue to work on identifying and stating main ideas all year, this lesson was a good one to begin with because it helped to make the concept of main idea a little more concrete.

As a follow-up to this directed reading lesson, I put the children in eight groups. Each group was to make a little flag for one of the eight places we had read about, write the place name and the main attraction on the flag, locate the place using the ever-growing supply of maps we now had in the room, and pin the flag to our giant map, which was no longer blank.

For readers to do together

Find a short selection. Use a primary typewriter to type it and make a transparency. Decide what word and concept problems this selection would present for most of the children at a particular grade level. Decide what you would do about those word and concept problems. Decide what area of comprehension you would try to strengthen by having a class read the selection. Set your purposes for reading and divide the selection to show which parts you would display together. Plan a follow-up activity.

● ● ●

We have taken two field trips this month. For the first, we went to visit the local newspaper. I bring daily copies of both the local and capital newspapers to school each morning, and since we began the unit on our state, the children have become quite interested in them. Before we took the field trip, I had the children put their chairs in a circle and we began to talk about the local newspaper and to formulate some questions to ask Ms. Daley, the editor. I listed these questions on a large sheet of chart paper, and on our return, we checked the chart to see how many of our questions had been answered.

We then got out a local map and looked at the various routes we could take to get from our school to the newspaper office. We tried to decide which route would be the shortest and which would be the quickest. Since there was much disagreement about the best route, I asked the children how we might plan an experiment to find out. After much discussion, the following plan was arrived at. Each of the four cars (Mrs. Penn, Mrs. Smith, and Daphne's grandfather had volunteered to drive) would take a different route. One person in each car would be responsible for writing down the beginning and ending mileage. Another person would time the trips. The other riders in the car would keep track of the number of lights, stop signs, intersections, and so on. It was agreed, of course, that each driver would drive carefully and obey all speed limits.

Finally, Friday arrived! The four cars set out at the same time. Mrs. Smith arrived first, but Mrs. Penn had taken the shortest route. I, of course, arrived last and my passengers were not too pleased about that, especially Butch!

The receptionist took us on a tour around the buildings and then took us to Ms. Daley's office. The children behaved very well, and because they had discussed and planned before coming, asked some very good questions. I was just beginning to relax and pat myself on the back for preparing them so well when the inevitable happened. A reporter came into Ms. Daley's office with some copy. She introduced him to the children and asked them if they had any questions. Hilda asked him a question about a story she had read recently in the paper and as he was answering her question, he turned to Ms. Daley and said, "Why don't you take them down into the morgue and show them some of the dead ones?" Roberta's head twitched with excitement; Betty fainted! The reporter quickly explained that the newspaper morgue had "dead" newspapers, not dead bodies, while Mrs. Smith and I revived Betty. A striking example of the multiple meanings of common words!

We then did go into the morgue, however, and spent a long time there. Ms. Daley showed us the newspapers which recorded such historic events as the end of the Civil War, the Lincoln and Kennedy assassinations, and the state's celebration of its 100th birthday. She pointed out the difference between history books which are written long after the actual events have occurred, and newspaper accounts which are written immediately. She also pointed out how newspapers are one very important source of historical data. The children were particularly impressed when she showed them a copy of a biography of a famous general and explained that the writer of that book had spent many days in this very morgue doing research about our town where this general had grown up.

Upon our return from the newspaper, we looked at our collected data, computed the mileages and times, decided that the shortest route in distance was not the quickest route and discussed reasons why this was so. We also looked to see which of our questions had been answered and decided that six had been answered quite thoroughly, three partially, and two not at all. Finally, each child composed a short note to Ms. Daley thanking her for her time and telling her what he or she had found most interesting about the visit. Here is Roberta's letter.

Dear Ms. Daley,

Thank you for letting us come down to visit your newspaper. There was lots to see and I can only apologize for Betty's fainting in your office. She is always doing things like that and I can't understand why. The dead newspapers were interesting but I would have liked to have seen some dead bodies since I never have. Being a newspaper lady, I bet you have seen hundreds of them.

Sincerely,

Roberta Smith

Our other field trip this month was to the county seat. This was an all-day field trip, and we packed a picnic lunch. Thank goodness it didn't rain! We prepared for this one as we had for the newspaper office, by having discussions and coming up with a list of questions we wanted answered. This time, Hilda wrote down the list to make sure that we came back with at least a partial answer to all our questions.

In the morning we visited the county court house. When we got to the county clerk's office, a young couple was waiting to get a marriage license. All the boys plus Pat and Roberta thought that was hysterical. The children were most fascinated by the sheriff. They wanted to know what happened when a person got arrested and what a sheriff and his deputies did. The sheriff showed them the county map, which was very detailed, and helped them to locate our school and some of their homes.

When we went into the court, the judge was hearing a traffic case. He revoked the license of a person arrested for driving recklessly and speeding. This impressed the children greatly. When we got to the tax assessor's office, Hilda was busily checking her list to see what we might have forgotten to ask. When her question was finally asked, it came out as, "We want to know how you decide how much taxes everyone should pay and my Dad says you must be a friend of our next door neighbor's because his house is twice as big as ours and he pays less taxes!"

That afternoon we toured the county historical museum. The children were especially intrigued by the original state flag and the lists of names of all the men who had died in the major wars we have fought. The restored log cabin behind the museum added much realism to our study of how people used to live in our state and, of course, the children were fascinated by the Indian artifacts.

Upon our return, we made a list of all the people we had visited or seen in the court house and what their functions were. We also referred to our question chart and, with Hilda's help, did indeed have at least a partial answer to all the questions we had raised. I then helped the children form five groups. Each group composed a letter thanking one of the people who helped us on our visit.

NOVEMBER

What a great month this has been! Normally, we don't go to the state capital. It is almost a two-hour trip, and the legislature is usually not in session during the fall when we are studying our state. Three weeks ago, however, the legislature was called into special session in order to consider a new water pollution bill. Everyone in the state has been debating this issue for some time now, but it took a tragedy to get the legislators moving. Four weeks ago, five people died in a small downstate industrial town. The cause of death was determined to be the high level of industrial chemical wastes in the water—way above the standards already set, but never enforced. The anti-pollution forces were able to rally support around this emotional issue and the governor called the legislature into special session to consider a more stringent water pollution bill with provisions for enforcement and severe penalties for lack of compliance.

The children came back to school on the Monday after the five people had died and they were all upset. Many of them brought the various newspaper stories and related the discussions they had had about this issue at home. The children, unlike the adult population, were almost unanimous in their insistence that the water pollution standards be much stricter. Not being burdened with financial responsibilities, they could see the need for clean water much more clearly than they could understand the financial strain the new controls would put on industry and, if industry is to be believed, the entire state population.

Of course, we put our chairs in a circle immediately and discussed the problem. I tried to raise questions and interject information which would allow them to consider the issue in its broadest terms. Many of the children were unclear about words like *chemicals* and *bacteria* and I began to make mental notes on which words we might want to explore more fully and add to our wall vocabulary. Later, I decided that the subject was such an important one and the children were so naturally motivated that a unit on ecology and pollution would be first on our agenda after Christmas.

It was Mrs. Penn who suggested that we take the children to the state capital. She came in after school that very afternoon and told me that she would be going over to meet with a citizen's action group later in the week and that she would be glad to make all the arrangements at the capital and to be one of our drivers. She added that she had seen Mrs. Smith that morning and had mentioned the possibility to her and that Mrs. Smith had agreed it would be a great experience for the children to see the legislature in session and that she, too, would be willing to drive. I told Mrs. Penn that I would talk it over with the children but that I was all for it!

The children, of course, were most excited. In addition to the general excitement of going on a trip that long and being "at the capital" was the excitement generated by the knowledge that Ms. Maverick had never taken any of her other classes to the state capital. They were not just doing the same trips all the other fourth grades did—they were doing something very special and very grown-up. As I watched their delight in this specialness, I vowed to try to think of something special for each class of children I taught.

The preparations for the trip took most of the month and many of the activities which I had planned for this middle part of the unit went by the boards. The transportation problem was solved by Mrs. Penn, who, in addition to commandeering Mandy's father as our fourth driver, also arranged for our tour through the capitol, our visit to the gallery while the legislators were debating, got our local representative to agree to come up to the gallery when the session broke for lunch and talk with us and answer our questions. Our list of questions for Mr. Stans took three sheets of chart paper and Hilda thought she would never get them all copied in her notebook.

Lunch was a problem. We were going to leave at 7:30 a.m. so that we could get there, park, and go on a 10 a.m. tour through the capitol building and be in the gallery from 11 a.m.–noon. A picnic lunch was a little risky at this time of year, and I thought it would be good for all the children to have the experience of eating in a real restaurant. They had all eaten at fast food drive-ins, but many of them had not been to a restaurant, ordered from a menu, or paid their own bill plus tax and tip! The problem with taking them to a restaurant, of course, was that many of them could not come up with the money and that many families who would come up with the money really couldn't afford it.

As I was thinking about the lunch problem, I was also gathering up the week's supply of newspapers to take them to the recycling drop point. I then remembered that some organizations had collected money for various causes by having paper and aluminum drives. It occurred to me that if our class could collect paper and aluminum for recycling as well as collect deposit bottles for return to the grocery stores, we might make enough money for everyone to have lunch. We might also become more personally pollution conscious.

In three weeks, we collected hundreds of pounds of paper and aluminum and returned $27.80 worth of bottles to the grocery stores. Several parents made voluntary donations to our lunch fund and we ended up with $72.60. The children thought this was a fortune until we divided by twenty-two and realized that each person's share of the fortune was only $3.30. Chip said that even that seemed like a fortune to him, and quickly went to work figuring out how many bags of peanuts that would buy!

Mrs. Penn had found an inexpensive restaurant close to the capitol and had arranged for the twenty-six of us to eat there. She had also gotten several sample menus and from these each child figured out the various combinations of food he or she could buy with $2.88 cents (which is what each child actually had to spend after paying the 4 percent sales tax and 10 percent tip).

In order to prepare them for their visit to the capitol and the legislature, I showed a film entitled "Your State Government" which is put out by the State Chamber of Commerce and the State Department of Education. Just as when I am going to have the class read something, I often do a directed reading lesson with them; when I am going to show them a film, I do a directed viewing lesson. First, I prepare my lesson just as I would a directed reading lesson. After previewing the film, I determine which unfamiliar concepts are introduced in the film and whether I will help them to build these concepts before, during, or after the film. I then determine my purposes for having them view the film and decide how much of the film I will show at a time. Unless it is strictly for entertainment, I never show a film all the way through. Rather, I set the purpose for viewing a particular segment, stop the film, and discuss the fulfillment of that purpose, set another purpose and begin the film again. If the film is one which the children seem to especially enjoy, I will often show it over again the following day in its entirety. I then try to think of an appropriate follow-up activity to the film. My purpose in this follow-up activity is to help the children organize and synthesize the new information gained from the film.

For the reader to do

In Ms. Maverick's curriculum, she integrates not only the teaching of reading and language with her social studies and science, but also the teaching of mathematics. Ms. Maverick has suggested several of the math activities in which her children have engaged so far while studying about their state (measuring distances, figuring mileage, figuring percents for tax and tip, calculating what $2.88 will buy). If you are thinking about trying an integrated curriculum approach, you will need to think about what mathematics activities you would include. Make a list of five mathematics activities, other than those mentioned above, which Ms. Maverick probably included in the state unit.

For readers to do together

Preview a film which is intended for use as an instructional aid in a classroom. Have in mind a particular group of students to whom you might show this film. After previewing the film, get into small groups and decide what concepts in the film might be unfamiliar to the students. What purposes might you set for various segments of the film? At what points would you stop the film? What might you do as a follow-up activity which would help the students organize and synthesize new information? Share your group's plan for a directed viewing lesson with the rest of the class.

When Ms. Maverick taught the directed reading lesson, she identified unfamiliar concepts and unknown words. In the directed viewing lesson, she only identified unfamiliar concepts. *Why* did she omit the unknown words part?

● ● ●

Mr. Peskins came this month before we went to the capital. He brought his routing slips and maps and talked to the children about all the reading he had to do in his job as a truck driver. The children were quite impressed! He also showed us the best route to take to the capital and told us some interesting things to watch for on the way.

The actual trip was exhausting but very exciting. We left promptly at 7:30 a.m. I provided some apples and crackers for each car so that the children could have a little snack when we first got there. The woman who escorted us on our tour through the capitol was very sweet and very pretty, so Betty and Daphne have decided to be tour guides when they grow up! Of course, while we were in the gallery, one of the "anti-the-more-stringent-bill" legislators was talking and the children were quite upset. I think they did begin to get some notion, however, that there are always two legitimate, defensible points of view. Mr. Stans was great! He spent almost thirty minutes talking with us. He commended the children on their paper/aluminum/bottle collection and told them that another way they could make a difference was by getting in the habit of writing to their legislator and letting him or her know how they felt. Larry asked him if telegrams weren't "a more effective media than letters." Mr. Stans agreed that legislators really notice when their constituents sacrifice time, trouble, and money to send telegrams expressing their views. He then gave us his address and promised to come to visit our class when he was next in our town.

Lunch was fun! The children were well prepared and most knew exactly what they wanted. The only person who overspent was Daisy. I didn't realize it at the time but Mandy's father had to bail her out with 34 cents. I told him he should have left her to wash dishes! We got back to the school at 4:30 p.m.

The next day as we began to discuss our trip and what we had learned, the children were all anxious to write to Mr. Stans. Larry suggested that in addition to our individual letters, we pool any money left from lunch and send a telegram from the whole class. His suggestion was applauded and the "telegram writing practice" that followed was great fun and a lesson in getting your money's worth of words.

For the reader to do

Here is the telegram Ms. Maverick's class finally decided to send to Mr. Stans. How was this a good language activity? What might the children have learned about words and sentences from doing this activity? Do you think the children worked in this in small groups or as individuals? Why?

MR STANS STOP 22 FOURTH GRADERS AND

TEACHER WANT BILL 7384 PASSED STOP

CLEAN WATER NOW STOP

● ● ●

This month marked not only the end of the year, but also the end of our state unit. No small feat, I can assure you! For culminating activities on this unit, I decided to have small groups work on several different activities: a timeline, a relief map, a mural, an historical drama, and a book about our state. I described the projects to the entire class, letting them know what they would be doing on each. I then had the children write down their first and second choices for the project on which they wanted to work.

Steve, Mitch, Butch, Hilda, and Jeff worked on the relief map. Actually I probably should add Ms. Maverick to that roster since I had to help this group more than any of the others. The children had already had many experiences with all kinds of maps throughout this unit, but constructing this relief map was still a big job. (When they had finished—finally!—the map was amazingly accurate.) I then sat down with the group and had them tell me the materials needed and steps to follow in making a relief map. This served as a good language and directions writing activity for the group, and the chart we made will help us in making relief maps in the future.

Making a Relief Map*

Materials needed:

opaque projector	varnish
contour map of area	paintbrush
sheet of paper	screen
ply board four feet long and cut as wide as needed	sawdust
nails	wallpaper paste powder
hammer	two-gallon pail
oil paint	

Steps:

1. Put the contour map in the opaque projector.
2. Put the plyboard in the chalktray.
3. Project the contour map onto the plyboard.
4. Trace the outline and all the markings onto the board.
5. Cover the board with a sheet of paper.
6. Trace the contour map on the paper like you did the board.
7. Decide what the highest point would be on your map and that will be three inches high.
8. Divide to figure out the scale.

_____

* Adapted from Preston, (1968).

9. Using the scale and the sheet of paper on which you traced the contour map, decide how high in inches each area should be built. Write these heights on the right place on the paper.
10. Hammer nails into the board along the contour lines.
11. Paint rivers and lakes on the board with blue oil paint.
12. Let blue paint dry. Then varnish.
13. Screen the sawdust.
14. Mix four quarts of sawdust with one quart of wallpaper paste powder.
15. Add just enough water so it can be shaped.
16. Build the map one layer at a time using the nails as a guide.
17. When it is all built and dry, varnish the whole map.
18. Paint the rivers and lakes blue again.
19. Paint the other areas.

For the reader to do

Making the relief map was a two-week project. At times even Ms. Maverick wondered if it had been worth it. She decided it was, however, when she considered all the language, mathematical, and social skills the group was practicing as they planned the map, carried out its construction, and made the chart you have just read. List some of the specific skills this group was practicing as they engaged in this project.

● ● ●

Paul, Manuel, Chip, and Carl worked on constructing a timeline for our state. The completion of this project was, indeed, much facilitated by the experience of making the lifelines which they had done in September. They began by listing important events in our state's history and verifying the dates on which they occurred. Miss Page, our librarian, helped them to find some of the references they needed for this part of the project. They then decided to use a twenty-foot piece of string and to let each foot represent ten years. While Paul was not much help on the researching end, he did work diligently to copy the dates and events onto the markers which would go along the line.

Rita, Mandy, Larry, and Horace made a lovely bound book entitled *Facts You Should Know about Our State*. They took much of the information we had gained from our discussions, reading, films, and field trips and wrote several topical stories. They also included maps, pictures of the state flower and bird, and representations of the several flags our state has had. Mrs. Mainstay was nice enough to type up their stories and I helped them to make a title page and a table of contents. They then bound it with a lovely cloth cover, as they had learned to do from

Mrs. Wise, and took it to the library to show to Miss Page. You can imagine their delight when she told them it looked good enough to be a library book. The children asked if it could really *be* a library book, so Miss Page pasted a pocket in the back, typed up a card, gave it an appropriate number, made a card for the card file, and shelved it with the other books about our state. Needless to say it doesn't stay on that shelf long. Every child in our room wants to check it out to read, and now they are all asking to make their own bound books to put in the library. Perhaps after the first of the year, we will begin keeping writing-notebooks in preparation for such a large project!

Mort, Tanana, Betty, and Daphne did the mural which covers the side of the room. This mural depicts the changes in the way people lived, traveled, and dressed in our state over the past 200 years. Again, Miss Page's help was invaluable in steering this group to reference works which contained many pictures. She also arranged for this group to view several filmstrips, including one film which helped them be accurate in their representations.

The drama group, Roberta, Alex, Pat, Daisy, and Joyce presented several short skits representing significant events in our state's history. The funniest one was their skit of the legislators debating the new water pollution bill. Pat was the "anti" senator and Roberta, Alex, Daisy, and Joyce sat and booed and hissed as she spoke.

For readers to do together

Ms. Maverick sees the relief map, time-line, book, mural and dramatizations as activities which help the children synthesize and organize the information they have learned throughout the unit. She also sees these activities as vehicles for growth in communication, computational and social skills.

Get together in small groups in your class. Each group should choose one of the culminating activities Ms. Maverick did and list the ways in which it served as a synthesizer and organizer, and a vehicle for skill growth. Then think up another culminating activity she could have done and list its educational values.

● ● ●

While these culminating activities occupied much of our time and energies this month, we did do some other things. We are now up to eighteen minutes of SQUIRT time each day, and many of the children are choosing to read from the our state books, magazines, pamphlets, brochures, and maps displayed on the back table. We have had lots of fun devising math word problems for each other to solve. The ground rules were that (1) each word problem had to involve our state in some way, and (2) the person who made up the problem had to be able to solve it. The children worked out the problems at odd times during the day, and then just before lunch, five children would come and write their problems on the board. The rest of us would then work at solving the problem. The children learned that writing clearly stated mathematical word problems which contain all the information needed to solve them is a difficult task.

For the reader to do

Here are some of the children's word problems. What information did Mort forget to put in his? Can you solve Mandy's problem?

When you drive from Merritt School to the capital, you have to pay tolls at three different toll booths. How much does it cost in all for tolls? (Mort)

At 4 percent sales tax, how much tax is there on a $1.57 lunch? (Betty)

Two new bond issues have been proposed. Three times the first bond issue is equal to twice the second. Together the bond issues would equal $8 million. How much is each proposed issue for? (Mandy)

● ● ●

We had a whole-school party on the day before school let out for the holidays. Mr. Sweep, the custodian, was retiring after being here since the day the school opened twenty-seven years ago. While we were all sad to see him leave, that sadness, for me, was lightened by the knowledge that Mr. Moppet, Chip's father, needed the job so badly. He has been out of work for months, and he and his family were too proud to accept "charity." I have, however, been seeing to it that Chip has some breakfast when he gets here in the morning and, now that his father is the school custodian, I know they will be all right.

Oh, I almost forgot! I am going to have a student teacher. I don't know quite what to expect, however. Dr. Link was here at the beginning of the month and told me about a young man named Donald Ditto. It seems that Donald started his student teaching in the fall but just couldn't get along with the teacher with whom they placed him. He dropped out of the program and was going to drop out of school entirely with only student teaching left to complete! Dr. Link assures me that the young man really has potential and that he had just been poorly matched with a very rigid teacher. At any rate, Dr. Link thinks he will be able to work with my program and that he will make a contribution. I hope she's right—for his sake as well as for mine. I guess we will just have to wait and see what this new year brings!

Mr. Ditto has been with us all month now and he is terrific! I am just so glad Dr. Link convinced him to give teaching another try and brought him out here. He has a very quiet, easy-going manner with the kids and will never be a disciplinarian, but the children respect and cooperate with him. He never talks about his other student teaching experience, but I'll just bet that in addition to the inherent problems created by matching him with an authoritarian teacher, he also experienced difficulties because of the expectations of what a male teacher is supposed to be like. I imagine that both the students and the other teachers expected him to behave like a drill sergeant. Mr. Ditto has no top sergeant qualities about him. I like him.

Our unit for most of this month has been on ecology. It was a lot of fun, and I found many ways to help the children become involved in the community. We discussed interviewing techniques and constructed a little questionnaire to find out what people are doing about energy conservation and pollution. The children interviewed neighbors, relatives, and business owners, and we prepared a report, sort of a miniature Harris poll, which we distributed to all the people interviewed. Newspapers, magazines, and television broadcasts provided much of the input for this unit because this information needs to be the most current available.

During one of our initial sessions, the children and I decided on some categories under the general heading of ecology and began a bulletin board for each of these subtopics. The children brought newspaper and magazine articles and pictures, shared them with the class, and put them on the appropriate board. I made tape recordings of the nightly national and local newscasts and played back for the children those parts which applied to our study. I also arranged for many members of the community who are involved in specific ecological concerns to come in and talk with us about their particular involvement. As a culmination to this unit, the children and I drafted a list of recommendations for conserving energy and preventing pollution which we sent to Ms. Daley. The letter was published with all the children's names under it. The children were pleased, but their parents were ecstatic! Copies of that paper with its fifteen suggestions for conserving energy and preventing pollution have gone to doting aunts and grandparents all around the country.

The children are very careful not to waste anything anymore, and are quick to point out wasteful habits in others. Sometimes, these others are not so pleased to have their faults aired in public. One day in the cafeteria, Mrs. Flame took her tray up to deposit it. She hadn't even touched her roll or her cake. Butch informed her that if she didn't want to eat something, she shouldn't take it in the first place!

The children are progressing quite well in their afternoon skills work.

Butch, Chip, and Daisy have mastered the first 300 words on the A and P list. Paul knows most of the first 200 most of the time. Larry, Horace, Pat, and Steve are now working together on an individual project. Miss Page, the librarian, is teaching them to locate information and how to use basic reference works. Alex, Carl, Mitch, and Roberta are learning to spell the words on the A and P list. Betty, Daphne, and Tanana are perfecting their cursive handwriting.

For several weeks now, I have been concerned about the inability of my children to remember the main points of what they read from one day to the next. Over the Christmas vacation, I picked up a copy of the *Journal of Reading* and found an article by a man whom I had heard speak at a seminar last summer. I then remembered that his "Guided Reading Procedure" was developed for the express purpose of helping children increase their ability to remember information for extended periods of time. With the article for review (Manzo, 1975), I vowed to try guided reading procedures with my children as soon as I returned to school.

To begin with, I chose a short selection from a magazine article on one city's successful attempt to clean up its waterways. I had this passage typed and duplicated and gave it to the entire class with the instructions to "read to remember everything." After approximately ten minutes when I observed that most of the children had finished the selection, I told them that if they had finished, they should turn the selection face down on their desks and that if they had not yet finished they should continue reading until they were finished. I then asked them what they remembered from their reading and recorded everything they told me on the chalkboard, numbering each response. Every once in a while when their responses seemed to stop, I would say, "Listen as I read what we already have on the board and see if you can remember anything else." Eventually they had exhausted their memories. I asked them to listen again as I reread what was on the board and told them that when I had finished reading I would allow them one minute to reread portions of the article to correct any inconsistencies or misinformation recorded on the board.

There was, of course, some misinformation on the board, and the children couldn't wait to get back to the text to prove it. When Hilda said, "Number 27 is not right. It should be. . . ," I responded, "Can you read me the part of the text which lets you know that?" Hilda then read that part aloud to verify her statement and the class agreed that number 27 was indeed incorrect. We then corrected it. In addition to correcting misinformation, the children added other bits of information they had missed or forgotten during the first reading.

Next, I asked them to listen again as I read the information on the board, but this time they were to listen and try to decide which ideas seemed to be the main ideas, the most important ideas, the ideas they would like to remember or tell someone else if that someone asked them what the story had been all about. I phrased "main idea" in this way so that the children began to conceptualize that very elusive concept of main idea. After I read the items one final time, several children suggested what seemed to be the main ideas, and I circled them. Different children had different notions about which were really the main ideas, but I circled all they suggested and then reminded them that we could all agree that each item on the board was written in the text. Choosing the main ideas was, to some extent, I explained, a matter of personal judgment: "What is most important to one person may not be most important to someone else." If the children had asked me to circle an inordinately large number of items, I would have done so, and as we finished, I would have said something like, "Now, as you know, not everyone would agree on which ideas are the most important. If I had to select the main ideas here, I believe I would select numbers 4, 6, and 27." I would then read those three items and explain that these three seemed to me to tell what the selection was primarily about, and that the other items explain these three. In this way, I would try to model for them the complex process of selecting main ideas.

Finally, I asked them to take out a sheet of paper and number it from one to five. While they were doing this, I erased the board. I then read them five true-false items which I had constructed prior to the lesson. The children responded by putting a T or F on their papers. When we had finished the five-item quiz, I reread the items and we decided whether each was true or false. Each child checked his or her own paper.

The children then recorded the number they got correct by coloring in the appropriate area on a graph. One week later, I gave them a delayed retention test on the same information contained in the selection. I used five different true-false items but I tried to make the two tests equally difficult. Needless to say, the children did not do nearly as well on the second test. This is exactly what I wanted them to observe. To us, as adults, it is obvious that unless we make an effort and review information, we forget. Children, however, are quite unaware of this natural phenomenon. Last week, in fact, when I gave them the delayed test and they did not do nearly as well as on the first test, they accused me of making harder items for the second test. No explaining of mine could convince them otherwise. Mr. Ditto settled the controversy by suggesting that next time I should make up all ten items ahead of time and put them in a hat. One child would then reach in and select five items which would be used for the immediate retention test and the others would be put away for the test one week later. I thought that was a brilliant suggestion, and I already have the ten questions made up for the guided reading procedure I plan to do tomorrow.

This guided reading procedure was developed by Professor Anthony

Manzo, who addressed a seminar I attended at the university last summer on the subject of comprehension. His theory is that many children do not comprehend a lot of what they read because they don't have many stored facts to which they can compare, contrast, and relate information being read. He suggests that if guided reading procedures are done every two weeks with a delayed retention test in the intervening week, children will, after several procedures, begin to develop a mind-set to try to remember more of what they read. About the fourth time they sit down to read a selection with the direction "Read to remember everything," a little voice inside their heads begins to say, "Hey, now I am going to remember this stuff well enough so that I can do as well on the test a week from now as I do on the one today." This is when, it is hypothesized, teachers begin to see some improvement in long-term memory of information read. Over the course of a year's time, it is hoped that this mind-set to remember what you read will transfer to material being read at times other than guided reading procedure times. As this continues, the child increases his or her store of facts with which to think about what he or she is reading.

I don't know how it will work, but I do plan to do a guided reading procedure every two weeks for the rest of the year and see what happens. I was at first concerned about giving everyone the same selection when I know that children like Daisy, Chip, and Paul couldn't read it. But Dr. Manzo pointed out that if the nonreaders sit quietly and look as if they are reading for the ten minutes and then listen carefully as the readers tell what they have remembered, they too will get the information and be able to do well on the test. This is the reason the test should be true-false. In this way, even the nonreaders in the class can learn the information and be successful. It seems to be working. Daisy got four right on the first test, and Chip got all five. He was so proud of himself. His chart appears on p. 233. As you can see, Chip has an unusually good memory. He only missed one item on the delayed test.

For readers to do together

Find a short article on teaching reading. Let a member of the class lead the class through a guided reading procedure. Remember to follow these steps.

1. Read the article to remember everything.
2. Record all remembered information on the board.
3. Return to the article for one minute to discover any inconsistencies.
4. Correct the information on the board.
5. Identify main ideas.
6. Give an immediate and a long-term memory quiz.

● ● ●

Chip's Progress Chart

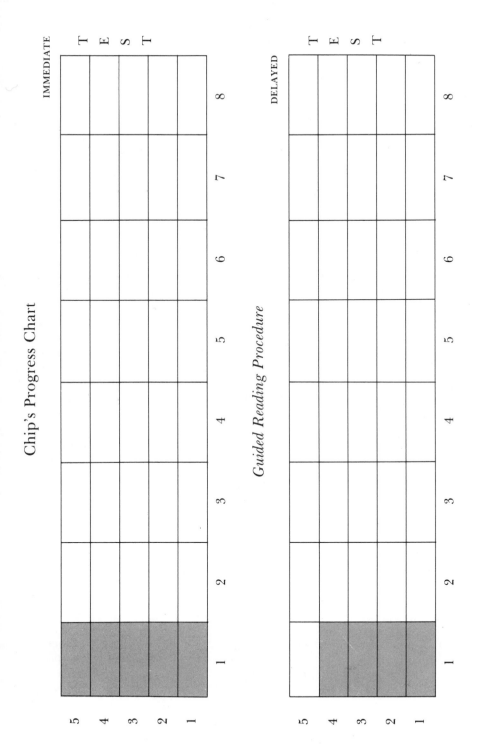

Guided Reading Procedure

FEBRUARY

What a strange month this has been! January, February, and March are supposed to be the calm, uninterrupted "teaching months" but so far they, like the rest of the year, have been extraordinary! I guess it all started when the legislature held the special session and we made our unexpected trip to the capital. The new water pollution bill was passed, by the way, and the timeline committee added this momentous occasion as a final event on their state timeline. Mr. Stans did come to visit our class as he had promised, and expressed astonishment at the children's political sophistication.

Then, Mr. Ditto came when I wasn't expecting to get a student teacher this year, and, as a result of his being here, I have been asked to leave my class in March and go to the university! It seems that one of the professors over there has been in the hospital for months and they are very shorthanded. She had been scheduled to teach a special seminar on the integrated curriculum during the spring quarter and there is no one else who can teach it. Dr. Link's plan is that Mr. Ditto should take over my class for the rest of the year and I should go to the university. She had already discussed this with Mr. Topps and the university administration before she let me in on her plans, so I guess the decision is mine. My first instinct was to say "no" immediately. How could I leave my children in the middle of the year? But, upon reflection, I had to admit that, with the exception of Daisy, the children would thrive under Mr. Ditto's continued tutelage. Next, I thought, "But I can't teach a university seminar. What could I tell them? How would I teach it?" But then I remembered some of the terrible graduate classes I sat through when I was working on my master's degree and I remembered wondering if the professors who taught our college classes could survive, let alone thrive, in a class of real children. At least I could bring some realism to that seminar. I am tempted . . . and I have one week in which to decide!

We have now completed four guided reading procedures and the children do, indeed, seem to be increasing their long-term memory of what they read. This month, I tried some "translation writing" experiences with Paul, Daisy, Butch, Jeff, Chip, Joyce, and Tanana. I got the notion for translation writing when I was reading through an old book which I stumbled across (Burton, 1952). Being curious about what educational methods were being expounded in the forties, I perused the book. One chapter was on the unit approach to teaching, which, while different in several ways, bears some striking similarities to what I call my "integrated approach." In one chapter a fifth-grade teacher describes some of the activities which she did with the children as part of her "colonial life unit." One of these activities she called "cooperative stories." To do a cooperative story, she sat down with the children who were not very able readers, read a portion of a book to them, and then had them tell her what they heard. She then recorded what they told her on the board and had them copy that "cooperative story" into their notebooks. In this way, the less able readers constructed a textbook at their own reading level.

As I was reading this, I thought of Paul, Daisy, Butch, Jeff, and Chip, whose reading skills are still not sophisticated enough to read the complex materials which we often need to read to gain information for our units. I vowed to try what I termed "translation writing" with them. I worried, however, that if I took these particular five children to work with me while the rest of the class worked with Mr. Ditto, the five I was working with might feel segregated because they don't read as well. I then hit upon the idea of including Joyce and Tanana in the group. While Joyce is a very good reader, her oral expression skills are not nearly as sophisticated. Tanana, while also a good reader, is hesitant to speak out in front of the group. I knew that with Joyce and Tanana added to the original five, no one would even think to label my translation writing group as a "slow group."

The lessons were fun. I, unlike the teacher in the forties, did not have the children copy the story into their notebooks. Rather, I wrote it as they all sat around the table, then I typed it and had seven copies made. Thank goodness for some aspects of modern technology! The other children were intrigued and the members of my group read their stories to everyone. Now, of course, everyone wants to do it. Hilda remarked that this was "just like we used to do in first grade." Roberta informed her that the topics we were discussing were, as Mr. Stans had said, "sophisticated!"

February was also parent conference month. I made it a point to include Mr. Ditto in all the conferences, both because he needs to build confidence in dealing with parents, and because if I leave, I want the parents to have met him. Daisy's mother will be furious if I leave. She just bragged and bragged about how well Daisy has done this year and how much more lady-like she has become. She is convinced that Daisy's only problem has been that she hasn't had a good teacher before!

Paul's mother didn't come, of course. The more I thought about that woman and that poor child the madder I got. So finally I determined that if she wasn't going to come and see us, I was going to go and see her. Mr. Ditto concurred and asked to come with me.

I wrote her a letter, which she ignored, asking her when would be a good time to visit. I then called her one evening and just about insisted that we had to talk with her and that we were coming. Finally she agreed, and last Thursday evening, we went! It was quite sad, really. She was stone sober and the house was modest but tidy. She invited us into the living room. The chairs and sofa all had new covers on them. She served us coffee and cookies. We then talked, or attempted to talk, with her. Mostly, she sat chain-smoking and nodding her head. She, like Paul, looked ready to burst into tears at any moment. She kept saying that it was hard to raise a child all alone and that she prays each night that Paul's father will come home. She said that Paul is a good boy and that he doesn't run around the neighborhood with the other hoodlums! She wishes there were some nice children around that he could be friends with. I asked her if she would go with Paul to the family services clinic and she said that she really wasn't very well and that she just couldn't depend on feeling well enough to do anything like that on a regular basis. Finally, we left. I drove Mr. Ditto home and as he got out of the car, he said, "You know, its even worse now because I don't have anyone to hate. That poor woman is doing the best she can!"

MARCH

I have always heard the expression, "Two heads are better than one." Now, I know it was referring to two teachers' heads! I really didn't realize how much I would miss Ms. Maverick, I was so excited about being able to stay with this class. But I do miss her. She comes in every Thursday afternoon and we plan activities together, but that is not the same as having her here every day. Just having another adult around sometimes is important, but I guess most teachers have to do it all, all day, every day by themselves. Maybe I'll team teach with someone next year! I guess the success of that would depend on who that "someone" is!

This month has gone well. Ms. Maverick seems pleased with what we've done here while she's been working at the university. Fortunately, she left all her materials here for me to use. I can see that if I try to do this type of program next year, I will have to spend quite a lot of time over the summer gathering materials on the topics around which I plan to build units. (Each week Ms. Maverick comes to our planning session and gathers up something to take with her and share with her students. She brings it back the next week, however, and so far I have not had to spend a great deal of time hunting material).

So far the children have adapted exceedingly well to the change. They miss Ms. Maverick, however, and for the first week, they were more unruly than usual. Ms. Maverick had warned me, however, that they would test me after she left, so I was prepared. I made a special effort to be fair and firm, and to continue the usual routines. In spite of my resolve, there were occasional laments of, "Ms. Maverick never did it that way!"

Daisy is the only one who seems damaged, perhaps even in some permanent way, by Ms. Maverick's leaving. Ms. Maverick is very worried about her, and even invited Daisy to her house after school to try to minimize the trauma. Daisy's mother refused to let Daisy go, however, and even wrote a very angry note to the school board concerning Ms. Maverick's unprofessional behavior in leaving her class. I try to be nice to Daisy and not to push her too much, but she simply does not respond positively. Her dislike of me is quite apparent. I just don't know what to do. I hope that by being gentle and patient, she will eventually come around.

Chip, on the other hand, is a delight! I can almost see him growing each day—physically as well as mentally. He has grown several inches since Christmas and has put on several pounds. He has mastered the words on the A and P sight word list and is beginning to get involved with books! We are now up to twenty-one minutes of SQUIRT time each day. Chip loves mystery stories and folk tales and takes a book home almost every night.

While I have tried to follow our routines just as we did when Ms. Maverick was here, I have experimented with a new teaching strategy. For some time now, I have been curious about why children seem to understand what they listen to so much better than what they read. Even when they can read most of the words, they often have a great deal of difficulty reading for a specific purpose. I discussed this with a friend who is still a student, and she directed me to a recent article in *The Reading Teacher* which discussed this very problem. The solution is a teaching strategy called a listening-reading transfer lesson (Cunningham, 1975). To do a listening-reading transfer lesson, the teacher uses two selections (or two sections of one long selection). (I chose selections which related to our unit.) One of these selections is read to the children and the other is used for them to read.

Although Dr. Cunningham did not suggest it, I identified several unfamiliar concepts in the selection that I was going to read to them, as well as some unknown words and unfamiliar concepts in the one they were going to read. I also decided what to do about these unfamiliar concepts and unknown words: as often as possible I try to lead the children to derive the meaning of unfamiliar concepts and the pronunciation of unfamiliar words from the context of the story, in order to encourage them to become independent readers. Usually, I write the unfamiliar concepts or unknown words on the board and ask them to see if they can figure out the meaning/pronunciation of these words. Often, after listening to or reading the selection and determining what the word seems to mean because of the way it is used and because of the other words around it, we look up the word in the dictionary, read the several definitions, and decide which one applies. We then compare our guess against the dictionary definitions and usually decide that the context of the story gave us a rather good notion of at least one meaning for that word.

Next, I decide on a purpose for having the students listen to or read the selection. To facilitate the transfer from listening to reading, I set the same purpose for both the listening and the reading part of the activity.

Last week I taught a listening-reading transfer lesson designed to help the children improve their sequencing abilities. I began by putting the word *rectify* on the board and asking the children to listen for this word as I read the selection and to try to figure out its meaning by the way it was used and by the other words in the story. I then taped to the chalkboard several sentence strips on which I had written the major events of the story. I read these events to the children and set the purpose for listening. "Listen as I read so you can help me put these events, which are now jumbled, into the order in which they occur in the story." After listening to the story, the children helped me rearrange the strips to put the events in their proper order and explained how they knew which should go first, second, and so on. We then discussed how *rectify* was used and several children suggested that it must mean "to fix something." We determined that the other words which let us know that *rectify* had to do with fixing were *broken, repair,* and *breakdown.* Hilda then looked up *rectify* in the dictionary and read us the dictionary definition. This ended the listening part of the listening-reading transfer lesson.

On the following day, I gave the children a story to read and a dittoed sheet on which I had written the major events of that story. I then put the words *candid* and *sword* on the board. I pronounced *candid* for them and told them that the other words in the story would help them figure out part of the meaning for *candid.* I told them that they all knew the meaning for the other word, but that many of them might not recognize it immediately and be able to pronounce it. I told them that as they read they would be able to figure out what the word was. Having alerted them to one unfamiliar concept and one unknown word, I then reminded them of the listening lesson we had done the day before and how we had reordered the events of the story after listening to it.

"That is exactly what I want you to do today, only today, instead of listening to me read, you will read the story and reorder the events. First, read the list of events, then read the story. Then use your scissors to cut the events into strips and reorder them just as we did with the strips on the board yesterday."

The children immediately formed reading pairs. These pairs have been set up for months now, and each pair contains a good reader and a less able reader. The children take turns reading and the better reader helps the less able one. This works out amazingly well and allows me to give the whole class the same selection to read. After reading the events and then the story, the children cut and pasted the events in order. We then discussed the order and the reasoning behind that order, and noted that *sword* was what knights carried, and that to be *candid* was to be outspoken or frank. Finally, I helped the children to observe that what they can do after listening, they can do after reading.

I have also done a listening-reading transfer lesson in which the children selected a main idea for each paragraph, and next week, I plan to do one in which they match certain causes with certain effects. Ms. Maverick says she always preached that a teacher must teach for transfer and that she can't imagine why she never thought about doing that. (It seems so obvious once you do think about it.)

APRIL

Our unit this month has been on Alaska. Ms. Maverick and I have long been concerned about helping Tanana adapt to our culture, and it occurred to us last month that one way to help her feel more comfortable with us would be for us to learn more about her and her home. Tanana was a great resource during this unit and helped us empathize with native Alaskans who see their traditional ways threatened by the advance of civilization.

After talking with Mrs. Wright, the first-grade teacher, I decided to try a "List, Group, and Label" lesson as a kickoff to our unit. I asked the children to tell me all the words they thought of when they heard the word *Alaska*, and listed these on the board. When the children had exhausted their Alaska vocabulary, I read the entire list to them and asked them to listen as I was reading for any that seemed to go together in some way. Mrs. Wright had suggested that the next step was to let individual children list the things they felt went together, tell why they put them together, and give a label to that group. I did this, but in order to get greater participation, I let each child write on a slip of paper the items he or she wanted to put together. Individuals then read their lists and responded to my questions on why they had put those words together and what they would call that group. When each child who desired to had read his or her group to us, had explained his or her reason for grouping, and had labeled the group, I suggested that each one of them make another group which was different from any they had already made. We then repeated the explaining and labeling process with these second groups.

This seems to be a very effective technique to use to begin a unit. I learned what kind of prior knowledge and preconceptions the children had about Alaska, and they began thinking about Alaska and using the specialized vocabulary: *caribou, Aleuts, pipeline*. I also think it helps their classification skills, and thus their thinking skills. I plan to begin each new unit with a "List, Group, and Label" lesson.

One thing that I tried this month was not quite successful, at least not at first. Ms. Maverick had always had the children in small groups to discuss various topics, so of course, I planned for some small group discussions, too. The first ones were awful. I let them form their own groups and told them to discuss the pro's and con's of Alaska's development. Absolutely nothing happened! They just sat there and looked at each other! When I told Ms. Maverick of my failure, she said, "The one direction which will ensure no discussion is to tell them 'Discuss!' If you want them to discuss, give them some concrete task to do which will require discussion for its successful resolution." She also suggested that I form groups which will remain constant over a period of several weeks so that the children in those groups will develop some group pride in what they accomplish. She further suggested that we spread the rowdy ones, the leaders, the quiet ones, and the "outcasts" among the groups. These are the five groups we formed.

Daisy	Paul	Butch	Mitch	Mort
Alex	*Betty	Carl	Chip	Daphne
*Rita	Hilda	*Joyce	*Pat	Horace
Larry	Manuel	Roberta	Tanana	*Mandy
		Steve		Jeff

We then planned the following structured discussion. The children were told which group they would be in and where their group would meet (the four corners and the center of the room). They then practiced getting quickly into their groups and ready to begin. Once they were in their groups, I gave them a card with their names on it and explained that the person whose name had a star next to it would be the recorder for that group for the day and would do all the writing for the group. (We picked the recorders according to their ability in spelling and writing.)

I then gave each group index cards and a felt marker and told them they had five minutes to list the resources of Alaska. They were asked to write only one resource on each index card because they would use the cards later. Since they had seen a film a few days before on Alaska's resources, and many had read about Alaska's resources in various source books, they had no difficulty thinking of resources. When the timer rang to signal the end of the five minutes, each group had a stack of cards and was still talking!

Next, I gave them two large sheets of construction paper and some tape. On the top of one sheet of construction paper, I had written "Resources which will be used up" and on the other, "Resources which will last forever." I explained the concept of renewable and nonrenewable resources to them, and gave them a few examples from our local resources. I then gave them ten minutes to tape each of their index cards to one of the construction paper sheets. The discussion which ensued was lively and topical! Ms. Maverick had been right again. Once they had a task to do which required discussion and a strict time limit in which to complete that task, there was no dawdling or silence. (Never again will I instruct a group to "discuss" unless, of course, I want a few rare moments of silence in this otherwise noisy room.) Once the ten minutes were up, we displayed the charts and compared the results. When two groups had put the same resource in two different categories, the groups explained their reasoning, and if we could come to any resolution, the resource was changed to the appropriate chart. In several cases, we decided we would have to do a little research to resolve a controversy—an unexpected bonus of our first successful discussion!

I have been continuing the guided reading procedures as Ms. Maverick began them, but have also initiated guided listening procedures. Every other week, we do a full procedure in which the children have ten minutes to read a selection, list what they remember, skim the selection to verify or correct inconsistencies, identify main ideas, and complete a five-item nonreading quiz. In the intervening week, we do the delayed retention quiz. The children have increased in their ability to remember information over a one-week time span and they are very proud of this growth, which is vividly displayed on their guided reading procedure charts.

I got to thinking that if the procedure was good for reading, it should also be good for listening! Last week, I tried it. I had planned to read to the class an editorial from an Alaskan newspaper. I brought a tape recorder to class and asked the children to listen to remember everything. I then read them the editorial and taped my reading. Once finished, I asked them what they remembered and listed what they told me on the board. When they had exhausted their memories, I replayed the tape, telling them to listen to make sure the information on the board was correct, and to raise their hands to stop the tape if they heard anything which contradicted the information on the board. They found several pieces of incorrect information and seemed to really enjoy this new strategy. We then circled main ideas, and I gave them a quiz. They all wanted to know if I was going to give them a delayed quiz next week and if they were going to keep a chart. I hadn't planned to be this systematic about it, but they seem to want to! They certainly did listen attentively and knew what that editorial said. I think I will do guided listening procedures on the off-week for guided reading procedures. I wonder what Ms. Maverick will say when I tell her about this!

For the reader to do

Compare and contrast the guided reading procedure and the guided listening procedure. How are they alike? different? When would you use a GRP and when would you use a GLP?

● ● ●

MAY

What a terrific month this has been. I started the month a little "down," realizing that this year was ending with so much left undone and that I still had to find a job for next year. I knew I would never find a school like this one. I had made up my mind, however, that I believed in the integrated approach to teaching, and that I would move elsewhere to find a school which would allow me to follow through on my beliefs.

You can imagine my surprise when, as I was relaying my concerns and convictions to Ms. Maverick, she informed me that she knew just the principal I ought to talk to—Mr. Topps! While conducting the seminar at the university, Ms. Maverick had become even more convinced of her approach to teaching and to children, and had decided that she would stay on at the university as a graduate student in administration and supervision so that she could get her principal's certificate. Although Mr. Topps was sorry to lose her, he agreed that the principal could be an effective change-agent in the schools, and admitted that this factor had weighed heavily in his decision to become a principal. I, of course, quickly applied for Ms. Maverick's job, and although the school board has not yet acted officially, Mr. Topps assured me that they will approve his recommendation. So, I have found a job in a school which will let me teach according to my beliefs! Ms. Maverick has even agreed to leave most of her materials here. While I am delighted at this turn of events, I am also somewhat apprehensive. Even with her materials, planning this program all alone and starting a whole new class of children in this approach will not be easy.

Ms. Maverick was away at a national reading meeting at the beginning of the month, and since then has been busy finishing up her seminar. The annual book fair thus became totally my responsibility. And while I survived and it got done, it was not as well planned as I would have liked. We ordered the books for the fair from several publishers of paperback books. We got catalogues and the children met in groups to decide how many copies of each title they thought we might sell. (Fortunately, the publishers take back and credit us for any books which are not sold!) Once the books were ordered, we began to plan how to organize and promote our sale. As is traditional, the books are first put on display for sale on the evening of the last parents' meeting. My children wrote flyers encouraging the parents to come to the final meeting and inform-ing them that many good, inexpensive paperback books would be on sale that evening. Parents were encouraged to buy the books for their children to have something new and exciting to read during the long summer months.

We then made posters which were hung in the various classrooms of our school and in the local supermarket and drugstore. A group of children composed an announcement about the book fair which they sent to the newspaper, and another group composed an announcement which was read several times a day on the local radio station.

With our advertisement campaign well under way, we began to plan how we would organize ourselves for the actual sale. After much discus-sion, it was decided that we would divide all the books according to topic and display them on cafeteria tables set up in the halls. We then began a lengthy classification procedure during which we looked at the titles of the books we had ordered and tried to place them in appropriate categories. After several days of discussion and argument about what the categories should be, I saw that we were getting nowhere except closer to the night of the fair. Obviously I had to provide some direction or we weren't going to make it! I then sat down with the lists and established eight categories, plus a ninth category for miscellaneous books. The next day I wrote the category names on the board and had the children get into the groups they had been in for the ordering. Each group took nine sheets of paper, put the name of one category on each sheet, and decided in which category each book they had ordered belonged. While we did have several disagreements and a lot of books relegated to "miscellaneous," we finally got our lists made. The children made a first or second choice for which books they would like to sell, and I formed them into groups of two or three based on these choices.

When the books finally arrived (only one day ahead of the fair!), it was a fairly easy job to sort them and put them in piles according to category. Then, on the afternoon of the fair, each group set up their displays. Several children who lived quite far away and I stayed at school until the parents arrived at 7 p.m., watching over our displays, doing some last minute "advertisement," and eating the three pizzas I had ordered. (The ones who had gone home for supper were not too pleased when the ones who stayed bragged about having pizza for supper, but you just can't please everyone no matter how hard you try!)

We sold books out in the hall that evening to the parents and all the next morning to the children who came out of their classrooms at scheduled times. We then took the 100-plus books we had left back to our room, put them on the back table, and sold about twenty more to children and teachers during the remainder of that week. Finally, on Friday, we boxed up the unsold books and shipped them back to the companies from which they had come. We also totalled our money and figured which books we would order with the profits. We decided that each child could order one free bonus book, and that with the remainder of the profits, we would order books for the classroom's already large paperback library. I didn't know until I was almost through with this project that I would be in charge of it again next year!

For the reader to do

Mr. Ditto obviously found the book fair a lot of work and found that it took more planning than he had anticipated. What did the children learn as they were planning and implementing the book fair? Specifically, what language, reading, math and social skills were they practicing? Can you think of ways that planning and carrying out the book fair improved the children's thinking abilities? List these and then decide if you think the time and effort was well spent. Remember the added bonuses—books for the whole school to read over the summer, extra books for Mr. Ditto's classroom library, and good public relations for the school with the parents and community.

● ● ●

We also spent a little extra time working on skills this month and I checked all of the children out so that I would know exactly what they had mastered and what they still needed to work on. All the children but Paul and Daisy have mastered the words on the A and P sight word list. Paul knows most of them most of the time, and Daisy, who had mastered the first 300 before Ms. Maverick left, has learned just a few more since then. Most of the children, with the exception of Daisy, Paul, Butch, Jeff, and Chip can also spell all of the words on that list. Butch and Jeff can spell the first 200. Chip can spell the first 300, and Paul and Daisy can usually spell the first 100 and some of the second 100. Paul and Daisy have mastered the addition and subtraction facts. Butch, Carl, Tanana, and Alex have mastered the subtraction facts and have almost mastered the multiplication facts. All the others have mastered the multiplication facts and are developing some facility with division and with fractions. Larry, Pat, Horace, Steve, Hilda, and Roberta have progressed tremendously this year in their ability to locate material in reference works, and synthesize and organize the material they find there.

We have been having SQUIRT time for twenty-four minutes for the last two weeks of this month. While this is a minute short of the twenty-five minutes Ms. Maverick thought they could reach, I think it is quite a long time for fourth-graders to sit still and read intently. I am proud of them!

Since Ms. Maverick was invited to the university, people in the school system have suddenly become curious about her approach to teaching. She has been asked to address the final meeting of one of the local professional organizations and has requested that I join her on the podium. At first I protested that I had nothing to say to teachers that they would be willing to listen to, but Ms. Maverick argued that I could answer some of their questions about beginning to teach with this method. When I hesitated, she asked whether I felt strange about going because I knew that my first supervising teacher and many of the other teachers in that school would be there. I had to admit that I wasn't looking forward to meeting those people who represented my failure as a teacher. She said that that was exactly the point: I was not a failure—simply misplaced—and that was precisely the reason I should be present at the meeting, even if I didn't say a word. I have had my orders and am going, and I have even begun to think I may enjoy it!

Mrs. Wright called the meeting to order, made a few business announcements, and then introduced Ms. Maverick.

"As many of you know," she began, "I use what is essentially a language experience approach to help my first-graders bridge the gap between the language they speak and reading the language of others. While I believe in this method for beginning readers, I realize that there are many valid approaches to the teaching of reading and that each teacher's approach must be one he or she is comfortable with and one which meets the needs of the children being taught. I have for the past five years been able to observe the results of Ms. Maverick's integrated curriculum. Often she teaches in fourth grade a group of children I had in first grade, and I am always pleased to watch these children grow in independence, self-awareness, and real-world concern under Ms. Maverick's direction. I must confess that until this year when Mr. Ditto took over Ms. Maverick's class and carried on just as she always had, I thought that Ms. Maverick's teaching method was really peculiar to her own style and personality. I have seen, however, that this was not the case, and that given the desire and the will, one can learn to teach an integrated curriculum. It gives me great personal pleasure, therefore, to introduce to you this afternoon my friend and colleague, Ms. Maverick, and her protégé, Mr. Ditto."

Ms. Maverick rose, but before she began her address made a confession to Mrs. Wright: "I must admit, Mrs. Wright, that I always thought your teaching was peculiar to *your* style and personality!" As the group nodded their appreciation of this humorous but candid confession, Ms. Maverick began her presentation.

"One of the main reasons why I teach an integrated curriculum is that there are never, for me, enough hours in the teaching day. When I help my children become better readers, more precise language users, and more competent mathematicians as they learn science and social studies content, I get almost twice the mileage out of my instructional time. I believe this is a principle which can be applied to learners of any age. Today, rather than lecture you about the wisdom of this economy, I am going to demonstrate it with you.

"While I use many teaching strategies in my integrated curriculum, a new one which I have tried out this year and which I am most impressed with is the guided reading procedure. Mr. Ditto is presently passing out to you copies of a summary of my instructional program which I wrote. I would like you to read this summary *to remember everything*. When you have completed reading this, I will demonstrate for you the steps in the guided reading procedure."

Ms. Maverick then sat down and after a few moments the teachers realized that she did indeed intend for them to read the summary and they settled down to do so. When most of the teachers had completed the summary, Ms. Maverick reminded them of the purpose she had set for reading and asked them what they remembered. At first no one responded, but Mrs. Flame finally responded: "You have a four-sided plan. Reading is real. SQUIRT. Skills time and the integrated block activity." Ms. Maverick smiled and wrote Mrs. Flame's responses on the board. Slowly, others began to volunteer bits and pieces of what they remembered reading. Ms. Maverick recorded their contributions, numbering each as she went along. (1) Each unit has three phases. (2) In the beginning phase, you provide much input and try to build interest in the topic being studied. (3) As much as possible, you use real-world reading materials from newspapers and magazines. (4) You do lots of directed reading activities with the whole class and the reading material on an overhead transparency. (5) At the end of each unit you do activities which help the children to synthesize and organize what they read. (6) You have a block of time in the afternoon when you teach reading and math skills.

Once the teachers got going, they, just like the children, were able to fill the board with their pooled remembrances from the summary they had read. Ms. Maverick continued through the steps of the procedure with them, having them go back to the summary for one minute to correct any inconsistencies or supply missing information, identifying the main ideas, and then giving them a five-item true-false quiz.

When she had finished the whole procedure, she explained to them the rationale for the guided reading procedure, that it was intended primarily to help children increase their long-term memory of what they read. She explained how Mr. Ditto had adapted this procedure to listening, and reported that the procedures did indeed seem to be effective in helping the children develop a mind set to remember more of what they read and heard. She showed them Chip's GRP progress chart which she had brought along.

"What I have just done with you is what I try to do with my children," Ms. Maverick went on to explain. "There was some content which I wanted to teach you—in this case, a summary of how my integrated curriculum works. At the same time, I wanted to help you increase your repertoire of teaching skills, so I used the guided reading procedure to teach you about my instructional program. Hopefully, you have experienced in the last forty-five minutes the kind of economy teaching I practice in my classroom."

The teachers seemed much warmer and more interested than they had when the meeting started, and Ms. Maverick reaffirmed her faith in the belief that a good teaching strategy is appropriate for learners of any age. Although there was not much time remaining, several questions were asked and answered. In one of the questions, an elderly teacher referred to Ms. Maverick's integrated approach as a radical approach. Ms. Maverick informed her that while her own version of it had certain unique characteristics, the notion that learning should be integrated was hardly new. She went on to cite references for this fact. She told them that Henry Morrison in 1931 had first pointed out the need for some external organization of subject matter to achieve internal learning products, and that he had condemned the fragmenting of the curriculum.

A young teacher indicated that he was very interested in trying the integrated curriculum approach, but that the intermediate grades in his school were departmentalized, allowing him only forty-five minutes of reading time for each of six classes. Ms. Maverick indicated to him that one of the greatest values of the self-contained classroom, as she saw it, was that teaching of the different subject areas could be integrated, but that she saw no feasible way of doing an integrated curriculum if a teacher only had the children for one subject a day. Ms. Maverick did point out to him, however, that he certainly could include SQUIRT and some "Reading is real" activities during his reading period.

The final question had to do with beginning an integrated curriculum, and since the time had nearly elapsed, Ms. Maverick referred the questioner to Mr. Ditto and informed the audience that both she and Mr. Ditto would be glad to stay and talk with anyone individually after the meeting. Ms. Maverick was delighted to observe that Mr. Ditto was still excitedly talking with a group of young teachers after everyone else had cleared out and gone home.

References

Burton, William H. *The Guidance of Learning Activities.* New York: Appleton-Century-Crofts, 1952.

Cunningham, Patricia M. "Transferring Comprehension from Listening to Reading." *The Reading Teacher* 29 (1975): 169–72.

Manzo, Anthony V. "Guided Reading Procedure." *Journal of Reading* 18 (1975): 287–91.

Morrison, Henry C. *The Practices of Teaching in the Secondary School.* Chicago: University of Chicago Press, 1931.

Preston, Ralph C. *Teaching Social Studies in the Elementary School.* New York: Holt, Rinehart and Winston, 1968.

Mr. Dunn

HIGHLIGHTS

Informal Reading Inventory

Diagnosing the Ceiling on a Student's
  Reading Ability:
  Word Identification
  Reading Comprehension
  Listening Comprehension

Ceiling Groups

Reading to Students Daily

SQUIRT

Jigsaw-puzzle Activities

Word Identification Instruction:
  Sight Words—Language Master
  Context Clues—Cloze Passages

Increasing Meaning Vocabulary:
  Context Clues
  Morphemic Analysis
  Direct Learning of Words

Translation Writing

Structured Overviews

Juvenile Series

Inferential Comprehension
  Instruction

Censorship

Critical Reading Instruction

Group Realignment

Four-step Vocabulary Building

Building Implicit Questioning

Asking Researchable Questions

Locating Information

Narrowing Research Questions

Using Subject Subheadings

Recording and Organizing
  Information

Mr. Dunn

The Parent Meeting

Ed Dunn sat at his desk waiting for the parents to arrive. The year before at this time he had been nervously rehearsing an almost-memorized speech, but this night he was more confident. His first year of teaching had begun as a challenge, but he soon found himself floundering. He faced discipline problems as well as he could, but every strategy he tried only seemed to make these problems worse. Many of his students had difficulty reading their textbooks, and he had had only one three-hour course in the teaching of reading. He tried teaching phonics during reading class, but the students hated it, calling it babyish and boring. When he asked Mr. Topps if he could paddle two boys who were fighting during recess, he thought the glare would kill him. Happily, with help and guidance from Mr. Topps and other teachers, he began to catch up with the challenge. He planned every period and class beforehand. At Mrs. Flame's suggestion, he made routines of those activities which were getting out of control. Using brightly colored paper to hide their real grade level, he covered easy content texts that he had found in the materials room. By the end of the year, he had survived, if not thrived, and he believed that the students too may have learned something.

Over the summer, Ed had taken two graduate courses in reading at the university. While there, he had asked specific questions of many professors and graduate students. He had read several books and articles beyond those assigned to him, and had participated actively in his courses. In short, he had attempted to learn everything he could about teaching reading.

"Hello, how are you?" he said to each person who came into his room. Not being a native of the community, he didn't know any of the parents personally. "Sit anywhere you like; make yourselves comfortable."

After everyone had arrived and was seated, he began: "Good evening and welcome to your child's fifth-grade classroom. I am Ed Dunn, and I hope to get to know all of you as I teach your children this year. So far we are just learning each other's names, but they do seem to be an interesting group of students.

"During this meeting, I hope to give you an overview of what we will be doing to improve reading, since that is the backbone of all our studies. Even in math, fifth-graders need to be able to follow written directions and to successfully deal with word problems. And in the middle school next year, your children will be expected to read well enough to be more independent.

"This week I am beginning a diagnosis of the reading ability of all the students. Since everyone can improve his or her reading ability, I'm not just trying to locate students with reading problems. Everyone can and should improve his or her reading, so I don't plan to label anyone as disabled or retarded in reading.

"I am going to try to plan instruction to help each student raise the limit on his or her reading. Some students will need to improve their ability to identify words; others will need to improve their ability to comprehend what they read; and some will need to improve their ability to comprehend spoken language. My goal this year is to help each one of your children improve in reading, regardless of where he or she needs to improve.

"Mr. Ditto and I have talked at some length about the type of reading program that your children had with Ms. Maverick and him last year. I was very impressed with their reading-to-learn approach. To some degree, my general approach to reading instruction can be seen as an extension of theirs, but I also hope to begin your children on the road to more responsive reading."

Noticing signs of confusion on several faces, Mr. Dunn moved to the chalkboard. "Let me show you what I mean by responsive reading."

On the board he wrote two sentences:

MR. DUNN WAS BORN ON JANUARY 22.

MR. DUNN WAS BORN EXACTLY ONE MONTH BEFORE GEORGE WASHINGTON'S BIRTHDAY.

He turned to the parents. "How are these sentences alike?"

After some silence, Mrs. Penn raised her hand. "They both seem to say the same thing or, at least, mean the same thing."

Several other parents nodded in agreement.

"All right," said Mr. Dunn. "How are they different?"

Mr. Moore spoke out. "One sentence tells you when your birthday is; the other one, you have to figure it out."

"Very good!" exclaimed Mr. Dunn. "You have to be more *responsive* to the second one if you are to understand what it says. Much of the reading your children will be asked to do in middle and secondary school will require them to read more responsively than they do now."

At this point, a woman dressed in a plain housedress raised her hand, stood up, and began speaking at the same time. "Mr. Dunn, I'm Daphne's grandmother. Don't misunderstand me, please. We've been very happy with Daphne's progress at Merritt Elementary and we've liked all her teachers. But from what we read in the newspaper, it seems like all anyone needs to improve their reading is some good old phonics. Does this other really matter?"

Remembering just the year before when he had thought the same thing, Mr. Dunn began. "There's no doubt that children must learn to identify words if they are going to learn how to read. But some children are 'word callers'; I taught a couple of them last year. One of my students could read orally from a fifth-grade book without missing a word, but couldn't understand what he was reading even from a third-grade book. To say that he needed more phonics, as I did at first, was to doom him to being a poor reader. I was trying to give him a bigger horn, when he couldn't play the one he already had!

"By the time someone reads as well as the average fifth- or sixth-grader, he or she usually can identify most of the words in what he or she reads. To some extent, then, if we don't teach a child to respond more meaningfully to what he or she reads or studies, we allow the child to become an 'advanced word caller'!"

For the reader to do

Obtain a copy of an advanced statistics book or theoretical mathematics book. Turn to the middle of the book and read orally.

Are you a word caller?

Is word identification placing a ceiling on your ability?

Would more phonics help you to read this passage?

● ● ●

"I'm Mike's mother and I just hope all of you realize how fortunate you are that your children have attended Merritt School. We lived here until two years ago when my husband got a promotion with his company and we moved away. Miss Launch, Mrs. Wright, and Miss Nouveau had Mike off to a pretty good start, even though he is a handful. In the other school we were constantly being called in for conferences with his teacher and the principal. We know he spent a lot of time in the principal's office!

"And he kept being referred for one kind of evaluation or another; a reading clinic one time, a school psychologist later. We appreciated all this concern and we know how much trouble he is to handle, but he didn't learn anything there.

"Last spring we decided that my husband would take the first opening in the firm back here even if it meant a cut in pay! That was soon after the day I took an old book off the shelves which Mike used to enjoy. I almost cried: after two years in school, he couldn't read that book a bit better."

Mrs. Penn broke the uncomfortable silence for everyone. "Yes, Mr. Dunn, we are all thankful that our children are here in Merritt Elementary, and we know that the program you have planned for our children will continue to help them grow as they have in the past. We don't always understand the philosophies behind what you do for them, but we know when our children are happy and learning."

Few questions seemed necessary after that, and the meeting came quickly to an end. Mr. Dunn left even more determined to improve the ability of all his students.

Monthly Logs

SEPTEMBER

The second week of school, I began giving Informal Reading Inventories to my students. During the time when I was testing, I scheduled activities for the other students to do as I sat in the back of the room administering the IRI to one child at a time. For one of these activities, they were asked to find all the words they could on a mimeographed sheet covered with rows, columns, and diagonals of letters. Hundreds of words were embedded in these strings of letters.

For another activity, I wrote ten words on the board and asked each student to write as many sentences as he or she could using all the words and only those words for each sentence. These activities had several advantages:

1. The students could perform these activities without my help, freeing me to complete the individual testing;
2. The activities were individualized across a wide range, enabling the poorest students some success, while remaining somewhat challenging for the best students;
3. The activities were interesting for most of the students;
4. The students gained practice in recognizing words and in manipulating syntactic elements;
5. By analyzing their performance on these tasks, I could get some additional information with respect to each student's sight vocabulary and ability to deal with syntactic structures; and
6. The activities did not lose their effectiveness as I interrupted the students for testing.

Mort and Paul put forth very little effort in completing these activities, but at least they did not disturb others who were working. I hope I am able to motivate them to work more than they do presently, but when I am with them individually, as during the IRI, they do exert themselves more than at other times.

Mike, Butch, and Daisy tried to take over the class at first, but, without overreacting, I continued to remind them of what I wanted them to do. I watched for signs of trouble and tried to prevent problems. I ignored what I could ignore, and when I made an assignment I insisted that it be completed.

I was able to average five IRI's a day, and within a week I had completed the testing. My IRI takes longer to give than the more traditional type, but I have more faith in the results. Over the summer, I randomly selected three 200-word passages from the middle third of each basal reader in the series Merritt School uses. One of the three passages from each book served as the passage for the word identification measure, the second passage served for the reading comprehension measure, and the third served for the listening comprehension measure.

During the first part of the testing, I obtained a word identification level for the student. He or she was given the word identification passage from the 2^2 book and asked to read it orally. As it was read, I made a written record of miscues. Based on how many miscues were made during this reading, I decided which word identification passage I would next use. A student's word identification level is the level of the basal at which the student makes no more than five uncorrected miscues per hundred words (not counting pauses or repetitions as miscues), before falling below the 95 percent word accuracy level on two consecutive passages.

After the student's word identification level was determined, I obtained a reading comprehension level for him. Beginning with the basal level two books below his word identification level, I asked the student to read the reading comprehension passage silently. When he or she finished, I removed the passage and asked the eight questions I had constructed from that passage. A student's reading comprehension level is the level of the basal at which the student misses no more than two of the eight questions, before falling below the 75 percent comprehension level on two consecutive passages.

The questions were difficult to make up because one must be certain that the student cannot answer the question unless the passage was understood. If a question is based on general knowledge, the student may know the answer to that question before reading the passage. For example, a question following a story which asked, "What were singing in the trees?" would only be a good question if the correct answer was not "birds." Otherwise, students who were unable to understand the story could still correctly answer the question because they know that birds usually sing in trees.

When I had determined the word identification and reading comprehension levels for the student, I obtained a listening comprehension level. Beginning at his or her reading comprehension level, I read the listening comprehension passage to the student and then asked eight questions which had been constructed the same way as the questions for the reading comprehension passages. The student's listening comprehension level was the highest level at which he or she answered six or more of the eight questions before failing to do so on two basal passages in a row.

For the reader to do

Compare and contrast Mr. Dunn's IRI with the one Miss Nouveau used. How are they alike in important ways? How are they different in important ways? Which one takes longer to give? Which one produces more information? Which one would you prefer to use?

● ● ●

After I had used the IRI to obtain profiles for each of my twenty-four students, I entered this information on a chart and began to analyze each profile to determine the probable limiting factor or ceiling on each child's reading ability.

Tentative Profiles Obtained from Informal Reading Inventory

Name	Word Identification Level	Reading Comprehension Level	Listening Comprehension Level
Alex	5	5	6
Betty	8	7	8
Butch	3^1	3^2	3^2
Carl	5	5	6
Chip	4	4	4
Daisy	2^2	3^1	4
Daphne	5	5	5
Hilda	7	8	8
Horace	5	6	7
Jeff	5	3^2	3^2
Joyce	6	6	7
Larry	8+	8+	8+
Mandy	8	8+	8+
Manuel	6	6	7
Michelle	6	5	8
Mike	1^2	2^2	5
Mitch	5	5	6
Mort	5	4	3^1
Pat	8+	8	8+
Paul	2^1	2^1	2^1
Rita	7	7	6
Roberta	6	7	8
Steve	5	5	6
Tanana	5	4	3^2

The step-by-step method by which I interpreted the profiles to estimate each student's ceiling works as follows:

1. I first look at the child's word identification score. If that score is fifth grade or above, I cross it out. (If word identification is fifth grade or above, it cannot be the ceiling.)
2. I then look at the child's reading comprehension score. If that score is sixth-grade level or above, I cross out the *listening comprehension score*. (When reading comprehension is sixth-grade or above, listening comprehension cannot be the ceiling.)
3. The limiting factor or ceiling on the student's reading ability is the lowest score of those which remain after Steps 1 and 2 have been completed.

   If there is a tie for the lowest score and if listening is involved in that tie, listening comprehension is the ceiling;

   If there is a tie for the lowest score and listening is not involved in that tie, word identification is the ceiling.

This breakdown is based on several assumptions. When a student is able to identify words in fifth-grade level material, he or she has mastered basic sight vocabulary in context and is able to visually sample the graphic information on a page. Additional word identification ability should come in conjunction with meaning vocabulary building and not in isolation from it. Meaning vocabulary building is an integral part of reading comprehension improvement.

At reading comprehension levels of sixth grade and above, listening no longer sets a limit on reading ability. At easier levels, material is less difficult to comprehend both literally and inferentially if students listen to it rather than read it. Material written at about sixth-grade level and above becomes as easy or easier to comprehend when read as when listened to.

Although Mrs. Flame and other teachers at Merritt School use an IRI to place students at their instructional level in our basal reading series, I do not use mine for that purpose since I do not use the basal in my class. Instead, I use my version of the IRI to determine what aspect of reading is limiting a student's growth at a particular time. Based on this type of IRI interpretation, I have placed my twenty-four students in four ceiling groups as follows:

1. Students with word identification ceilings:
   Daisy   Butch

2. Students with listening comprehension ceilings:
   Jeff   Tanana
   Chip   Mort
   Daphne

3. Students with reading comprehension ceilings, and reading comprehension scores equal to fifth grade or below:

Alex   Michelle
Carl   Mitch

4. Students with reading comprehension ceilings, and reading comprehension scores equal to sixth grade or above:

Betty   Larry
Hilda   Manuel
Horace   Mandy
Joyce   Roberta
Pat

For the reader to do

Mike, Paul, Rita, and Steve have not been placed in the ceiling groups. Determine which group each belongs in based on his or her IRI profile.

● ● ●

It took me a hectic week to complete giving the IRI's and several hours during my weekend to check and chart the scores, and to interpret the profiles. By this time, we had already established some routines. Every day during the last fifteen minutes before lunch, I read to the whole class from a work of children's literature. The book is chosen based on my estimate of its quality. I believe every student should be read to daily from interesting, high-quality literature, even in the upper grades!

At 1 p.m. every day, of course, we participate in school-wide SQUIRT. We started out reading fifteen minutes, but it is apparent that we will be able to increase this amount of time without difficulty. Everyone, even Mike, seems to look forward to this quiet and relaxing time after lunch. Miss Page, the school librarian, is very willing to cooperate in helping me to have a wide choice of books for the students to choose from. I bring my morning newspaper from home each day, and when I finish with a magazine I bring it to school as well to add to the school's current reading materials. We do have a stack of comic books, but few students ever choose them now. At first, several students did read comic books, but only Butch and Mort still do. All in all, I try to have at least 100 different books, magazines, and newspapers for my twenty-four students to select from.

My reading program is actually a mixture of whole-group, small-group, and individual activities. The sustained silent reading of SQUIRT and the follow-up voluntary discussion of what individuals are reading is conducted in a group setting, as is my reading to the students.

We engage in a variety of small-group activities, each type of activity requiring a different grouping pattern. The majority of activities are designed to raise the various ceilings which the students seem to have on their reading ability. For these activities, the students are instructed in ceiling groups. The word identification and listening comprehension ceiling groups receive instruction in improving word identification and listening. The reading comprehension ceiling group with reading comprehension scores of sixth grade and above receive instruction in meaning vocabulary, inferential comprehension, critical reading, and study skills. The reading comprehension ceiling group with reading comprehension scores of fifth grade and below receive instruction in meaning vocabulary and in literal and inferential comprehension taught through listening-to-reading transfer lessons like Mr. Ditto uses. Occasionally we have skills instruction where students are grouped according to the degree of mastery of a skill they indicate. At other times, we have interest grouping where the students group themselves by choosing from several alternative activities. Also, we have random groupings and mixed groupings. These latter types of groupings are designed to make groups which have a maximum range and variety of abilities within each group. Jigsaw-puzzle activities (Aronson, 1975) are most appropriate with mixed groupings. The other day, for example, I noticed that many of the students were becoming unusually competitive. Competitiveness certainly has its good side, but so does cooperation, and it appeared to me that the relationship between the two was out of balance. Butch attacked Larry with a stick after Larry had gotten a science experiment to work when Butch had given up on it. Daisy and Mike jumped on Paul, verbally and physically, when the three of them were reading silently and Paul dropped his book on the floor.

To build a spirit of cooperation, I first put the students in four mixed groups of six. Each of these groups had a common experience unique to that group. The first day, the lesson centered on Dwight D. Eisenhower. One group heard me read a section from a biography of Eisenhower which described his boyhood. Another group heard a taped section from that same biography about Ike's days at West Point. The third group listened to excerpts from a record about World War II which told about Eisenhower's role as Allied Commander, and the fourth group watched a film-strip about Eisenhower's presidency.

Following these activities, six new groups of four were formed by taking a member from each of the four previous groups to make a new group. In the new groupings, each of the four had one—and only one—piece of the whole picture of Eisenhower's life. These groups of four were instructed to share what they had learned in the other groups so that every member would know all four parts of the puzzle.

After the discussions were completed, each student was given a multiple-choice/true-false test on the life of Eisenhower. I constructed the test so that my students with reading or writing problems would still be able to show that they had learned the content. Almost everyone did well on the test, even Paul, Daisy, and Mort.

The next time we grouped for "jigsaw puzzle activities" around four different experiences, I noticed slightly more cooperation. All the children had begun to realize that they had to learn what each member of the group knew. Questioning improved, and the students began treating each other somewhat more courteously in their groups. As September draws to a close, I believe that a trend toward more cooperation and less competitiveness has begun in my classroom.

OCTOBER

Compared with last year, my discipline problems have been minimal. The jigsaw-puzzle activities have helped make the class more cooperative, and the classroom meetings (Glasser, 1969) which we began this month have given the students an outlet for their concerns as well as a method of solving both personal and academic problems.

As I get to know my students better, I wonder just how typical they are! Larry is every bit as intelligent as I am, and his knowledge of science is actually astounding. Occasionally I wonder if he couldn't teach the class. The students ask him for help as often and as willingly as they ask me.

Mike either cannot or will not stay at any task or in any one place for more than a minute or two. He does not defy me, but he does require constant reminding. Regularly, he finds mischief of such a devilish kind.

Betty, Tanana, Daphne, and Michelle are fast friends, which is not unusual of course, but individually they are such diverse people. Betty is a perfectionist who almost always succeeds. Tanana's interest in nature has dominated all her other interests. Daphne has a tremendous imagination. And Michelle has developed a flair for all the arts and crafts projects.

This month I have tried to help Daisy, Butch, and Mike with their word identification problems. By looking at Butch's word identification level (3^1), I could tell that he probably knows basic sight words. Daisy knows most of these basic words, also, but Mike does not. Every day this month, Mike has been taking a stack of twenty-five A and P words to the Language Master* with the instruction to come to me when he could read all twenty-five. At first, he would come back in just a few minutes and say that he knew them all. When I shuffled them and went through them with him, he would usually miss several—he was not staying with the task. That was when I began to use the kitchen timer with him. At first I set the timer for five minutes and told Mike that he had to sit at the Language Master until the timer rang. He is able to sit relatively still for SQUIRT when the timer is on fifteen minutes, but that may be because it's right after lunch.

---

* Piece of equipment often used to provide drill on basic sight vocabulary.

When the timer rings, he is allowed to do another activity. Later, he goes back to work with the Language Master and I set the timer for five minutes again. When he seems to be comfortable with five minutes, I put the timer on six minutes. By adding a minute at a time, and only when he is comfortable with the time period already set, we have worked up to the point that Mike is now able to sit for eight minutes, and he is learning the A and P words. He knows the first 200 perfectly, and he is reading some high interest, low vocabulary novels.

Daisy and Butch do not work well together but they do not fight either, and so they have been paired for completing cloze passages to improve their mastery of context clues. The advantage of having them work together is that with only one cloze passage between them, they must agree on their choice for a blank. Their discussions on what to put in each blank is the real lesson for them. At first, I used either Steve or Horace as tutors to get them started, but now the two usually work independently.

For the reader to do

A cloze passage is one in which certain words have been deleted (and replaced with a uniform blank) or blacked out, so that students must use context clues to figure out the deleted word. (Leaving out every tenth word or every third noun are two of many possibilities.) Construct a cloze passage.

● ● ●

For the students who have listening comprehension as the apparent ceiling on their ability, I have been structuring daily directed listening lessons as well as weekly guided listening procedures. Mr. Ditto has helped with the listening. I read to them for the guided listening procedures, but for the directed listening lessons, I check out records from the library. After a few minutes of readiness building, they can listen to the record through earphones while I work with other groups.

The students receiving listening-to-reading transfer lessons are making great progress. Steve and Alex are so good at following the sequence now when reading that even tricky flashbacks do not throw them. All the students in this group are very capable, and this transfer type of lesson really makes it clear just what they are being asked to do when they read to satisfy previously stated purposes. I could be wrong, but I believe these five students have already raised their comprehension ability beyond where further listening-to-reading transfer can help them. Soon they will be included in the activities that Betty's group are doing.

As for Betty's group, this month has been a time of building meaning vocabulary. Both Larry and Pat have tremendous vocabularies, but in some respects still have skills they can learn. The rest of them definitely have improved their meaning vocabulary skills. I have taught them three ways of dealing with meanings of words in difficult material: (1) use of context clues; (2) use of morphemic analysis; and (3) direct learning of specific words and their meanings.

All of the students in Betty's group are capable users of context already, so they do not need basic context clue instruction. On the other hand, there are still some subtleties of context clue usage which I have attempted to teach them this month. The first week, each student had a dictionary from the set of school dictionaries in our room. I projected a transparency of a passage with several words I was sure most of the children did not know. The following is a selection from one of those transparencies:

> Whenever Bob writes *lyrics*, he uses lots of *tropes*. For his mother's last *occasion*, he recited one of his *ditties*. Her guests, however, took him *literally* and threw him in the pond.

The students individually looked up each underlined word and decided which definition of that word matched its use in the passage. The students discussed their choices for each word and defended their reasoning. Eventually, students were given individual activities to complete before discussion took place. Hilda enjoyed these activities the most.

These lessons gave way to lessons in using morphemic analysis, although I never called it that in front of the students! We began by learning the meanings associated with each common prefix, but we did not simply memorize them as that is the way they were taught to me, and I was never able to use them comfortably until now. In other words, the students and I learned them together.

At first we restricted our work to prefixes, then worked on suffixes, and then finally worked on roots. Harris and Sipay (1975) have recommended that the seventeen prefixes that together account for the prefixes in more than 82 percent of the words with prefixes be taught:

ab	ob, of, op
ad, ap, at	pre, pro
be	re
con, com, col	post
de	super
dis	trans
en, em	sub
ex	un
in, im	

Rather than teaching a definition or synonym for each prefix, I presented pairs of sentences which allowed the students to speculate on the contribution of a prefix. For example, when teaching the prefix *dis*, I wrote these sentences on the board:

On the first night in the castle, a ghost *appeared*.
After that, the guests *disappeared*.

The soldier *charged* the gun by loading it.
The soldier *discharged* the gun by firing it.

The contribution of *dis* in each sentence pair was discussed by the group. When all sentence pairs had been covered, the students were asked to suggest rules or definitions which generalized the contribution of the prefix to all the root words. Following the recording of several possible generalizations, new words were written on the board and the students speculated on their meanings:

dis*close*
dis*seat*
dis*part*
dis*serve*

Similar lessons were taught around the other prefixes, as well as the most important roots and suffixes (Harris and Sipay, 1975). Pat, Horace, and Larry have been using the prefixes, suffixes, and roots which we have been studying to make up words not in the dictionary. They present these words to the group and try to come up with definitions for the word which are compatible with the contributions of the parts. Horace said, "I hope we don't get 'aborteous' (carried away) with this thing!"

Most of the direct teaching of vocabulary has taken place in the content subjects we study. For the seven students who are simply unable to read the textbooks we have for social studies and science, we do translation writing. I select portions from a chapter which I really want to get across to the students, and present these portions orally as part of directed listening lessons. Of course, as part of readiness for a DLL, new and important vocabulary terms used in that selection are introduced. This directed listening lesson then acts as the common experience for a group language experience story. The students dictate what they believe to be an accurate retelling or translation of the passage they have heard me read to them and I record their dictation on the board. As they use vocabulary in their retelling which was introduced to them in the DLL, I point out this usage and we discuss the words. The students copy the group experience story from the board in their notebooks as I record it. This copy serves as a textbook they can read and study.

For the rest of the students, we discuss groups of related words at the same time. The words are selected by me based on the importance they have in the transmission of content material we are studying. Rather than looking up definitions for these words, we use the words to discuss the topic which the words have in common. These structured overviews (Barron, 1969) help build readiness for learning a content unit as well as build meaning vocabulary particular to that unit. When I recently introduced a unit in math on metric measurement, I began by writing the word *measurement* on the board. We discussed what measurement is and why it is necessary. Then under *measurement* I wrote the words, *volume, length,* and *weight,* and we discussed each of those terms. Then under each type of measurement, I wrote the various metric units of measure. Of course, they soon noticed that the root word for *volume* is the liter; for weight, the gram; and for length, the meter. And they also noticed that the same prefixes are used in all three types. Following this overview, they were ready to learn the content and were already somewhat familiar with the basic concepts and terminology with which that content would be expressed.

good!

For the reader to do

Diagram Mr. Dunn's structured overview for metric measurement as it probably looked. Use straight lines to show the relationship between a word and its subdivisions. Design a structured overview of your own.

● ● ●

NOVEMBER

This month started with two visits: Daphne's grandmother came to school, and I went to see Daisy's mother. Mrs. Field was concerned that Daphne was developing some very bad habits. "Mr. Dunn, maybe you can help us decide what to do. This fall my husband and I have noticed that Daphne is hard to get up in the morning. Every year before, she's always jumped right out of bed. The other night I went to her room after midnight and there she was under the cover with a flashlight reading a *Nancy Drew* book!

"I asked the public librarian and she said that Daphne has checked out over fifteen of them in the past two months. We want her to read better books than that. What do you think we ought to do?"

I tried to reassure her. "Yes, Daphne has been reading *Nancy Drew* in SQUIRT every day since school started."

Mrs. Field frowned slightly. "You mean you allow them to read those series? Aren't all the books alike anyway?"

"Juvenile series do have some positive attributes," I explained. "They interest many children in reading. Once the reading habit is formed, books of greater literary quality can be introduced. These books also provide lots of easy reading which is the way many children practice the skills they have learned in reading instructional time at school. Don't worry, every good reader I've known read both comic books and one or more juvenile series at Daphne's age. If these books didn't cause them to be good readers, they at least didn't prevent them from becoming good readers.

"I would suggest that you give Daphne time to read before she goes to bed so that she won't miss her sleep. I agree with you that she needs proper rest, but please don't be alarmed about these juvenile mysteries."

I haven't heard any more about it, but Daphne has continued to read *Nancy Drew* during SQUIRT. Whether that nineteen minutes a day is all the *Nancy Drew* she gets is another question!

For readers to do together

Survey your class to see how many of those who now enjoy reading used to read juvenile series books. Let those who read juvenile series books talk about them and explain why they read them. *Ask these questions to my students*
Do the same with comic books.

● ● ●

My trip to see Daisy's mother was a failure, I fear. I had watched Daisy refuse to eat anything that wasn't sweet or starchy during lunch every day. She had been growing noticeably larger around the middle and subsequently more lazy with her assignments, but her mother was not concerned about Daisy at all. In fact, all I heard in the time I was there was how awful all her teachers had been: Daisy could do no wrong, and her teachers had done no right. I hate to think what she will say about me. Poor Daisy, destined to be fat and lazy, I'm afraid. I am requiring her to work and learn in my room, but I doubt if she will become self-motivated.

On the bright side, the students have loved the book I have read to them this month, *Mrs. Frisby and the Rats of NIMH* by Robert C. O'Brien (1971). It had everyone writing stories about these and other rats. By reading to them just before lunch, we all seem to relax and enjoy eating better. Certainly, I seldom have any discipline problems in the cafeteria. After lunch, we all enjoy a quiet time for our own reading.

In social studies, math, and science, we are continuing to build meaning vocabulary through structured overviews and directed listening lessons in combination with translation writing. Unlike last year, I haven't allowed the reading problems of some of my students to prevent them from learning these content subjects.

Daisy, Butch, and Mike are still working on improving word identification, although Mike has really made a lot of progress. He knows the first

250 A and P words without hesitation, and has read five high interest, low vocabulary novels. Even though he is still active and mischievous, when I am reading to the class and during SQUIRT, he is almost a model student. Butch and Daisy have finally refused to work together and I have stopped requiring them to, except for very short items and specific purposes. Generally they work individually on cloze passages which have every tenth word deleted and which have the initial sound in each blank. They work together in this case to see how many they do not agree on! They talk about those and come to me if there is one they cannot agree on.

The other students have worked on improving inferential comprehension this month. Since no one seemed to be very good at making inferences, I combined the listening comprehension ceiling group with the listening-to-reading transfer ceiling group. The listening group worked on making inferences while listening, and Betty's group worked on making inferences while reading. The type of lessons the two different groups got were not different, except that one group listened to a story while the other group read a story. For several of the lessons, the story was the same for both groups, enabling the whole class to work together. On these occasions, I included Mike, Butch, and Daisy in the listening group so they would not feel that they were the only ones left out of the lesson.

A typical lesson went this way. The ones who would read the story went to the corner of the room where we sit for SQUIRT. The others gathered in the opposite corner of the room where they listened to me read them the story. In the beginning I picked stories which were mostly characterizations. Following the reading/listening phase, everyone was given a copy of the story and sat facing the board. I began by asking, "What do you know about the character? Tell me everything you know."

As different students raised their hands or expressed facially that they knew some characteristics of the person, I first called on those I knew would only know a few things to say. After they made their contributions, Larry, Hilda, and Pat would be sure to point out things that even I had missed. Soon we had a sizable number of features and facts about the character written on the board. When our list was fairly complete, I asked everyone to take five minutes to locate in the passage the place where each feature or fact had been given to them by the writer.

After five minutes, I asked for hands and, again, called first on those who wouldn't have anything left to say after others had contributed. Each time someone would read a part which really did make a characteristic clear, I would draw a line through that item on our list. Eventually, all the items which remained on the board without lines through them were the features and facts which the students had inferred about the character. I then asked, "How did you know these? Tell me how you came up with these."

A good discussion usually followed, and I made sure that students were clear as to how they really had been able to figure out those items. I then asked, "What did you have to know before you read the story that would allow you to figure out these things about the person?"

Soon we had a list of prior concepts which the students believed they had used in making the inference about the character. Then we tried to use that list of prior concepts with the lists of inferred characteristics to infer other, more complex characteristics. Finally, I asked questions like, "What political party would he belong to today?" and "What color clothes did he wear, do you think?" In each case, when a student made a guess or prediction, I would require an explanation of what the student knew, either literally from the passage or prior to reading the passage or both, which led to that guess or prediction.

Of course, these lessons were all designed to teach the students to synthesize background information with literal understanding of the passage in order to go beyond the passage. The guidance which I provided was to allow divergent and creative responses while requiring a clear explanation of the thinking behind each response.

We extended this kind of approach to the reading of poetry later on in the month. In this case, the procedure helped the students to see that poems often require more prior concepts than they do literal comprehension. And since we have gone through several poems in this way, there seems to have been a rekindling of interest in poetry among the students. I even received an anonymous love poem the other day! Alas, the handwriting tells me that Roberta has a crush on her teacher.

For readers to do together

Go through a poem or passage, following the steps in Mr. Dunn's inferential comprehension lesson. Become aware of how concepts are synthesized to make inferences.

● ● ●

DECEMBER

Poor Roberta! I now know the meaning of the word *pine*. I asked Mr. Topps what to do about student crushes, and whether I should call Mrs. Smith to talk to her about the situation.

"No, Ed. I don't believe so. You will have a certain amount of this happening to you as long as you're in teaching. Why, it may surprise you to know that even I get an occasional anonymous love letter. The important thing is to continue to treat Roberta fairly and positively. You can't lead her on by giving her extra attention; you shouldn't hurt her feelings by belittling her or by ignoring her. And don't make a big thing of it. Calling her mother might just do that."

In effect, he had asked me to walk a tightrope, and so far I have done so. She still smiles at me a lot when she thinks I don't see. Unfortunately, Hilda seems to be coming down with the same malady. If only I had this kind of luck with more mature women!

This month began with a controversy over a book. Near the end of November, I began reading *The Little Fishes* by Erik Haugaard (1967) each day before lunch. Never have I had such interest in a book on the part of the students. It is a sad tale about orphan beggars in Italy during World War II, and it is beautifully told. When I read it, everyone was totally still and quiet. It was not unusual to see tears in certain eyes when the story became especially intense.

One day when we were a little over half finished with the book, an office messenger brought a note from Mrs. Mainstay. Daisy's mother had called and wanted permission to come and have lunch with our class. Of course, I returned a message to the office that she was welcome to come.

Just as I opened *The Little Fishes* at our place and began reading, there was a knock on the classroom door. The door opened and in came Daisy's mother. Naturally, she was invited in and was given a chair; then I continued with our reading. Part of what I read included a part in which the main characters are captured by a cruel and unscrupulous man. The students were on the edge of their seats, including Daisy. Even Paul seemed interested in what was going on. In the middle of my reading, Daisy's mother stood and stalked out of the room. I didn't hesitate in my reading. Daisy sat glued to her chair.

After we were seated with our trays in the cafeteria, I was called to the office. When I arrived, Mr. Topps and Daisy's mother were there. I went in and closed the door behind us.

Daisy's mother was seething as Mr. Topps turned to me. "Mr. Dunn, Daisy's mother is disturbed about the book you are reading to your students." Facing her, he asked, "Would you please tell us both your objection to the book?"

"I certainly will! I try to protect Daisy against this kind of book. When she told me what she was hearing at school, I just had to hear it for myself."

"And what is she hearing?" asked Mr. Topps.

"About beggars and wars and cruel people. Sad, unhappy stories. Children are supposed to be happy. They should always have what they need to be happy."

("And be spoiled and lazy like Daisy," I thought, but didn't say.)

 Mr. Topps paused momentarily and then explained. "If you do not want Daisy to hear the rest of the book, she may come to the office during that time and study her lessons here. Meanwhile, I will read a copy of the book and I recommend that you do the same. When you have read the book, if you are still concerned about it, you may come and we will discuss it."

I left the office and returned to my room. Each day when I was to read from the book, Daisy had to go to the office to sit. I felt sorry for her because she cried every time she had to leave. But she didn't have to hear anything unhappy; she only had to be unhappy.

This incident led me to begin the teaching of critical reading. I felt that the students needed to be able to make value judgments about what they read if we were ever going to get beyond the stage of dealing with books as propaganda for or against somebody's cause.

Our first discussion of critical reading issues occurred in a classroom meeting soon after the incident with Daisy's mother. These meetings are conducted on the basis that the students are free to express and work out problems. The teacher guides the discussion with questions but does not use the meeting to further his or her own opinions or to correct the opinions of the students. We have had daily classroom meetings since September, and by now the meetings are active, thoughtful sessions in which almost everyone regularly participates. It is our last activity during the school day.

On this occasion, I began the meeting with the question, "Do you like *The Little Fishes*?" Everyone did. Some, like Betty, said it was too sad; others, like Pat, Horace, and Larry, said it was too short. But all said they liked the book.

Next I asked, "What if someone didn't like the book?"

"They would be wrong," said Mitch. Almost everyone else agreed with him.

"But how do you *know* that person is wrong? How would you convince that person to like the book?" I needed to ask no more questions. The rest of the meeting was a lively discussion which raised several important issues:

Is the quality of a book just a matter of opinion?
Is everyone's opinion as good as everyone else's?
Is it enough to say you like or don't like a book?

This discussion served as the groundwork for the unit I taught on critical reading. The books which students were reading or had read for SQUIRT served as the raw material for that unit.

Our first task in becoming more critical readers was to deal with the standards we use to measure whether or not a book or story is a good one. Every student in the class was asked to pick two books that he or she had read or was reading. Each student was asked to choose the book he or she had liked most and also the book he or she had liked the least. When everyone had selected two books, we examined them to determine ways in which they differed that made one book better than the other.

Pat chose between her books by saying: "For one thing, the pictures are really pretty in this one, but they are dull and flat in the other one."

I wrote *quality of illustrations* on the top of one side of the board.

Butch chose the thinnest of his two books "'cause it's short."

Larry said that he liked long books better, although both of his books happened to have been of the same length.

I added *length of book* to the list on the board.

After a few days, we had a list of fifteen standards which the students seemed to understand, and which at least one person in the class used to decide which of two books or stories he or she liked best. At no point did I try to eliminate any standard which anyone had suggested, even though we did combine some similar suggestions.

Our second task, then, was to determine the relative importance of these standards. Is the length of a book, for example, as important as the characterization in that book for determining its value? For this part of the unit, we talked about books or passages which I presented to the class. If the book was short, I read it to them; if we used a selection that was short enough, I put it on a transparency and used an overhead projector.

The first selection we talked about was *My Grandson Lew*, a picture book by Charlotte Zolotow (1974). After I presented the book to them, I asked Larry if he liked it. When he said yes, I asked him if he didn't like longer books better. He said, "I like a lot of long books, but a book can still be good even if it is short."

By this process of discussion, the students were constantly asked to make choices between two or more standards. I tried to present selections which differed markedly, depending on which standards were to be examined. I picked books with great illustrations and dull characterizations, and books with dull illustrations and great characters.

Finally the students were asked to rank the fifteen standards we were using in the order of importance. They were totally unable to agree. Butch was actually going to hit Larry at one point, and Roberta was constantly heard exclaiming, "Oh, Betty!" After all, even professional critics cannot agree on which criteria to judge pieces of writing!

Each student then was asked to individually rank the fifteen standards and keep this ranking in his or her notebook. The remainder of the critical reading unit was spent by having the students choose books to read for SQUIRT and to take home. Each book the child read was to be checked off against each of the fifteen standards as good or bad. Whenever we met for our one-to-one conferences, which I try to have every two weeks or so, we discussed what the student was reading in terms of the standards and the ranking he or she had given them.

The day we let out school for the holidays, I asked Mr. Topps what had ever happened about Daisy's mother, if she had come back or called.

"No, Ed, I think we defused that situation pretty well. Censorship is a deforming and incurable disease, and, once, caught, there is nothing that can be done about it. The only thing that can be done to try to prevent it is to have parents place their faith in the school, and by handling individual complaints in a firm and reasonable manner the way I tried to in this case. Once people come looking for ideas and books to censor, it is no longer possible to have a good instructional program."

All I could say was, "Thank you for standing by me," but he was already walking toward a child who was trying to give him a present that I'm sure was a tie.

For readers to do together

Compile a list of different standards on which members of the class claim to evaluate books.

Ask each person to rank the standards by their importance. Randomly group and have students compare rankings.

● ● ●

JANUARY

I began this month by realigning the ceiling groups. Mike still requires word identification instruction but Daisy and Butch now listen and identify words better than they comprehend when reading. I placed them in the reading comprehension ceiling group which receives listening-to-reading transfer lessons regularly. There they should begin to learn that they can understand what they read in the same way they understand the books I read to them.

Everyone who received listening comprehension instruction in the fall is now also in that listening-to-reading transfer group with the exception of Daphne. She has improved her reading so much that she is certainly ready to join Betty, Pat, and the others. (I wonder if all those *Nancy Drew* books might have helped!) This realignment is intended to help Jeff, Chip, and the others to transfer their improved listening abilities to reading. I have also moved Alex, Michelle, and Steve to Betty's group because they did so well during the first four months of school. With these changes the ceiling groups are now:

1. Students needing word identification instruction:
   Mike

2. Students needing listening-to-reading transfer instruction:
   Daisy   Tanana
   Jeff   Mitch
   Butch   Mort
   Chip   Paul
   Carl

3. Students needing vocabulary and study skills instruction:

Alex	Larry
Betty	Michelle
Daphne	Manuel
Hilda	Mandy
Horace	Roberta
Joyce	Rita
Pat	Steve

As soon as these group realignments were made, we began intensive reading instruction. Of course, we continued to do SQUIRT as a whole group; we read for twenty-two minutes now each day without interruption. Each SQUIRT session is regularly followed by five to ten minutes of voluntary discussion of what individuals are reading and enjoying.

I also am continuing to read to the whole class each day. During January, I read several of my favorite Sherlock Holmes stories to them. Everyone seems to have enjoyed them, especially Hilda and Larry, who usually figure out the ending ahead of time. That boy is a genius; I am sure of it.

Mike knows basic sight words, but is unable to do mediated word identification (decoding). In addition to being read to and participating in SQUIRT, Mike's reading program now consists of lots of easy reading with exercises in completing sentences, and cloze passages which require him to use context clues plus initial consonant letters to figure out the missing word. As often as I can, I work with Mike individually on inductive phonics lessons to teach him to use initial blends and digraphs as word identification clues.

The listening-to-reading transfer group continues to have directed and guided listening lessons with specific purposes to listen for, followed immediately by directed and guided reading lessons with the same purposes to read for. We also do four-step vocabulary building exercises which teach them to read, spell, and understand new words. We add these word meanings to both their reading and listening vocabularies (Crist, 1975).

As a group we select a theme for each week of vocabulary building. The theme may come from a content-area unit with which we are presently dealing, like weather or Australia. Or the theme may be a topic which the students are especially interested in, like food or sports. Once a theme is adopted, each lesson has four parts:

1. For the first third of the lesson, we sit as a group and discuss the theme we have chosen. I have prepared for the discussion, and some students have as well, by selecting words which the students probably do not know but which I feel they should learn. As we discuss the theme, we make a conscious effort to introduce these words in meaningful context, however ridiculous a turn the conversation may take. Each time a new word is introduced I write it on

the board and each student copies it on a page in his or her notebook. We discuss each word until everyone feels he or she understands its meaning.

2. For the second third of the session, the students pair off for one-to-one talk sessions. The requirement is that each student use each one of the new words in a meaningful context at least once in talking to the other.

3. For the final third of the time, each student writes a theme trying to use every one of the new words in a meaningful context. These papers are collected and are corrected only for spelling and proper inclusion of the specific words being learned.

4. The beginning of the next vocabulary lesson is spent by having me read two or three themes aloud. I select these on the basis of how cleverly and how well the students used the words being studied. Of course, this fourth part serves as review of the words studied in the previous lesson.

The remainder of the students had already worked on building vocabulary, inferential comprehension, and critical reading during the fall. Over the holidays I decided that the time had come for them to become independent learners. Beginning this month and for the rest of the school year, they will be improving their skills with respect to asking and answering major study questions. While their comprehension abilities are remarkable, they have not learned how to use these abilities to extend their own knowledge. Most of them read a lot from books on various topics, but when we have a question in social studies class, they refer to the encyclopedia and copy from it. My goal is to move them beyond this meager level of study skills development.

In this case a technique was used to build implicit questions in the mind of both questioner and answerer. Each student in the group was asked to write down a topic which he or she was most interested in and which he or she knew something about. Larry chose scientific crime investigation, while Mandy chose computers. Hilda wanted police duties as her topic, while Michelle chose human biology, of all things. The other choices, for the most part, were equally diverse and unusual.

After I had collected and made a record of each topic chosen, I made an assignment. Each day, three of the group were to bring in objects, pictures, or other examples with which they could demonstrate their knowledge about their chosen topics. Each one of the three students was given one half-hour and a corner of the room in which to exhibit his or her object or picture. The rest of the class was divided into three random groupings. Each group spent ten minutes at each exhibit and then all the groups moved to the next exhibit. The activity at each exhibit went like this: the students could ask the exhibitor any question about the object or picture, and the exhibitor had to try to answer the question. If the exhibitor could not answer a question satisfactorily about the exhibit, he or she had to write that question on a sheet of paper. At the end of the exhibition period, I had an individual conference with the student to discuss why the questions might have been impossible or difficult to answer. In most instances, the students seemed unaware that there was so much they didn't know about the things they thought they knew about!

At the end of a week, each of the fourteen members of this group had participated in this activity. Most had found it interesting and informative. Everyone had enjoyed trying to stump the exhibitor even though the exhibitor did know quite a lot about his or her object.

This activity gave way to a more sophisticated form of question formulation. At the beginning of the next week after the daily exhibits, I put a box with a slit in the top by the desk in the back of the room. On the box was written, "Stump Mr. Dunn!" The students were each allowed one question about their topic which they were sure I would not know the answer to. At the end of each day, I would choose two questions blindly from the box. I had until first thing the next morning to find an answer to each question and to have some source for my answer to back it up. If I was unable to answer the question, but the student who had asked it could answer it, I had been "stumped" by that student. Competition ran high. Some of the questions were dillies. Daphne asked me how many people were living in Rhode Island in 1900; Manuel asked me the name of the style of type used to print the daily newspaper!

In every case except two I was able to find the answer to the questions. Pat stumped me over a detail of Louisa May Alcott's life, and Mandy stumped me on a detail in computer hardware! (I found information about Mandy's question, but couldn't understand what it said.) In answering each question, I explained where and how I had found the answer and how long it had taken me. I was trying to model or simulate for the students how to go about finding answers to questions, and to demonstrate that if one knows how, he or she can find the answer to most questions, even "stumpers," in a relatively short time.

After these three weeks or so of activities, I felt that I had accomplished several goals:

1. The students had selected topics which interested them and which they already knew something about;
2. The students had discovered specific areas of these topics which they knew little about and they had discussed reasons for their gaps of knowledge;
3. They had practiced asking stimulating and difficult questions of each other and of their teacher;
4. They had witnessed how successfully one can learn answers to difficult and stimulating questions if one has the ability to use sources where the answers are stored.

For the rest of the month, the fourteen members of this group and I spent at least thirty minutes per day asking researchable questions about suggested topics. A topic would be selected and we would list possible questions. When questions were exhausted, we would select the most interesting questions which we felt could be answered by research. We made no attempt to answer the questions, only to ask them during the session. To minimize frustration, at the end of each session I answered the questions that I knew and suggested a source in which interested students might find an answer for those questions which I could not answer.

This has been the month of caterpillar jokes! What monster have I created?

Early in the month during science class we were discussing the four stages of metamorphosis of certain insects. As a part of this lesson, Butch and Mitch each brought in live caterpillars in a jar. In a moment of weakness, I asked the class, with a straight face, "What do you call a baby caterpillar?"

When no one responded, I answered, "A kitty-pillar!"

Everyone laughed loudly at the joke and we went back to discussing insect development. Before long, Horace raised his hand, "When does a caterpillar go the fastest?" After a short pause, he said, "When it's being chased by a dogerpillar!" This, of course, brought a new round of laughter.

Ever since, during recess, lunch, and occasionally, in class there has been an epidemic of caterpillar joke-telling. Some of my favorites have been these:

Q: What did the caterpillar say when it climbed into its cocoon?
A: See you next moth!

Q: What do you call a caterpillar who finks on his friends?
A: A dirty raterpillar!

Q: Where do crazy caterpillars go?
A: To the cuckoo cocoon.

Q: What is green and breaks into your house?
A: A caterpillar burglar.

There were many more. Why children at this age love jokes like these, I don't know. When I was in the fifth grade, we told elephant and grape jokes. (Why was the elephant hiding in the grape tree? He had welched on a bet and gotten himself into a jam.)

This month, the study skills group extended their work from formulating interesting, researchable questions about topics to locating information about these topics. This extension took us to the school library on a daily basis. Miss Page said we could have a thirty-minute period each morning from 9:00 to 9:30.

On the first day in the library, Miss Page taught the class for me. She taught everyone about the concept of subject indices. First, everyone was given a mimeographed copy of the index of a book on the federal government. To see if everyone could use the index, she dictated ten topics for each student to find in the index and write down the page numbers where information on that topic could be found. Everyone then traded papers and she read out the correct answers. No one missed any, of course, since this task only requires the ability to spell the word dictated, the ability to alphabetize, and the ability to copy.

Next she showed them the *Reader's Guide to Periodical Literature*. As they grouped around her, she would take a topic suggested by a student and look it up for them as they watched. This task, too, seemed simple enough for them.

Finally, Miss Page demonstrated the use of the subject card catalogue. Again students would suggest topics for which she would search and show them what she found. If a subject was not listed, she asked for another one and searched for it.

At the end of the lesson, everyone was asked to write the answers to two questions:

1. How are the index of a book, the *Reader's Guide to Periodical Literature*, and the subject card catalogue alike?
2. How is each one different from the other two?

For the reader to do

Answer the two questions which Miss Page asked Mr. Dunn's students after her lesson.

● ● ●

When all the students were finished writing, they discussed the answers to the two questions.

Following this lesson, Miss Page and I knew that this group of students had the prerequisites for learning to locate information. They could find key words in any type of alphabetized subject index and copy the sources indexed there. They knew what subject indices were and the principle on which they work. And they knew the three major subject indices available in most school and public libraries.

For the next few days, either Miss Page or I taught the students how to locate a book given as a source by the subject card catalogue, or a periodical given to them by consulting the *Reader's Guide*. Most of the students could already find books by Dewey Decimal System number, which reflected their experience with this and other libraries.

After these different areas of readiness were established, we began building the more sophisticated locational skill of predicting key words to use in locating information with the help of subject indices.

Like many cognitive skills, the ability to postulate and select key words is a complex one. The strategy I used with my students had two parts. First, we tried to think divergently of all the possibilities for key words given a particular topic. Then we tried to think critically to determine which of those possibilities would seem most likely to yield the desired information.

One of several lessons designed to teach this process was concerned with the upcoming Valentine's Day. Using a chalkboard, we brainstormed all the possible key words which, regardless of source used, might yield information about Valentine's Day. The following list is representative of what we wrote:

hearts	Cupid
St. Valentine	romance
Valentine's Day	February
holidays	February 14
love	red
candy	saints
greeting cards	

After compiling the list, we considered each item as a possible key word for use in researching Valentine's Day. After the discussion, everyone wrote down three sources to consult and handed in these choices. I sorted the ballots and placed votes by the items in our list as they had been chosen by the group.

Four possible key words received the most votes by far: St. Valentine, Valentine's Day, holidays, and February 14. As a group, we then discussed why these four might be better than the others.

The follow-up activity for each one of these lessons was to go to the library with the key words the group had selected, and to use those key words to see if information could be found about that topic.

After several sessions in which we brainstormed possible key words for a topic, evaluated and selected a few of those key words for use, and actually tried to use them in the library, the students worked individually. I still had the list made in January when each student had picked a subject he or she was interested in and knew something about. After being reminded of the subject he or she had chosen, each student was asked to brainstorm on a piece of notebook paper all the key words which might be used to learn more about the subject. At the end of the brainstorming period, the students each chose five key words they thought would yield the most and best information.

No matter how much you reason through something, you can always overlook important considerations! After I had worked with the study skills group in asking stimulating, researchable study questions, and then in locating information about those questions with the help of subject indices, I thought they were ready to ask questions and find information about individual topics of interest. When each student independently attacked the library in search of knowledge with nothing but the five key words, it soon became obvious that they were not yet properly prepared.

Michelle was the first one to come back empty-handed. "It seems like *everything* had to do with the human body!" Joyce came soon after to complain that "half of this drama book is on acting. Do I have to read all of that to find the answer to my question?"

When this happened to two-thirds or more of the students in the group, I panicked. Horace asked me. "Mr. Dunn, when we tried to stump you on all those questions, did you find the answers this way?"

Horace's question was an excellent one and I thought about it. In fact, we talked about it in a classroom meeting during one of our morning sessions in the library. After that meeting, I knew what I had done. Everything I had taught them was right, but I had left out two concepts, the lack of which was reflected in the two major problems the students were having. They were asking interesting, researchable study questions, but those questions were generally so broad that they would have required a book or a dissertation to answer them. And they were quite good at generating and selecting key words, but they were unable, for the most part, to use subheadings with main entries to arrive at the specific books and parts of books where the exact information they wanted might be. This month began with a series of lessons on narrowing topics and using subheadings in subject indices.

We were able to narrow the questions we were asking by a simple procedure in which we asked each other to expand on specific words in the study questions we had formulated. Joyce, for example, was researching the question, "How to Act?" As a group we asked her the following questions and received the following answers:

HORACE: What kind of acting are you interested in?

JOYCE: What do you mean?

PAT: Well, would you rather act in radio plays, on the stage, or in movies?

JOYCE: Oh! I think I want to act on the stage.

MR. DUNN: What kind of stage plays would you like to be in?

JOYCE: I'm not sure. We went to see a play once at the University Theatre by a Greek playwright who lived a long time ago. We sat all around them and the actors wore masks. And there were a group of people off on one side who kind of said their lines together.

LARRY: That's Greek drama.

JOYCE: Okay, that's the kind of acting I would like to do.

MR. DUNN: And why are you trying to find information about acting in the school library?

JOYCE: So I can learn how to do it!

At that point, I stopped the discussion and asked each member of the group to write down the exact question he or she thought Joyce was asking. I took these suggested questions from the students and read them to the group. When one was different from the ones read previously, I wrote it on the board until every different type of suggestion was recorded. Then the group discussed and reworded these possibilities until everyone could agree on a final wording. In this case, the question which resulted was, "How does one learn to act in classical Greek dramas?"

Similarly, we discussed the research question of each of the fourteen group members. Near the end, the group was capable of hammering out a specific unambiguous research question on almost any subject. I must admit that if I ever go to graduate school I will be better able to formulate research and study questions from having helped these students to do so.

For our lessons with subheadings, I used transparencies made from the subject indices of various books. For entries like this:

Uganda   6, 89, 114, 335; area, 234–38; government, 256–65; natural resources, 237–43; population, 233; weather, 241–42

I asked a series of specific questions and each student wrote the number of the page on which he or she would first look to find the answer to each question. After they had recorded these numbers, we discussed each one of the consensus choices and why it made sense. At first, several students put "page 6" as the first place to look regardless of the question. Soon, however, students gained a good bit of practice with subheadings and became able to zero in on the specific page where an answer was most likely to be found. Of course, you can buy commercial workbooks with this kind of exercise in them, but the way students really learn to use subheadings is by discussing why they made certain choices. No commercial material can provide this kind of group interaction.

I'm afraid that caterpillar jokes have continued to plague us during March. Larry has edited a book of them with the help of Horace and Pat. Naturally they call it, *An Encyclopedia of Caterpillar Jokes*. Some of the new ones this month are really ridiculous:

Q: What did the butterfly sing when it flew out of its cocoon?
A: The old green caterpillar ain't what she used to be!

Q: What kind of caterpillar do you find in the refrigerator?
A: A cool caterpillar!

Q: What do you call a caterpillar who eats hamburgers?
A: A pattykiller.

Q: What kind of hat did Davy Caterpillar wear?
A: A cocoon's skin cap.

Q: Where does a caterpillar go to wash up?
A: The larva-tory.

Q: What do you call a caterpillar when he goes to school?
A: A pupa!

My question is, of course, "Will this nonsense ever end?"

APRIL

When spring comes, the sap rises, and it has certainly risen in my students! Pat and Horace are obviously in love, and Hilda is constantly following Larry around and writing him notes. Daisy seems to have her eye on Mitch but he pays no attention to her.

By the beginning of this month, everyone had gone caterpillar crazy. The joke-telling showed no signs of subsiding, and I, for one, was getting pretty sick of it. Both Daphne's grandmother and Manuel's father had been to see me about the jokes. Apparently they had the notion that we did an inordinate amount of playing in my room.

Several of the boys were bringing live caterpillars to school and throwing them at the girls. Mike put one down Roberta's blouse and she punched him hard, right in the nose.

Soon after that I heard the following interchange between Butch and Rita:

RITA: What did the two doting aunt caterpillars say the first time they saw the newborn baby caterpillar?

BUTCH: I don't know.

RITA: What a darling little cute-rpillar!

BUTCH: Okay. Why was the cocoon embarrassed?

RITA: I give up.

BUTCH: Because his butterfly was open!

Well, that did it. I got the class together in one group and ordered them to be silent and pay strict attention. "Look. I've tried to be a nice guy about this, but I have heard my *last* caterpillar joke. Is that clear?"

It apparently was clear and the caterpillar craze has died out as far as I can tell. Everyone is still interested in affairs of the heart, but at least the caterpillars have been left out of it.

The listening-to-reading transfer group works almost exclusively with reading now. I teach regular vocabulary lessons to them using both structured overviews and the four-step procedure outlined in January. I also teach directed and guided reading lessons to them. Occasionally, to still build on their strength in listening while building vocabulary and comprehension, I read them something which they could not read and have them write it in their own words, a variation on translation writing.

The study skills group now seems very capable of asking specific researchable, and interesting study questions, and of locating information about those questions through the use of various subject indices, including subheadings under main entries. During April, my lessons with them have centered on recording and organizing information once that information has been located. This ability will be invaluable to them later in fulfilling research assignments which require them to submit a written report of what they found.

To begin with, I wrote a research question on the board: "What part did our state play in the Civil War and how was it affected by the Civil War?" Everyone took several minutes to develop an individual set of key words and then went to the library to find two or three pieces of information which would help us begin to answer the question.

The next day we met as a group and I wrote the different bits of information on the board. In all, we had over twenty bits of knowledge, ranging from individuals from our state who had been important officers in the war, to the battles fought within our state, to the political stance our state's representatives had taken on the slavery issue before the war. After I recorded this information on the board, I instructed each student to use that information to write the answer to the question I had given them the day before.

Soon it became obvious that it was a very difficult task for almost everyone. When Mandy said that she didn't know where to start, several nods indicated that she had expressed the sentiments of the others as well. Then I asked the group, "Would it help you if each piece of information were on a card and you could shuffle the cards to put things in the order that you wanted to write about them?"

All the students said or indicated that it would probably help. Each student then wrote the pieces of information on index cards which I provided. I collected them and we sat together in a semi-circle. As a group, we discussed several possible orders for the cards. As it turned out, each order was based on several sortings of cards as to type of information on the card. We finally agreed on these piles of cards:

1. military leaders of the Civil War from our state
2. Civil War battles fought in our state
3. our state's stand on slavery before the Civil War
4. our state's Civil War industry

When I asked which of the four categories our answer should begin with, Manuel suggested that we start by describing our state's stand on slavery, since "what caused the Civil War should come before the Civil War." I then had the students dictate the answer to our question, line by line, and I wrote it on the board. When we were finished, we had a detailed answer to the question which included all the pieces of information we had started with.

For the reader to do

Describe how Mr. Dunn's lesson is similar in purpose to a lesson in how to outline. Describe how it is different. Discuss why outlining is so hard to learn how to do.

● ● ●

Following this lesson, the students were given a major assignment which entailed the following steps:

1. Choose an area of interest to you.
2. Ask a study question which relates to that area of interest.
3. Brainstorm and select possible key words to help you locate information in answering that question.
4. Record relevant information in your own words on index cards, one piece of information to a card.
5. Group those cards into piles which go together and label each group.

Miss Page allowed the students to ask her for help as they needed it while in the library, and I tried to give supervision to their work as well. This assignment was the true test of whether they could put everything that I had tried to teach them together. Everyone required some assistance, but all in all they did very well. Considering that they are fifth-graders, I am extremely proud of their research abilities.

MAY

Oh, no! The mushroom jokes have started. The students and I need the summer off in the worst way.

Q: What is a frog's hammer called?
A: A toad's tool!

Q: Where do Alaskan huskies go when they're hungry?
A: The mushroom.

Q: What were all the toadstools gossiping about?
A: A mushrumor.

Q: What do you call two toadstools who live together?
A: Mushroom mates.

Q: What do you call a toadstool who drinks?
A: A lushroom!

My second year of teaching has been a good year and I feel that I have met the challenge of this very capable group of students. Mike has made really extraordinary progress. If he continues to read *Hardy Boys* books over the summer the way he does now, I don't believe he will have as many reading problems next year in the middle school.

Daisy is still overweight and lazy, but I believe she shows some signs of breaking out of the pattern she is in. She obviously is interested in the opposite sex and this interest may provide the motivation she needs to shape up.

I have failed with poor Paul. I believe he has made some progress, but at times he is totally unable to respond in any way. Whatever is to happen to him, I don't know, but at this rate I fear he may never be literate.

I am extremely proud of the rest of the students. Tanana, Mort, Carl, Chip, Jeff, Mitch, and even Butch will be good students next year and will be able to read well enough to master their content-area materials. And with Mr. Topps in the middle school as principal, I know they will have a good instructional program from which they will continue to benefit.

As the school year has drawn to a close, the study skills group of students has been making individual oral reports on the study questions they began researching at the end of April. Mr. Topps came in on the days that Alex, Betty, and Daphne made their reports and was so impressed that he has asked me to come to the middle school to address the last planning session with the language arts teachers there. I wish he were not leaving Merritt Elementary for we shall miss him mightily, but I will worry less about the students we send to the middle school from now on.

I have read over twenty complete books to the students this year and in SQUIRT we were reading twenty-six minutes per day by the end of the school year. The vocabulary instruction seems to have paid off; the students certainly use more precise words in their conversations. All in all, except for the caterpillar joke fiasco, it has been a great year!

Q: Where should tired, vacationing caterpillars go?
A: They butterfly to Cocoon Beach.

The Meeting at the Middle School

Ed Dunn sat quietly by Mr. Topps as the language arts teachers filed into the small meeting room at the middle school. The expressions on their faces indicated that they were as excited about going on vacation as he was. They were smiling and kidding each other about what they would do with their upcoming vacation. For most of them, it seemed that their families and summer school at the university would take much of the time, and they were enthusiastic about the change.

Mr. Topps had been meeting with small groups of teachers at the middle school ever since he knew for certain that he would be moving there the following year. He thought it would help make for a smoother transition, and, so far, everyone was very positive about the coming September.

When all the teachers were present, Mr. Topps closed the door and introduced Mr. Dunn. "Ed has done an excellent job with his students this year and I wanted him to share some of his ideas with you. He has emphasized some of the areas with which you teachers are most concerned, like critical reading and reference skills."

Ed, in his usual serious and business-like manner, stood to address these smiling teachers. "To demonstrate how my type of reading program fits in with other types, it might be useful to talk about stages in the development of reading ability. I believe there are five stages in that development:

1. The Reading Readiness Stage
2. The Beginning Reading Stage
3. The Independent Reading Stage
4. The Reading-to-Learn Stage
5. The Responsive Reading Stage

"The Reading Readiness Stage begins at the birth of the child, continues through the development of oral language, and ends when the child knows what reading is, knows what it is for, and desires to learn how to do it. A kindergarten program like Miss Launch teaches at our school is really an attempt to bring this stage to a successful completion.

"Upon completion of the Readiness Stage, the child is able to benefit from regular reading instruction. For some children, the Beginning Reading Stage starts in kindergarten; for others, it does not start until much later. A first-grade teacher like our Mrs. Wright would have most of her students at this stage, although she would still have some students at the Readiness Stage.

"The Beginning Reading Stage is over when material exists which the student can and does read silently, without instruction or help from anyone. Mrs. Wright tells me that many of her students are reading pre-primer and primer stories independently by the end of the first grade.

"The Independent Reading Stage continues from the first successful attempts at independent, silent reading until students become quite adept at seeking out, selecting, and self-pacing their reading through a variety of books. Most second- and third-graders are becoming more sophisticated in their ability to read independently.

"Reading independently, however, is not enough if students are to thrive academically; they must become able to learn from what they read independently. Mr. Ditto, who teaches fourth grade at Merritt School, tries to take students from the Independent Reading Stage into the Reading-to-Learn Stage.

"Now we have reached the point where I come in. By the time many of my students reach fifth grade, they have had such excellent instruction year after year that they have reached the Reading-to-Learn Stage. Given an assignment or study question, they are able to read, comprehend, and recall information from written material. If all we wanted were students who could fulfill specific assignments, that would be enough. But I believe we want students who can create their own assignments; who can, and do, ask their own questions, locate information, and formulate answers.

"Eventually, we want students to go beyond the literal, to respond inferentially, critically, and even creatively to what they read. I hope that I have started my students on their way through the Responsive Reading Stage. It is a stage which, once begun, will never be finished. The ultimate goal of reading is to become more and more responsive to what is read, and to seek out more and more stimulating material to respond to."

Mr. Dunn sat down. One of the language arts teachers spoke up, "I have a question, Mr. Dunn. What do you do when you have students who are at different stages of development in their reading ability?"

"Yes, Miss Stern," Ed responded, "that is a very important question. It would be an unusual class without students from several stages. In my class this year, for example, I had at least one student still in the Beginning Reading Stage, and possibly one still in the Reading Readiness Stage.

For the reader to do

Decide which two children Mr. Dunn is referring to in this instance.

● ● ●

"There are several approaches to individualizing instruction, and instruction must become individualized to some degree if students at differing stages of reading development are all to benefit from that instruction.

"My particular approach to this problem was to give instruction based on general weaknesses which seem to limit growth in reading. Regardless of teaching method used, most children learn to read. Among the vast majority of people who can speak and understand their spoken language, there seems to be a strong impetus to learn to read in that language.

"Given this impetus, one who is not progressing in reading must have some obstacle preventing his or her progress. And, because everyone can improve in reading, it could be said that everyone has a limit on his or her ability. That limit can never be eliminated but it can be raised, allowing the student's ability to rise until it once again finds a limit.

"In reading, I believe there are three possible limits to improving the rate of progress: listening comprehension ability, word identification ability, and reading comprehension ability.

"For many years, listening comprehension has been thought to place a ceiling on a child's reading ability; many diagnosticians have used a measure of listening comprehension as a measure of potential. Yet language arts researchers have assured us that listening ability can be improved. Why not combine these concepts to conclude that if listening is limiting a particular student's progress in reading, give that student instruction in raising that listening level and then transfer that improved listening ability to the reading act.

"That word identification ability places a ceiling on reading ability has never been seriously questioned and is almost universally accepted. It seems obvious that meaning cannot be gained by a reader if he or she is unable to recognize the words by which that meaning is conveyed.

"Reading comprehension certainly acts as a ceiling for those learners who comprehend when they listen but who are word callers when they read. Certainly reading comprehension is limited in those instances when mature readers are confronted with materials so difficult for them that they can only call the words. Finally, reading comprehension acts as a ceiling on reading ability because comprehension is the goal of reading ability.

"A diagnostic strategy which is not limited to 'poor readers' or, in fact, to any subclass of readers, may be based on this rationale. Each student, regardless of reading ability, should be diagnosed to determine what is placing a limit on that ability at that time. When the area of limitation is discovered, the student should receive specific instruction in that area in order to raise the limit.

"Students in the Beginning Reading Stage will almost always have word identification as the limit on their reading ability. Students in the Responsive Reading Stage generally will have passed the point at which word identification or listening comprehension can be the limit."

"What about materials?" Miss Rule asked. "What materials do you use?"

"That's a good question, because it underscores the nature of the Responsive Reading Stage. For SQUIRT, reading to my students, inferential comprehension lessons, and critical reading lessons, I use children's and adolescent literature. Good children's books have so much for intermediate students to be responsive to.

"For building research-study skills I use the school library. If students are going to be responsive readers and learners, they must not be limited to one section of an encyclopedia or to the viewpoint of one textbook. Responsive readers must have access to a quality *and* quantity of information on which to base their responses."

Mr. Topps stood up from his chair. "I'm sure Ed will be glad to talk with any of you individually about his reading program. Don't take too long though. On my way in, I noticed that his car is packed and seems ready to head for the coast."

As some teachers left and others moved toward Mr. Dunn for further discussion, Mr. Topps whispered, "Ed, I hear there's not mushroom at Cocoon Beach!"

References

Aronson, Elliot, et. al, "The Jigsaw Route to Learning and Liking." *Psychology Today* 8 (1975): 43–50.

Barron, Richard F. "The Use of Vocabulary as an Advance Organizer." From Herber, Harold L., and Sanders, P. L. (eds.). *Research in Reading in the Content Areas: First Year Report.* Syracuse, N.Y.: Reading and Language Arts Center, Syracuse University, 1969.

Crist, Barbara I. "One Capsule a Week—A Painless Remedy for Vocabulary Ills." *Journal of Reading* 19 (1975): 147–149.

Glasser, M. D., William. *Schools without Failure.* New York: Harper and Row, 1969.

Harris, Albert J., and Sipay, Edward R. *How to Increase Reading Ability,* 6th ed. New York: David McKay, 1975.

Haugaard, Erik C. *The Little Fishes.* Boston: Houghton Mifflin, 1967.

O'Brien, Robert C. *Mrs. Frisby and the Rats of NIMH.* New York: Atheneum, 1971.

Zolotow, Charlotte. *My Grandson Lew.* New York: Harper and Row, 1974.

Further Readings

Kindergarten

Bruck, Margaret, and Tucker, G. Richard. "Social Class Differences in the Acquisition of School Language." *Merrill-Palmer Quarterly* 20:204–20.
This article reports research done with children of lower socioeconomic status. It was found that these children have the same ability to comprehend grammatical structures, but more trouble reproducing them spontaneously. Other equally interesting finds were reported.

Eisenhower, Julie. *Julie Eisenhower's Cookbook for Children.* New York: Doubleday, 1975.
This book has many recipes for young children to cook at home or in school. Very clearly written.

Fisher, Carol J., and Lyons, Patricia A. "Oral Interaction: Involving Every Child in Discussion." *Elementary English* 51(1974):1100–1101.
Various ways that the teacher can involve all children in classroom discussion are detailed in this article.

Glovach, Linda. *The Little Witch's Black Magic Cookbook.* Englewood Cliffs, N.J.: Prentice-Hall, 1972.
The cookbook includes many easy recipes for children to follow. Suggestions for holiday foods are also given.

Hall, Mary Anne, and Matanzo, Jane. "Children's Literature: A Source for Concept Enrichment." *Elementary English* 52(1975):487–94.
The importance of enriching children's conceptual backgrounds through children's literature is discussed at length. An excellent annotated bibliography is provided, along with suggestions for using the books with children.

Ploghoft, Milton H. "Do Reading Readiness Workbooks Promote Readiness?" *Elementary English* 36(1959):424–26.
Dr. Ploghoft disputes the commonly held notion that readiness for reading can be enhanced by the use of workbooks in kindergarten.

Ross, Ramon Royal. "Frankie and the Flannel Board." *The Reading Teacher* 27(1973):43–47.
Storyteller Ross discusses how he uses the flannel board for storytelling in the classroom. He details the parameters he sets and why.

Smith, Rosalind Bingham. "Teaching Mathematics to Children through Cooking." *Arithmetic Teacher* 21(1974):480–484.
Smith explains some of the many things that children learn from classroom cooking experiences.

Weaver, Susan W., and Rutherford, William L. "A Hierarchy of Listening Skills." *Elementary English* 51(1974):1146–50.
Various skills of listening-environmental, discrimination, comprehension are discussed as they apply to different grade levels.

Wilkinson, Andrew. "Oracy and Reading." *Elementary English* 51(1974):1102–1109.

Wilkinson presents a discussion of the relationship between language skills and reading acquisition. Myriad examples of various phases of his thesis are provided.

Willems, Arnold, and Willems, Wanda. "Please Read Me a Book." *Language Arts* 52(1975):831–35.

This article stresses the importance of reading to children with the "how," "when," and "what" discussed. A fine bibliography is included.

First Grade

Ashton-Warner, Sylvia. *Teacher.* New York: Simon and Shuster, 1963.

Describes the author's experience in teaching "organic" reading to Maori children. Children write their own books and compile their own "key" vocabulary of "essential-to-the-individual" words.

Askland, Linda C. "Conducting Individual Language Experience Stories," *The Reading Teacher* 27(1973):167–70.

A very brief description of the step-by-step procedure used by volunteers and paraprofessionals in conducting and recording individual language experience lessons.

Cunningham, Patricia M. "Investigating a Synthesized Theory of Mediated Word Identification." *Reading Research Quarterly* 11(1975–76).

Describes the results of research which supports the compare-contrast theory of word identification.

Hall, Maryanne. "Linguistically Speaking, Why Language Experience?" *The Reading Teacher* 25(1972):328–31.

Presents seven "statements of linguistic rationale" for using the language experience approach in beginning reading instruction.

Lee, Dorris M., and Allen, R.V. *Learning to Read Through Experience.* New York: Appleton-Century Crofts, 1963.

Describes a plan for integrating the learning of reading with the development of all the communication modes and with the total development of the child. Provides examples of experience charts and related skills development activities.

Madison, John P. "The Language Experience Approach to Teaching Reading. NCTE ERIC Report." *Elementary English* 48(1971):682–88.

Gives a brief summary of and references to books and papers which trace the history of the language experience approach, outline its application and discuss its empirical validity.

Mulligan, Joseph P. "Using Language Experience with Potential High School Dropouts." *Journal of Reading* 18(1974):206–211.

Describes a language experience reading program with preliterate inner-city high school students.

Stauffer, Russell G. *The Language Experience Approach to Reading Instruction.* New York: Harper and Row, 1970.

Describes both the theoretical background for and the practical application of the language experience approach to reading instruction. Gives detailed suggestions for stimulating dictated stories, building word banks, integrating the language curriculum and utilizing the language experience approach in varied situations.

Second Grade

Goodman, Kenneth S. "Effective Teachers of Reading Know Language and Children." *Elementary English* 51(1974):823–28.
Goodman argues that teachers must be aware of the tremendous language potential of children before they can begin to assess, diagnose, and remediate reading problems.

Hollander, Sheila K. "Why's a Busy Teacher Like You Giving an IRI?" *Elementary English* 51(1974):905–907.
Hollander discusses the reasons for giving IRI's, and the kinds of information that they can give a teacher.

Hopkins, Lee Bennett. *Let Them be Themselves.* New York: Citation, 1969.
Many ideas are given for providing children with a broader, more varied language arts program. Though it is especially good for use with the disadvantaged, there are implications for use with all children.

Livingston, Howard F. "Measuring and Teaching Meaning with an Informal Reading Inventory." *Elementary English* 51(1974):878–79, 895.
Livingston's article outlines the aspect of IRI's that is often incomplete—comprehension. He makes a plea for the incorporation of more material to deal with comprehension.

Moffett, James. *A Student-Centered Language Arts Curriculum, Grades K–13: A Handbook for Teachers.* Boston: Houghton Mifflin, 1968.
Moffett's book has become a classic in the field of language arts because of the concern with individual students and the provision of multitudes of materials and ideas for each grade.

Rodenborn, Leo V. and Washburn, Earlene. "Some Implications of the New Basal Readers." *Elementary English* 51(1974):885–88.
The authors provide an interesting discussion of the changes in the basal programs of the seventies. Core vocabulary, vocabulary load, and vocabulary frequency are investigated.

Spache, George and Spache, Evelyn. "Using the Basal Reader Approach (Chapter 4)." *Reading in the Elementary School.* 3rd ed. Boston: Allyn and Bacon, 1973.
The Spaches provide a complete discussion of the advantages and disadvantages inherent in basal readers. Excellent.

Third Grade

Allington, Richard. "Sustained Approaches to Reading and Writing." *Language Arts* 52(1975):813–15.

Allington proposes that USSR (Uninterrupted Sustained Silent Reading) be supplemented with *Can't Stop Writing,* an approach to sustained silent writing in order to strengthen children's writing skills.

Criscuolo, Nicholas P. "Parents: Active Partners in the Reading Program." *Elementary English* 51(1974):883–84.
The benefits of using parents are manifold. This article discusses how and why.

Garry, Vee. "Add a Dash of Poetry Seasoning." *Language Arts* 52(1975):950–52.
Creative, innovative uses of poetry in the classroom encourage teachers to do more with poetry.

Hill, Charles H., and Methot, Kathleen. "Making an Important Transition." *Elementary English* 51(1974):842–45.
The article relates the results of a study done to determine if children could change from reading a programmed series to trade books. Interesting to read, particularly if one is contemplating making such a change.

Jernigan, Mary L. "Centers Approach to Reading Instruction." *Elementary English* 51(1974):858–60.
One description of teaching reading with learning centers is given in this article. Though there are many in the literature, this one has some unique features.

Koch, Kenneth. *Wishes, Lies and Dreams: Teaching Children to Write Poetry.* New York: Random House, 1971.
The author details many of the poetry formats which he has used in working with children. Many samples of children's poetry are included.

Meehan, Trinita. "An Informal Modality Inventory." *Elementary English* 51(1974):901–904.
The use of the Aids to Psycholinguistic Teaching (APT) book by Bush and Giles enables the teacher to create a learning modality test to use with children.

Stauffer, Russell G., and Harrell, Max M. "Individualizing Reading-Thinking Activities." *The Reading Teacher* 28(1975):765–69.
The authors reiterate the necessity of challenging the thinking of children and suggest many ways in which the teacher can do so.

Fourth Grade

Aulls, Mark W. "Relating Reading Comprehension and Writing Competency." *Language Arts* 52(1975):808–812.
Discusses the nature of the relationship between reading and writing and suggests that integrated reading-creative writing instruction may enhance reading comprehension and promote writing fluency.

Burns, Paul C. "A Re-examination of Aspects of Unit Teaching in the Elementary School." *Peabody Journal of Education* 40(1962):31–39.
Examines the unit approach to teaching in terms of topic, objectives, motivation, activities, and evaluation. Suggests some cautions to be observed when teaching with a unit approach.

Cox, Carole. "The Liveliest Art and Reading." *Language Arts* 52(1975):771–75.
Suggests ways in which film and reading can be woven together to provide motivation for reading and promote vocabulary growth, comprehension, critical reading, and creative reading.

Cunningham, Patricia M. "Transferring Comprehension from Listening to Reading." *The Reading Teacher* 29(1975):169–72.
Describes listening-reading transfer lessons for sequence of events, main idea and inferences, and suggests three ways of adapting these lessons to the varied reading levels found within a particular classroom.

Manzo, Anthony V. "Guided Reading Procedure." *Journal of Reading* 18(1975):287–91.
Describes the guided reading procedure, a "new strategy to improve reading comprehension" and outlines six steps to follow in teaching a GRP lesson.

McKee, Paul. *The Teaching of Reading in the Elementary School.* Cambridge, Mass.: Houghton Mifflin, 1948.
Describes a program of reading instruction in the intermediate grades which includes instruction in basic reading skills and the integration of reading instruction with instruction in science and social studies.

Wilson, Robert M., and Hall, Maryanne. *Reading and the Elementary School Child.* New York: D. Van Nostrand, 1972.
Discusses the nature of comprehension and its relationship to thinking. Provides examples of purpose setting and follow-up activities for the directed reading lesson.

Fifth Grade

Manzo, Anthony V. "Reading and Questioning: The ReQuest Procedure." *Reading Improvement* 7(3), (1970):80–83.
Manzo's ReQuest (Reciprocal Questioning) Procedure builds implicit questioning in the learner, thereby making him or her more responsive to what he or she reads. The article outlines the steps in the procedure as well as kinds of questions a teacher may use with the learner.

Manzo, Anthony V. "The ReQuest Procedure." *Journal of Reading* 13(2), (1969):123–26, 163.
The original article which outlines the ReQuest Procedure and presents a rationale for it.

Robinson, H. Alan. *Teaching Reading and Study Strategies.* Boston: Allyn and Bacon, 1975.
This book describes many strategies to help students improve their ability in study-research skills. Higher-order comprehension and critical reading abilities are fostered by many of these strategies.

Root, Shelton L., Jr., ed. *Adventuring with Books,* 2d ed. New York: Citation Press, 1973.
A thorough, annotated bibliography of books for primary and intermediate students, ranging from picture books to books concerned with the biological and physical sciences. Books are included to meet almost any interest possible.

Appendix A

Professional Organizations and Addresses

These are only a few of the professional organizations which you should consider joining. Most of them have local chapters near you.

Association for Childhood Education International (ACEI)

Journal: *Childhood Education*

Address: 3615 Wisconsin Avenue, N.W.
Washington, D.C. 20016

International Reading Association (IRA)

Journals: *The Reading Teacher*
The Journal of Reading
The Reading Research Quarterly

Address: 800 Barksdale Road
P.O. Box 8139
Newark, Delaware 19711

National Council of Teachers of English (NCTE)

Journals: *Language Arts* (formerly *Elementary English*)
The English Journal

Address: 1111 Kenyon Road
Urbana, Illinois 61801

Appendix B

Revised A and P Sight Word List*

First fifty words (according to frequency of occurrence):

the	that	at	be	each
a	was	as	can	will
to	on	have	but	up
and	for	she	there	many
of	are	what	not	we
in	they	one	when	then
you	I	this	how	her
is	with	all	were	or
he	his	had	your	out
it	said	from	do	some

Second fifty:

them	make	did	go	back
write	into	people	get	first
their	him	an	now	way
about	other	which	long	over
by	word	could	find	too
like	would	time	look	than
see	water	more	made	good
so	little	down	just	use
if	two	my	big	day
these	has	no	very	where

Third fifty:

me	right	does	why	another
went	air	say	work	number
put	sound	same	through	our
around	think	been	here	must
new	tell	take	place	off
know	after	only	before	name

---

* This list is adapted from that presented by Wayne Otto, and Robert Chester in "Sight words for beginning readers," *Journal of Educational Research,* 65 (1972): 435–43. All numerals, proper nouns, and duplicated inflected forms were deleted from the original list of 500 words. Reprinted by permission.

come	Mr.	old	three	mother
who	man	away	home	asked
its	may	children	house	picture
came	much	help	again	most

Fourth fifty:

part	line	men	need	along
food	because	read	still	night
saw	thought	left	keep	took
different	next	hear	together	sentence
live	small	show	sun	story
well	every	end	us	land
any	want	don't	got	never
school	something	found	Mrs.	always
even	earth	eat	great	play
under	last	boy	father	began

Fifth fifty:

give	white	dog	told	ran
below	soon	door	country	page
also	let	once	white	world
head	hard	enough	large	eyes
grow	hearts	near	I'm	high
set	side	kind	year	ever
paper	until	oh	letter	might
it's	should	top	fish	four
morning	sometimes	didn't	car	few
I'll	own	draw	city	move

Sixth fifty:

sure	vowel	far	red	both
miss	almost	today	means	turn
feet	ground	cold	hand	warm
tree	sea	inside	green	without
knew	heard	run	gave	between
often	try	cried	across	short
add	money	fast	yes	stop
better	box	answer	learn	family
room	cut	best	can't	form
such	thing	light	change	black

Seventh fifty:

those	stood	girl	animal	stay
am	table	sat	important	toward
horse	moon	bird	really	feel
front	song	town	soil	young
seen	miles	cannot	ball	himself
ready	baby	fire	hot	fly
eggs	beautiful	call	sky	cat
body	second	plant	study	hold
whole	above	talk	ago	face
blue	leaves	that's	spell	wind

Eighth fifty:

window	open	winter	fine	happened
done	book	milk	nothing	everything
half	six	goes	catch	gone
true	glass	gold	everyone	order
walk	ice	rain	legs	sleep
dark	start	river	grass	strong
sing	ten	garden	listen	anything
summer	five	Indian	someone	try
outside	watch	piece	happy	let's
behind	road	boy	being	snow

Final thirty-two:

tall	class	slowly	tiny	against
round	fun	woman	friend	covered
care	street	hole	kept	wood
store	space	remember	ride	bright
built	bed	ship	tail	game
hit	complete	stand	seeds	rest
maybe	carry			

Appendix C

The Dolch Basic Sight Word List

	Preprimer		Primer		First grade		Second grade		Third grade
1.	a	1.	all	1.	after	1	always	1.	about
2.	and	2.	am	2.	again	2.	around	2.	better
3.	away	3.	are	3.	an	3.	because	3.	bring
4.	big	4.	at	4.	any	4.	been	4.	carry
5.	blue	5.	ate	5.	as	5.	before	5.	clean
6.	can	6.	be	6.	ask	6.	best	6.	cut
7.	come	7.	black	7.	by	7.	both	7.	cone
8.	down	8.	brown	8.	could	8.	buy	8.	draw
9.	find	9.	but	9.	every	9.	call	9.	drink
10.	for	10.	came	10.	fly	10.	cold	10.	eight
11.	funny	11.	did	11.	from	11.	does	11.	fall
12.	go	12.	do	12.	give	12.	don't	12.	far
13.	help	13.	eat	13.	going	13.	fast	13.	full
14.	here	14.	four	14.	had	14.	first	14.	got
15.	I	15.	get	15.	has	15.	five	15.	grow
16.	in	16.	good	16.	her	16.	found	16.	hold
17.	is	17.	have	17.	him	17.	gave	17.	hot
18.	it	18.	he	18.	his	18.	goes	18.	hurt
19.	jump	19.	into	19.	how	19.	green	19.	if
20.	little	20.	like	20.	just	20.	its	20.	keep
21.	look	21.	must	21.	know	21.	made	21.	kind
22.	make	22.	new	22.	let	22.	many	22.	laugh
23.	me	23.	no	23.	live	23.	off	23.	light
24.	my	24.	now	24.	may	24.	or	24.	long
25.	not	25.	on	25.	of	25.	pull	25.	much
26.	one	26.	our	26.	old	26.	read	26.	myself
27.	play	27.	out	27.	once	27.	right	27.	never
28.	red	28.	please	28.	open	28.	sing	28.	only
29.	run	29.	pretty	29.	over	29.	sit	29.	own
30.	said	30.	ran	30.	put	30.	sleep	30.	pick
31.	see	31.	ride	31.	round	31.	tell	31.	seven
32.	the	32.	saw	32.	some	32.	their	32.	shall
33.	three	33.	say	33.	stop	33.	these	33.	show
34.	to	34.	she	34.	take	34.	those	34.	six
35.	two	35.	so	35.	thank	35.	upon	35.	small
36.	up	36.	soon	36.	them	36.	us	36.	start
37.	we	37.	that	37.	then	37.	use	37.	ten
38.	where	38.	there	38.	think	38.	very	38.	today

Preprimer	Primer	First grade	Second grade	Third grade
39. yellow	39. they	39. walk	39. wash	39. together
40. you	40. this	40. were	40. which	40. try
	41. too	41. when	41. why	41. warm
	42. under	42. who	42. wish	
	43. want		43. work	
	44. was		44. would	
	45. well		45. write	
	46. went		46. your	
	47. what			
	48. white			
	49. will			
	50. with			
	51. yes			

0–75 known	Pre-primer reading level
76–120	Primer
121–170	First Reader
171–210	Second Reader or above
Above 210	Third Reader or above

From: Guszak, Frank J. *Diagnostic Reading Instruction in the Elementary School* (New York: Harper and Row, 1972; Learning Disabilities Center, University of Texas).

Appendix D

Kucera-Francis List

	Set 1		Set 2		Set 3		Set 4
1.	more	1.	men	1.	place	1.	less
2.	than	2.	between	2.	American	2.	public
3.	other	3.	life	3.	however	3.	almost
4.	time	4.	being	4.	home	4.	hand
5.	such	5.	day	5.	Mrs.	5.	enough
6.	man	6.	same	6.	thought	6.	took
7.	even	7.	another	7.	part	7.	head
8.	most	8.	while	8.	general	8.	yet
9.	also	9.	might	9.	high	9.	government
10.	though	10.	great	10.	school	10.	system
11.	back	11.	year	11.	untied	11.	set
12.	years	12.	since	12.	left	12.	told
13.	way	13.	against	13.	number	13.	nothing
14.	should	14.	used	14.	course	14.	night
15.	each	15.	states	15.	war	15.	end
16.	people	16.	himself	16.	until	16.	called
17.	Mr.	17.	few	17.	something	17.	didn't
18.	state	18.	house	18.	fact	18.	eyes
19.	world	19.	during	19.	though	19.	asked
20.	still	20.	without	20.	water	20.	later
						21.	knew
						22.	late

From: Johnson, Dale D. "The Dolch List Re-examined," *The Reading Teacher* 24 (1971). Reprinted with permission of Dale D. Johnson and the International Reading Association.

Index

A and P sight word list, 207
Alphabet, 10, 20, 27, 28, 43–44
ARRF (Average Reader Readability
    Formula), 152, 156, 157
Assignment cards, 157–58, 163, 165
Attendance plan, 12
Auctioning, 92–93
Auditory discrimination, 32, 45–46,
    70–71
Auditory screening, 114

Basal readers, 63–64, 80, 84, 89–90,
    102–103, 105, 120–21, 122–23,
    125, 134, 142, 146–47
Behavior modification, 125–27
Book awards, 172
Book fair, 93, 242–44
Bookmaking, 79, 82, 176–77, 226–27
Book reports, 152, 153, 168–70,
    171–72
Bulletin boards, 101, 103–104, 136–37

Card catalog: see Subject indices
Card catalog, preparing a, 180–81
Categorization skills, 90–91, 239, 240,
    243
Ceiling groups, 259
Ceilings on reading ability, 252–59,
    285–86
  listening comprehension, 261, 286
  reading comprehension, 261–64,
    286
  word identification, 260–61, 286
Censorship, 268–69, 270–71
Centers, 7–8, 16, 24–26, 36, 45, 46–47,
    66–68, 83–84, 89, 94, 132–33,
    163, 167
  listening center, 66–68, 94
  magazine center, 66, 68, 89, 94
  math center, 66, 68, 94

reading games center, 84
story center, 66, 68
writing center, 83–84
Children's literature, 13, 41, 152,
    172–74, 176, 185; see also
    Literature response activity
Classification skills, 90–91, 239, 240,
    243
Classroom management, 111–12, 113,
    116, 120–21, 122–23, 125–26,
    128–31, 132, 138–39, 141–42,
    143–46; see also Discipline
Classroom meeting, 269
Classroom organization: see
    Organizational patterns
Cloze passages, 261, 272
Comic books, 265
Comprehension questions, 255
Comprehension-reading, 8, 9, 14, 17,
    35, 36, 38–39, 40, 46–47, 49, 74,
    77, 128–29, 133, 138–39, 140–41,
    145, 156, 165, 215, 216–18,
    230–35, 237–39, 245, 255, 261,
    262, 263, 266–67, 272, 285; see
    also Critical reading, Meaning
    vocabulary
Concept development, 8, 9, 10, 16–17,
    21, 23, 28–29, 32, 33, 38–39, 40,
    42–43, 46–47, 49
Conferences with parents: see Parent
    conferences
Conferences with students, 95, 152,
    156
Consonant-plus-context, 74, 77, 266,
    272
Consonant substitution, 74–77, 88–89
Context clues, 74, 77, 261, 262, 266
Cooking in the classroom
  recipes, 18, 24, 26–27, 34, 37, 40–41,
    44, 48, 49
  value of, 9, 10
Cooperative stories, 234–35

Creative writing: *see* Writing
Critical reading, 269–71

Decoding: *see* Word identification
Diagnosis, 21, 34–35, 49–53, 55,
    105–10, 114–15, 117–18, 123–24,
    134–35, 138–39, 142, 146, 225–
    29, 285–86; *see also* Informal
    Reading Inventory
Dialects, 95–96
Dictionary, 87–89
Dictionary, preparing a, 181–82
Directed learning, 16–17, 21, 27, 35,
    38–39, 42–43, 44, 46–47, 105–
    106, 111, 115, 117, 118, 122,
    123, 125, 128–29, 130–31, 133,
    134–35, 136–38, 139, 142
Directed listening lesson, 261
Directed reading activity, 215
Directed reading lesson, 215
Directed viewing lesson, 222–23
Directions, giving and following, 9,
    28–30, 31, 32, 37–38, 42–43,
    225–26
Discipline, 82, 89, 94, 251, 254–55,
    260, 265; *see also* Classroom
    management
Discussion, 221, 239–41, 278–79
Ditto sheets, 10, 55–56, 125, 163–64
Dramatization, 14, 174

Early reading, 16–17, 34, 35, 38, 51,
    52–53
Experience charts: *see* Language
    experience approach

Field trips, 8, 17, 23–24, 25–27, 30–32,
    36, 43, 45, 48, 218–24
Flannel board, 63, 79, 84
Four-step vocabulary building
    exercises, 272–73

Games, 14, 27, 28, 42–43, 43–44,
    46–47, 70, 74, 84, 134, 136–38,
    154, 159–60,167, 170, 174–75,

179–80, 182–84, 186–87, 190–91,
    198, 207–208
Grade-level meetings, 53–57, 93–97,
    195–99
Grading, 64, 116, 117, 125, 129, 142,
    146
Grouping, 12, 17, 27–28, 35, 65, 66,
    94, 104, 108, 111, 115, 117, 120,
    122–23, 128, 131, 132, 138–39,
    142, 144–46, 159, 163, 165, 166,
    177–79, 196–97, 198, 259
Guided listening procedure, 241, 261
Guided reading procedure, 230–33,
    245

Hardy Boys, 283
Homebox, 134–35

Implicit questioning, 273–74
Index: *see* Subject indices
Individualization, 115, 118, 122,
    123–24, 127, 128–29, 131, 133,
    145, 146, 152–53, 155, 161–62,
    187–89, 190, 196–99, 285
Individual testing, 254
Inferential comprehension, 216–17,
    266–67
Informal Reading Inventory, 102,
    105, 106–110, 142, 144, 145, 155,
    190, 192–95, 254–58
Integrated curriculum, 9, 14, 16, 120,
    122, 127, 128, 129–30, 140, 142,
    205, 247
Interest inventory, 155–56, 197
Interviewing, 229
IRI: *see* Informal Reading Inventory

Jigsaw puzzle activities, 259–60
Juvenile series, 264–65, 283

Key words, 276–77

Language experience approach, 8, 17,
    23, 25, 31, 33, 61–64, 67–72, 79,
    93–97, 135, 145

Language master, 260–61
Lap story, 15–16, 54
Learning Activity Packet (LAP), 189–90
Learning centers: *see* Centers
Letter names: *see* Alphabet
Library, classroom, 127
Lifelines, 210–11
Listening comprehension, 66–67, 107, 109, 241, 261
Listening comprehension test, 107, 109
Listening-reading transfer, 237–39
List, group and label lesson, 90–91, 239, 282
Literature response activity, 9, 14–15, 16, 18, 38–39
Locating information, 274–75, 275–79

Main ideas, 217–18, 230–31
Maps, 211–14, 225–26
of school, 212
Materials-skills checklist, 197
Meaning vocabulary, 33, 54, 90, 237, 239, 257, 262, 272–73
context clues, 74, 77, 261, 262
direct teaching of, 213–14, 221, 263–64, 272–73
morphemic analysis, 262–63
Motivation, 108, 116, 117, 122–23, 125, 127, 128, 129, 131, 133, 134, 136–38, 142
Mural making, 227
Mutter reading, 141–42

Nancy Drew, 264–65
Newspaper, classroom, 122

Oral language development, 96
Oral language stimulation
activities, 28–30, 38–39, 40, 42–43
value of, 3, 8, 13
Oral reading, 9, 34–35, 64, 114, 141–42, 145
Oral reports, 283

Organizational patterns, 111, 113, 115, 117, 118, 120–21, 122–23, 124, 125, 128, 129, 130–31, 132–33, 138–39, 142, 144–47, 152, 161–63, 172, 184, 187–89, 190, 196–99
Organizing information from sources, 281–82
Outlining, 281–82

Pairing students for reading, 238, 261, 273
Parent conferences, 64, 86–87, 131, 235–36
Parents, 61–65
meetings with, 7–11, 61–65, 101–104, 151–53, 203–206, 251–54
volunteers, 11, 21, 22–23, 70, 114–15, 124, 132, 136–38, 151–52, 190, 205
Parents, reporting to; *see also* Grading, Parent conferences
written reports, 49–53, 192–95
Phonics, 63–64, 70–71, 73–77, 88–89, 94–95
application level, 74, 94–95
association level, 73–74
blends, 63
consonant substitution, 74–77, 88–89, 94–95
consonants, 63, 73–74
digraphs, 63
discrimination level, 70–71
inductive teaching of, 272
Picture-word cards, 73, 94
Poetry, 19–20, 33–34, 40, 46, 69, 139–40, 152, 179, 184–86, 267
Polysyllabic words, 88–89
Prefixes, 262–63
Professional organizations, 127

Readiness, 8, 9, 24–25, 43–44, 45–46, 56
Reading comprehension: *see* Comprehension-reading

Reading is real, 204
Reading to children, 79, 258, 268–69
Real world reading materials, 203–204
Record-keeping, 9, 10, 12, 21, 32, 54,
     153, 165, 166–68, 175
Recording information from sources,
     281–82
Reference books, 276
Relief map, 225–26
Research questions, 273–75, 278–79
     asking, 273–75
     narrowing, 278–79
Responsive reading, 252, 285
Rhyming words, 69, 75
Ring of words, 124, 129–30, 146
Rule of thumb, 191–92

Schedules, 12, 16, 68, 84–85, 111, 117,
     120–21, 125, 130, 131, 138–39,
     157–58, 161–62, 172–74
Self-concept, 13, 20, 24, 26, 45, 48–49
Self-corrective material, 189–90
Self-discipline, 156, 157–59, 197; see
     also Discipline
Sequencing, 237–38
Sight vocabulary, 35, 63–64, 71, 78,
     83, 87–88, 94, 110, 123–24,
     129–30, 134, 136–38, 142, 146,
     213–14, 221, 257, 260
Silent cheer, 13
Skills, 205, 226, 229–30, 244; see also
     Word identification, Compre-
     hension, Study skills
Small group discussion: see Discussion
Snacks, 102, 112
Sociogram, 208–209
Spelling, 142, 214
SQUIRT (Sustained QUIet Reading
     Time), 9, 64, 72, 92, 112–113,
     115, 118–19, 125, 134, 140,
     204–205, 258
Stages of reading development, 284
Story parties, 64
Storytelling, 15–16, 39–40
Structured overviews, 263–64
Student aides, 155
Student crushes, 267–68

Study skills, 273–79, 281–82
Subheadings of index entries, 279
Subject indices, 276
     subheadings, 279
Survival reading, 203
Survival skills, 10, 12, 17, 20, 21
Sustained quiet reading time: see
     SQUIRT

Tape recording, 152, 156, 158
Telegram writing, 224
Testing, 10, 34–35, 154, 155–56; see
     also Diagnosis
Timeline, 226
Timer, 64, 66, 260–61
Translation writing, 234–35, 263

Units, 212, 246

Vision screening, 114–15, 116–17
Visual discrimination, 16–17, 20, 21,
     24, 27–28, 43–44
Vocabulary: see Sight vocabulary,
     Meaning vocabulary

Wall vocabulary, 213–14, 221
Word banks, 63–64, 71, 78, 87–88, 94
Word books, 174
Word identification, 73, 74–77, 88–89,
     94, 207, 260–61, 266, 272; see also
     Context clues, Phonics, Sight
     vocabulary
Word meanings: see Meaning
     vocabulary
Word problems, 227–28
Workbooks, 10, 102–103, 113, 116,
     117, 118, 123, 145–46
Work folders, 156, 157, 158, 165,
     166–67
Writing
     creative, 9, 17, 23, 31, 33, 36, 44, 45,
          83–84, 92, 95, 167, 168, 174, 184
     readiness, 8, 20, 27, 32, 44